Sept. 10, 2016

Tell Me
Your Story

To Tais,

Thank you for journeying
with me through this last
decade — for loving and
encouraging me, and for
telling me to keep writing...
There would me no book
without you my friend!
With love and gratitude,
Tuya

*A guide to overcome anxiety, depression,
compulsions, addiction, fear, grief, obsessions,
confusion, and self-doubt*

Tell Me Your Story

How Therapy Works to Awaken, Heal, and Set You Free

by

Tuya Pearl

SHE WRITES PRESS

Published 2016
Printed in the United States of America
ISBN: 978-1-63152-066-2
Library of Congress Control Number: 2016932190

Book design by Stacey Aaronson

For information, address:
She Writes Press
1563 Solano Ave #546
Berkeley, CA 94707

She Writes Press is a division of SparkPoint Studio, LLC.

CONTENTS

∾

The hardest thing for human beings to do is to know themselves and to change themselves.

—ALFRED ADLER

This book is dedicated to the brave storytellers who change hearts and lives by courageously telling the truth.

INTRODUCTION

Ⅽ∾○

We are each born with an open, magnificent spirit, but life seems to trip us up somehow. For many, something happens that rewires or covers up the perfect program set inside us at birth. As if our navigational systems lose connectivity along the way, we seem unable to stay the course; we get lost, separated from the system encoded within our deepest selves, the one meant to direct us toward a life of joy and freedom.

As a therapist, I have witnessed how, as social beings, we are impacted and short-circuited by the experiences we have in our relationships. Those who come to see me, and plenty who don't, are greatly in need of feeling loved and valued. Most come because they have been on the receiving end of betrayal, abuse, or animosity, and what they all have in common is that they have been wounded by the disdain or insensitivity of other people. I witness the damage story after story, year after year, and can't help wondering why we go on hurting one another.

It seems strange to me that, even at this point in our evolution, we haven't yet figured out how to stop mistreating our children or maligning and killing one another. True, we each strive to find our place and purpose in the world, sometimes using and abusing others to selfishly elevate ourselves. But we are spiritual beings, too, with the capacity and choice to plug into a Higher Power and source of goodness. Hatred, greed, and heartbreak may not yet have gone away; and even though I am sometimes tempted to say that the world is worse now than it has ever been before, it is just not true.

What *is* true is that we receive our information from an industry in which "no news is good news." Through a combination of words, sound bites, and images, we are bombarded with *bad* news—atrocities and corruption that depict the worst of humankind. Though we're regularly exposed to what's dark and disturbing, the world is also constantly being enriched and brightened by generous spirits and magnanimous acts that rarely make headlines. For many of us, the hope is that as we become more *aware* of newsworthy injustices and brutal hierarchies, we will commit to being more civilized, more benevolent citizens of the universe we share.

But how? Many today are seeking ways to treat one another with greater care, reconnecting to the original source of compassion and inner guidance. Maybe it doesn't have to be the way it has always been. Change is in the air; plenty of people are reattaching to a deeper sense of wisdom, moving past pain and ego and resentments, searching for a path to peace and divine love. As we grow spiritually, we are able to *feel* and extend love to ourselves and others and take responsibility for our actions, recognizing that love is what heals us from the inside out. And love begets love.

At best, therapy is soulful work. It not only restores troubled relationships but also returns us to the beloved, unblemished self we barely remember. It always begins with humility—pushing pride aside and reaching out for help. The people who come to therapy are often considered by those who never do as the sick or crazy ones. But, in reality, those who engage in this process are the strong and brave ones, wiser than even they realize, the seekers of truth who are willing to *really* know themselves.

Therapy is a journey to the true self, the place beyond defenses, wounds, and baggage. It is a place where—in a safe relationship built on empathy and understanding—the spirit of truth clarifies and transforms us with new perspectives nurtured by grace. Tenderness and honesty change those who come to therapy, and can, one person at a time, improve the planet. I'd like you to join me and see exactly how this happens.

So, for those who have been, as well as those who may never have the opportunity, I invite you behind the door and into this private realm to eavesdrop on the human struggle, get acquainted with this therapist, and experience the transformational process yourself. And I hope that by coming inside, you, too, will grow in insight and clarity, reconciled to the truth that heals and unites us all.

sad, sad stories
pull me in
to a world of secrets
and untold sin
where shadows hide
the master key
to unlock the truths
that set us free

ONE

The Beginning

1.1 | HOW IT BEGAN

The past is but the beginning of a beginning.
—H.G. WELLS

For as long as I can remember, I have been attracted to sad stories. I am not talking about the well-crafted variety that make their way into best-selling novels or the kind that get circulated in tabloids and neighborhoods like dreadful, juicy gossip. The ones that have always fascinated me are not printed, nor spoken, but are secretly lingering all around us, trapped beneath the surface of ordinary lives in a visible ache that weighs countless people down . . . and draws me in.

Now, I confess, these real-life sagas have always been hard for me to ignore. They are painfully obvious—written on faces in furrowed lines etched at the corners of mouths and jaded eyes, and engraved across weary brows. And due to circumstances beyond my control, these are the very kinds of stories that show up everywhere I go—I have found them in grocery stores and on park benches, at airports and in restaurants—or, somehow, they have an uncanny way of finding me.

Buried in grimaces and somatic burdens that bend and bloat and debilitate, they dim the glow of enthusiasm under heavy layers that grow increasingly difficult for people to carry. And with a sixth sense for misfortune and the dedication of a first responder, I find that whenever one of these stories is about to surface—ready to spill from a heart that has finally broken open—I am seized by the fateful opportunity to lend a hand and lighten the load, and invited in by the bold, refreshing veracity that, frankly, I find irresistible.

For years, I've had an affinity, and odd relationship, with this covert world of quiet sorrow, where tears are harbored in overwrought cells and tender lymph nodes, sagging shoulders, and tired sighs. I can't seem to stop myself from spotting those who need a listening ear or word of encouragement, and have always felt a pull—like a noble mandate—obliging me to scout for pain that is stuck, begging to be released by the medicinal simplicity of a caring listener and no-frills, utter candor.

At times, I've wondered if I am depressed, or just naturally curious, or whether I have a twisted compulsion, like that of a germaphobe to sanitizers and excessive hand washing. But what I've come to believe is that this proclivity to pluck tragedies and survivors from the depths has been a personal pilgrimage, a search for my own truth and autonomy. It's been a way for me to heal, discover keys to transformation, and offer the curative gift of empathy that fuels a more compassionate world.

And what I realize now, as well, is that the lure of these living tales and the compelling desire to attend to them stem from my own wounds and messed-up childhood. Like the soulful connection of a cellist to a symphony or a botanist to a hybrid rose, our drives and natural inclinations—

whatever they may be—are the very way in which providence links the story of who we are and where we've been with our individual passions and personal calling.

It makes sense that I would become a psychotherapist, where pastime and profession meet in an office with quiet music, a sofa, and an invitation for storytellers to come and share their most heartbreaking secrets, struggles, and grief. With a breathless pause and eyes moistened by a sensitivity that lingers for just a moment before being wiped away, each disclosure flows directly from a rarely opened inner sanctum, in the intimate language of a private journal entry.

With childlike transparency, these unrefined narratives melt away all of the usual fluff of pretense and soften the ego-sharp competitive edges we normally erect to defend our sensitive spots and vulnerable insecurities. And what comes alive in straightforward, unadorned detail when masks and embellishments are removed is an incredible sight and a privilege to behold: the pure, dazzling *essence* of a lightened, unencumbered soul.

Though it can be embarrassing for any of us to open up, and confusing even to know where to start, here—behind the door—we simply go back to the beginning. What we recall about yesterday offers invaluable information about what might be happening today and helps us to make changes for a better tomorrow. And while we all have a tendency to unconsciously deny, distort, and even lose touch with troubling memories through the years, unless we are willing to revisit our history with curiosity and an open mind, we will likely repeat it in some disconnected, unintentional, and *crazy* way.

Facing the truth about our life isn't about blaming or being ungrateful; it's about accepting the reality of our experiences and clearing away obstacles that stand in the way of our freedom—starting with an honest assessment of what happened in our childhood home and what it felt like growing up there. Awareness is the first step to setting ourselves free from our baggage and emotional wounds, and it usually involves opening a few doors or sharing a secret or two.

What I remember about the place where I grew up— that place where my intrigue and compassion for sad stories began—is stored in my mind like a blurred black-and-white video with a strong, clear soundtrack. From shadowy shades of gray comes the loud, lurid audio that makes me want to cover my ears, as I am transported back inside the home of a conscientious little girl and a mother she wanted desperately to please . . .

1.2 | LOOKING BACK

How we remember, and what we remember, and why we remember form the most personal map of our individuality.
—CHRISTINA BALDWIN

Mommy is screaming again, and has been screaming for a long time. I don't like when she screams like this. Especially the curse words. I don't want the neighbors to hear them. I am afraid that they won't like what they hear. The words feel bad in my ears, and I think the neighbors will feel bad, too, if they hear her. And she is yelling just about as loudly as any person can ever yell. I've been to other kids' houses, and their mothers have nice voices. I don't think they yell. I'm not really sure what they do when they get mad, but I'm pretty sure they don't use curse words. I can tell.

Nobody ever comes to play inside my house, because my mother doesn't like messes. She gets really mad about messes, so mainly I play outside or in Beverly's basement. Sometimes I play with dolls in my bedroom, which I clean up right when I'm finished. "In or out!" my mother shouts whenever I open the door. She likes "out" the best and clicks the lock behind me when I leave. When I get back home, I wait until she opens the door and checks my shoes. Then I head to the sink, wash my hands, and go straight to my room.

This was one of those rainy, inside, doll days when I had to come back home. I am not exactly sure what I did wrong. I get in trouble a lot. She just shows up at my bedroom door with wild eyes and starts calling me names with lots of curses strung together in a row. I wish she didn't use the f-word or the c-word. And I don't like it when she uses God's name in vain. She usually puts God's name and "damn" together in front of everything when she's yelling.

I wish she wouldn't call me worthless and filthy and good for nothing and a pain in the ass all in one big, long sentence. It makes me want to cry or disappear. Sometimes I hide in my closet, hoping that she'll wonder where I am. But mostly I just get tired of waiting for her to come and find me. My dad says she can't really help herself and she doesn't really mean any of it. Still, I wish she wouldn't say any of those words ever again.

Once, when she was doing a really long yell, I tried to sneak out. But it didn't work. She got even madder and louder and chased me until she could grab my ponytail and pull me back inside. Then she screamed in my face for so long that she got bright red and sweaty. Spit came out of her mouth. Blue veins stuck out of her neck so far that I was afraid they would pop and she would die right then and there. I never, ever tried to escape again.

Usually when my mother starts screaming in my bedroom, her face gets all wrinkled up and she points at me. She says I did something that made her mad, really mad. . . . "YOU sit in this room until your father gets home. YOU better not make any noise or mess." She says all of it at the top of her voice, with curses in between the words. Sometimes she smacks at me, but it never really hurts that bad. "And YOU better not bother me." Then she goes down the hallway to the kitchen, ranting and cursing the whole way.

I listen as she opens the cupboard and gets a glass. That's when I make my move, like Bambi, darting into other rooms, dodging danger and silently lowering windows that are open. By the time my mother pours herself a drink, I have made it back to safety and she is on her way, getting closer for another round of yelling. After a while, she gets all shouted out, then reads the newspaper or takes a nap. Funny, she never seems to notice how the windows magically close themselves.

No one knows about my secret mission to keep those dirty words trapped in my house, away from the neighbors. But maybe, because of my good deed, they will never have to hear them for themselves. They will think we have been inside, playing jacks or sipping tea, with nice voices. My mother reminds me often, "Sticks and stones will break your bones, but names will never hurt you." For some strange reason, those mean words do hurt, and I feel sad. I want to cry when I hear them, but I don't. And I do not want anyone else to hear them, either.

My mother always tells me that I am just a big baby, a jackass, and too damn sensitive for my own good. She's probably right. But sometimes, even when I cover my ears, get under the covers, or hide in the closet, those words grab onto me like Scotch tape stuck on tight. Then I have to peel and scrub and tug the words away one by one, but they are never all gone. Usually, bits of glue hold on like shadows of the words and won't let go. They seem to cling to me, like dirt that won't wash off.

Someday, I will do my best deed. I will find a way to capture those words and lock them in a box forever. And maybe, if I'm really good, my mom won't say them anymore. Then they will never be loose to stick on skin, or float in air, or fly out of windows.

1.3 | A THERAPIST IS BORN

Home is where one starts from.
—T.S. ELIOT

Like all children, I wanted the world to be a better place and had young ideas about how to make it so. Simplistic and childishly egocentric, I mistakenly thought it was my responsibility to spare people from painful experiences. Growing up in a home where I was often dismayed, I became sensitive to the world of suffering, where I watched and resolved, with the young mind of a determined superhero, to liberate others trapped in the clutches of despair.

I may have been confused, or maybe I was hoping to exhume a solution to unlock my own autonomy, but, like many children, good codependents, and fellow therapists, I wanted to fix and save *other* people by helping them find the freedom that I longed to have myself. Through the years, I have been completely smitten with the ache mirrored in others, familiar to me and essential to the renovating process of transformation.

But what continues to draw me into this world of sad stories, even today, is the unadulterated *sincerity* that comes with the telling: the willingness and courage to pull back the conventional drapes that shroud our secrets and keep them, and us, hidden from the world. There is something about opening these darkened rooms, drawing in fresh air, and cleaning stagnant, murky spaces with the unfettered breeze of pure honesty that mitigates pain, sets us on a course of healing, and changes us from the inside out.

Without instructions or a map to chart our private journeys, stories become a vital source of information and a new way of life. They shine a light that can point us in the right direction or warn us to turn back and take a different path. They show us the world from angles and experiences beyond our own, taking us inside other children's homes and adult predicaments. They mentor and guide us through dark stretches and new paradigms. Told by everyday heroes, stories have the power to cheer us on with inspiration that propels us toward higher ground and grander views.

Each of us has a story that began years ago in the place we called home. It was there that we watched, listened, and learned. As social beings, we all need love and nurturing—a sustaining connection with our own kind—just to survive. Our character, and our entire orientation to life, develops within a human family, within the society in which we are raised.

Unlike other animals, nature did not equip us to live without the cooperation and support of others within our species. Human infants are completely defenseless and entirely dependent on the dedicated care and guidance of someone else—for *years*! As children, we had no way to provide for ourselves, no resources to raise ourselves alone. By design, we attached to our human guardians for our very existence, and much more.

Naively, we relied on those guardians to show us our worth, the ways of the world, and how best to live. We studied them. We asked questions, got answers, and, in the earliest of our relationships, assumed that what was being

taught—or caught—was the absolute truth. With little awareness, my decision to become a psychotherapist was made a
long time ago, by a young girl hungry to bring some good
out of a confusing reality. In an attempt to be set free from
damning words and memories, she and I formed an alliance
to search for fellow strugglers and unlock their stories.

Together, we would find keys to release us from the
debilitating patterns that began in childhood and followed,
with ruthless determination, into our adult lives. After
twenty years as a therapist, with hundreds of stories behind
the door, I know that what is said and done to us as children can cause internal damage that lingers and is not easily
repaired. But within an honest, empathic relationship, we
can unlock denial, clarify distortions, and be set loose to
enjoy the glorious freedom that is our birthright.

1.4 | A PLACE CALLED HOME

A home is not a mere transient shelter; its essence lies in
the personalities of the people who live in it.
—H.L. MENCKEN

While our stories technically start on the day of our arrival in the world, there is a backstory developing before we are ever conceived—one that gets woven into our fiber as mysteriously and intricately as strands of DNA. The slate that is supposed to be clean at the time of our birth is actually filled with an assortment of hopes and shattered dreams, family secrets and expectations.

Upon delivery, we entered smack dab into the *middle* of a story that would influence our growth and worldview yet likely never be mentioned or examined. Every family has its own background, traditions, and rules. As children, we didn't question our environment. We adapted. The ecosystem in which we developed may have been arid, lush, or nearly intolerable; regardless, its flora and fauna were the familiar territory we knew simply as home.

The landscape we saw around us every day was our reality; its climate, rules, and messages were the truths we accepted and got used to. Left unexamined, the conditions of our upbringing remain the familial facts that continue to inform us about what is true and how we should live. The greater the sense of restriction and lack of open communication within our family back then, the more resistance arises when we attempt to revisit and objectively evaluate it later, even after many years have passed.

There are certain directives found in these restrictive homes, imperatives that inhibited the individual growth of those who lived there. From rules that were never discussed came powerful, unwritten principles that governed the family system without question and that continue on in legacies through the ages, unless we intentionally bring them to light, inspect and amend them.

In these dysfunctional systems, childish mistakes and self-expression are equated with willful disobedience. There is a mistaken notion that children become spoiled or overly confident if they are allowed too much freedom. So, rather than using discipline to teach cooperation and contribution, parents focus on maintaining power and control, using punishment and humiliation to demean a child until he or she feels *bad,* and, eventually, becomes confused about what is true.

Years ago, parenting education and resources were not prevalent; parents simply repeated what *they* experienced, even if it was hurtful. It's no wonder that, without a new model or honest evaluation, unhealthy family practices live on in rules and messages inside grown children who continue passing them along. The imperatives from these old systems are about constraining who you are and are infused with a contaminating shame that impedes individual development and brings people to therapy for release.

1.5 | DYSFUNCTIONAL ORIGINS

Over and over, we have to go back to the beginning. We should
not be ashamed of this. It is good. It's like drinking water.

—NATALIE GOLDBERG

Many of us come from homes in which it was difficult for the family to function properly. A dysfunctional system is one that is unable to provide a healthy, safe environment in which a child can develop. Though no family is perfect, an impaired family system results when there is a parental deficit involving alcohol or drug use; mental or physical illness; or a self-absorbed immaturity that leads to physical or sexual abuse, emotional mayhem, dogmatic intolerance, abandonment, or neglect.

One thing all dysfunctional families have in common is an implicit set of rules that thwarts emotional growth and ultimately damages the self-worth of those who live by them. These unspoken decrees, infused with guilt and shame, discourage open, honest communication. Squelching feelings and needs is the hallmark of such impaired systems, in which appearances and denial become more important than being real, and maintaining control supersedes the expansion of its members.

In a dysfunctional home, talking about what goes on is taboo. Imperfection or vulnerability threatens to expose internal issues and secrets, and so, in time, the less-than-perfect true self hides itself away. When simple necessities are treated like reprehensible burdens to the system, and innocent mistakes or limitations are handled like willful defiance, the line between unacceptable behavior and *being unacceptable* becomes shamefully distorted.

From the guiding principles of childhood, we learn how to act, think, and feel. Unless we become aware of restrictive rules and messages that may have taken root years ago, they will usher us into adulthood and will continue informing us about how to behave and relate with others.

In 1986, Melody Beattie popularized the term codependency when her modern classic *Codependent No More* sold over eight million copies and educated the world about the concept. From her own experience and insights, she clarified how impaired systems undermine our sense of worth, contributing to codependency and other compulsive behaviors. She has written more than a dozen books, workbooks, and daily meditations, guiding millions to re-evaluate and let go of the need to focus on opinions and actions of other people for *our* self-esteem. In *Beyond Codependency,* Beattie identifies the rules and messages at the core of crazy, dysfunctional systems:

> People don't make these [dysfunctional] rules. Addictions, secrets, and other crazy systems make these rules to protect the addictions and secrets and keep the crazy systems in place. But people follow these rules. And people mindlessly pass them on from generation to generation. The rules are the guardians and protectors of the system—the crazy system.

TEN COMMON RULES OF A DYSFUNCTIONAL FAMILY

1. Don't feel or openly express feelings.
2. Don't think or make decisions on your own—you don't know what's best.
3. Don't be who you are—be good, strong, and perfect.
4. Don't take care of yourself—it's selfish.
5. Don't ever make someone else angry or hurt their feelings.
6. Don't have fun, be silly, or enjoy life—it is unnecessary.
7. Don't trust—yourself, God, people, or life.
8. Don't be direct, honest, or open—guess or let others talk for you.
9. Don't get close to people—it isn't safe.
10. Don't grow, change, or rock the boat—it will disrupt the system.

What comes from these dysfunctional rules and crazy systems are messages that get deposited and carried inside our heads. Though they were never spoken aloud, and though they were originally formulated within the mind of a receptive child, their destructive dogma continues coloring the way we live and feel *today* with commanding words that are difficult to silence.

COMMON DESTRUCTIVE MESSAGES

* It's not okay for me to feel.

* It's not okay for me to have needs or problems.

* It's not okay for me to have fun or be spontaneous.

* I'm not lovable.

* I'm not good enough.

* I don't deserve good things.

* I'll never succeed.

* If people feel bad or disappointed or act crazy, it's my fault.

The imperatives from our early years are carried in our thoughts and beliefs, out of awareness. Though we do not *hear* the messages in actual words, we accept them with the same mesmerizing authority of hypnotic suggestions that enlist agreement and drive our behavior. An honest look at the system of personalities and convictions in which we were planted is where psycho-clarity and healing start—at the *beginning* of our stories.

1.6 | FAYE'S STORY

> *It's the awareness . . . of how you are stuck*
> *that makes you recover.*
>
> —FRITZ PERLS

Faye has come to see me because she is suffering from anxiety and depression. She has no appetite, inconclusive test results, and a stomach that has been rebelling since childhood. Though she has been to several doctors and is taking antidepressants, she is getting little relief.

Tall and lanky, with magnificent, wavy auburn hair, Faye is wearing a black tailored suit, impressive gold jewelry, and a dusting of freckles across the bridge of her nose, remnants from the little girl she once was. On the outside, she looks impeccable, like the successful attorney she is hoping to become.

She positions herself gracefully at the arm of the couch, closest to the end table and box of tissues. And then, after the usual pleasantries and protocols, she welcomes me into the desolate place where rejected and motherless children live.

"Some days are so bad that I can't get out of bed," she tells me. With a heavy sigh and sense of urgency, Faye traces her symptoms back to a time when they sprang to life and took hold. "I don't really remember the actual day my mother left," she continues. But what she does recall is dark and obscure: the sense of having been a nuisance, alone and unwanted, and loud, unsettling threats about leaving. And how, one day, it really happened. Her mother bought a bus ticket to somewhere out there and disappeared.

Today, thirty-two years later, Faye still has no idea of her mother's whereabouts. "My dad and I never saw or heard from her ever again." In a flash, this eloquent law student becomes two years old, as years of abandonment trickle over those steadfast freckles. The memories and emotions of a frightened toddler lie just beneath the skin of this beautiful young woman, making their way back to the surface.

Her teenage dad was more interested in partying than in caring for a two-year-old in need of a mother, and no one else in the family wanted to be bothered, so Family Services found her a home with a foster family. Papers were signed, and when Faye was just three years old, she was sent out into the world, like Mom, to find a new life away from all that was familiar.

Faye has no recollection of the move, but what she does remember is the yelling, sleeping on couches in cheap motels, and sobbing deep into her pillow at night. She remembers put-downs and punishments, and the ache in her belly when she determined that she was a nuisance, alone, and unlovable. She remembers the repulsive sexual advances, the molestations, and a desperate urge to get away.

Sitting in the room as she describes her abuse, I feel my stomach twist and turn, and I want to get away, too. Somehow, I am here to catch her pain and offer hope, but now I am feeling anxious and sad. What I really want to do as I watch her sob is to cry along, to tell her that life sucks, that she got a raw deal. I want to let her know that she deserved so much more.

Welling up, as I frequently do in the face of tragedy, I am triggered by grief, overly focused on her sorrow. I feel depressed and angry. Inadequate. I want to scream in protest, fix all the world's injustices. As that empathic lump for helpless children and our grown-up selves grows in my throat, I pause long enough to pull myself together, silently pray, and remember why I am here. And then I quietly surrender.

I have lost myself in another story—in the unfairness of it all, and in the familiar depths of despair trapped inside another casualty. It is beyond me to cure Faye or to take away her anguish. But what I can do, as a still inner voice gently reminds me, is to be a believer in the human capacity to be restored and transformed, to rely on the source of healing to provide hope that transcends understanding. So, with a cleansing breath and renewed assurance, I return once more to the present, to trust the process of renovation, to be available, and to listen.

When Faye turned eighteen, she disappeared from her foster family and never looked back. Like her mother, she created a new life for herself and eliminated her history. By nineteen, she was planning an expensive wedding and dream life with her Prince Charming, Alex, a life that would crumble amid doubts, familiar reprimands, and feelings of not being loved enough, or at all.

With unstable adults as her teachers, she confesses, "It was hard to know about love," and so, eventually, she found her way out of the confusion. She packed up a few belongings, bought a bus ticket, and left her husband, exactly as her mother had taught her to do years earlier. "I didn't even leave a note."

Like Faye, we all tend to reconstruct some version of what was demonstrated for us. Stories told in therapy are sometimes uncanny replays of something witnessed in childhood. It doesn't always make common sense, but, strangely, it can make perfect sense to *us*. As if there is a program running in our heads, we reenact what we saw and experienced, a model that we emulate in our relationships.

Sometimes we repeat, and sometimes we avoid or even do the complete opposite of what we observed as children. But on some level, we react to our earliest archetypes in behaviors that get played out in our most intimate connections. We do it because it is our reality through and through, because it's what we have lived and learned, and what we know how to do for sure.

If home doesn't make sense, nothing does.

—HENRIETTA RIPPERGER

Many of us, like Faye, did not have a positive role model growing up. I knew I didn't want to act like the one I had, so I studied other people, imitating their personas and trying to fill my head with new messages, but I couldn't rid myself of my mother's words. I had a difficult time keeping them out of my mind and off my skin. For years, I was irritated by the cling of their old sticky adhesive, reminding me that no matter what I did, deep down I was a disappointment, a "bad girl," and a "jackass."

I couldn't seem to shut down the program that evaluated my worth by scanning the reactions of those I strove to please. I didn't want to be so tuned in, so dependent, but maybe it was true—maybe I *was* just "too damned sensitive." Through the years, I told myself that my mother was just being harsh in her assessment, or that maybe other people were just too damned callous. But lately, with her words still ringing in my ears, I have been rethinking all of this.

We all need boundaries to shield our innocence and protect sacred spaces, but, like many raised in abusive environments, I am not sure I ever had the opportunity to erect them. As a child, I wasn't allowed to say no, was never encouraged to have an opinion. It didn't matter what

I felt or wanted. I wasn't permitted to close a door or help myself to food when I was hungry. Messes were out of the question. I was a nuisance, plain and simple—a lot of work —and I was reminded of that fact regularly. And I bruised easily.

As if my skin lacked protective padding or had been peeled away altogether, I walked around feeling raw, vulnerable to every breeze or salty tear. My mother may have known something that I did not (bullies do seem to have a sixth sense for defenseless victims and the tenderhearted); it is dangerous to be overly sensitive, porous, in a world in which equity gets exploited by those who prefer to dominate and turn relationships into self-serving hierarchies. Perhaps she was just trying to toughen me up.

As a child, I tried my hardest to have no needs, no desires, no voice. And though I felt bumped and prodded, beaten up by statements and sorrows that I didn't know how to erase or avoid, I was called a "selfish brat" if I tried to speak up, protect myself, or have any self at all. There was no point in dodging bullets, trying to escape, or attempting to defend myself. The only armor I may have had was stripped away early on, and, like a prisoner of war, I became an expert at complying, tolerating attacks, and enduring their sting.

I grew to be a talented perfectionist, demonstrating my value with impressive accomplishments. I finished college with honors, became a dedicated wife and schoolteacher— but tacky remnants from childhood had bonded onto me like cumbersome cement, weighing me down with a dread I couldn't shake. Without warning, the past would spill into the present, and I would be reminded in a flash that I was "worthless," "good for nothing," and "a waste of time." No matter how hard I tried, fear of failure loomed around every corner along with a lurking anxiety that the terrible truth would be exposed.

I often felt like a child in grown-up clothes, acting the role of a successful, confident adult. As though I were an actress in a play, I created a woman on the outside but could not figure out how to grow myself up on the inside. Commanding voices joined with the disapproving voice of my mother in a chorus of disparaging words that often intimidated me and turned me into an obliging five-year-old scrambling to find a solution or make someone happy. Though no longer confined to my room, I struggled to be free from the mind and memories of the little girl I held inside.

Any hint of criticism or anger suggested that condemning eyes were scrutinizing my every move. So I kept a cautious lookout for signs of contempt, with a tender ego that found opportunities to compare and lift me to a flawless place of merit. Conflict scared me, so I eagerly set about making things right, often adding insult to injury as I scrubbed away simple mistakes, defended my intentions, or picked at misunderstandings that needed time to heal on their own.

Funny, but the words of my mother never ceased to astound me. Her criticism entered without a buffer, and I seemed unable to completely discount or deflect her hurtful remarks. Strange as it seems, I never got used to their sting. As an adult, I eventually realized that the attacks weren't about *me*, that my mother was unstable. But when I was a child, it felt more like *I* was unlovable or unable to ever get it right. And even as a grown-up, whenever I suffered from a crisis of confidence or faced a new challenge, I could, in a moment, become the self-conscious child I had carried with me into adulthood.

Of course, I had no way of knowing at the time that I, like many who come to therapy, was dealing with a bona fide *crazymaker*, someone impossible to please who was detrimental to healthy development. So, no matter how hard I tried, I had little influence over an authority with weapons used regularly to drain, bludgeon, or manipulate anyone who got a little too close.

And little did I know that my personal healing from the bruises of a dysfunctional crazymaker would take a lifetime of research, a degree in psychology, and hundreds of courageous people—mentors, clients, friends, and colleagues —willing to share their transformational journeys with me.

1.8 | THE CRAZYMAKERS

Crazymakers are emotional manipulators. They come in various packages, but the bottom line is, they demand their own way and use every opportunity to get it. They insist on running the show, and, like it or not, you don't get a vote. Emotional manipulation can be distastefully aggressive or sweetly wrapped in a coating of sugar and tears. Some crazymakers victimize with power and punishment, while others use the victim stance and guilt, acting helpless and needy to get exactly what they want. Emotional manipulators will use and abuse with little concern for how their self-absorption impacts others.

Unbalanced adults, crazymakers manipulate and hurt others through their choices and actions. They are insecure, usually wounded children themselves. They push their agenda and invade boundaries, even when those boundaries are meant to protect the fragile outer edge of a tiny, developing child. Everyone is a potential target to a crazymaker. They are somehow entitled, and you are there to fulfill their wishes and be in their service. No one is immune.

The wants and demands of a crazymaker always come first. They are voraciously needy and will engulf, use, or abandon anyone to get their way. They are attempting to save themselves with compulsions linked to words that describe irrational, hurtful behaviors guaranteed to leave casualties—terms like alcoholism, drug addiction, narcissism, mental illness, and abuse. Though clients come to therapy for a variety of reasons, I have found that the majority of my clients have been significantly impacted by the actions and energies of a crazymaker: a parent, relative, sibling, partner, or close friend of the family.

Living with a manipulative crazymaker and their destructive fallout is beyond confusing, especially to a child. At times they may be loving and kind, even playful. At other times, however, they are exceedingly egocentric and *crazy*, exhibiting thought disorders and troubling behaviors. They are the ringleaders of dysfunctional family systems, and—intentionally or not—crazymakers inflict damage on the children who are in their care. Sadly, the injuries suffered in childhood do not necessarily heal and go away.

Internalized messages from crazymakers get under our skin and stubbornly follow us into adulthood. Unless we are willing to examine and remove the splinters left behind from their acerbic sticks and stones, we are prone to bouts of psychic infection, accepting abuse from others or from our own distorted minds. *Wounds inflicted on crazymakers' children require treatment.* Mine certainly did.

Obviously, damaging words and hurtful behaviors cannot simply be locked in a box or wished away by a hopeful child. The stories that they write can be covered up and may even seem forgotten for a time, but—like shameful secrets or dirty fragments trapped beneath a healthy surface —painful memories often fester for years, contaminating the minds and bodies of those who have sealed them inside.

While "crazymaker" is not a clinical diagnosis, being in

connection with one is sure to create anxiety or other neuroses. Dealing with a crazymaker demands a symbiotic obsession with another person, a loss of self, and a process of growing steadily accustomed to guilt, chaos, abuse, or hostility. Scanning for signs of emotional upset and walking on eggshells become customary in homes where a crazymaker resides. Frequent mood changes and explosive outbursts provide a tumultuous, unpredictable roller coaster of drama and adrenaline—a wild ride that begins to feel "normal" and even strangely exhilarating.

Beneath the skin of a crazymaker are anguish and a lack of inner strength. Due to their chronic feelings of emptiness, fear of abandonment, and impulsivity, they create unstable, intense relationships in which control is the core issue. According to Julia Cameron, the iconic queen of creativity and author of *The Artist's Way*, crazymakers are especially destructive to anyone attempting to cultivate a sense of identity and their own creative gifts.

Plain and simple, being the child, sibling, or partner of a crazymaker stifles individual development and self-worth. Crazymakers insist on being the center of attention, controlling and influencing others with little regard for anyone else's opinion or well-being. In power plays that exploit and create confusion, they engage in behaviors that get them exactly what they want.

According to Cameron, "Crazymakers like drama. If they can swing it, they are the star. Everyone around them functions as supporting cast, picking up their cues, their entrances and exits . . ." With the precision of a journalist, and artistry of a playwright, Cameron details how crazymakers:

* break deals and destroy schedules
* expect special treatment
* discount your reality
* spend your time and money
* triangulate those they deal with
* are expert blamers
* create dramas—but seldom where they belong
* hate schedules—except their own
* hate order and thrive in chaos
* deny that they are crazymakers

Not only is life with a crazymaker sure to inhibit creative development, it also impacts our ability to value and protect ourselves. We spend our time striving to please —looking for ways to be helpful, to feel significant and earn approval. We learn to seek our worth from others who usurp our vitality or invade our boundaries, but we don't mind; we don't even seem to notice. Destructive relationships that are sacrificial feel acceptable to us because the alarm system meant to safeguard us, to divert us from exploitation, has been damaged and is in need of repair.

In order to build healthy relationships in which we respect others, and ourselves, we need to take a look at the crazymaking behaviors and dysfunctional systems that required us to disconnect from our internal sensors in the first place. Then we can reassess, plug back in to the Source of guidance and inner wisdom, and find ways to treasure our time and growth. And no, this does not mean that we will become the self-absorbed, demanding crazymaker we know all too well.

1.9 | BREAKING FREE

The secret of happiness is freedom,
and the secret of freedom is courage.
—GILBERT MURRAY

Those of us who grew up in crazy, dysfunctional homes learned to be curious spectators, voyeurs constantly trying to figure out what normal is supposed to look like. Confused, we found ways to hide behind a regular life, all the while keeping a watchful eye for subtle and blatant deviations from the norm. Crazy's survivors observe how other people live in an effort to break from the stranglehold attaching them to the psychic energies of a crazymaker and the damaged, crazy perceptions of ourselves we come to accept as a result of that attachment.

Here in the office, though strangers when we meet, we are clumped together, connected by the courage to share our experiences and pain. We have all witnessed the confounding influence of crazy and its ability to ostracize prisoners to a life of exile, bound by secrets and self-doubt. We have seen how crazy demonizes and shames its victims and keeps them in solitary confinement. But as we break our silence here and tell our stories, the door to crazy is unlocked, and those of us who have been stuck in its aftermath gain liberation from its grip.

For years, I longed to know why people viciously wound one another with judgments, a look, or blunt instruments, and why the sticks and stones of the unstable hold such power and venom years later. To this day, I have not been completely able to delete certain expletives from my heart, nor have I managed to gather all of them into a box for safekeeping.

Though I have tried to dispose of hurtful messages, they still find a way to sneak back into my head if I let them. At any time, they can threaten to become my reality or simply serve to remind me of my beginnings and the arduous journey from self-condemnation to freedom. Since childhood, I have wanted to understand why people have such power to damage those who love them, and how we heal and transform ourselves once they do.

What better place for this human research to occur than in the safety of a therapy office, where authentic bits of regular life are unearthed and examined with sworn secrecy? Like an archeologist, I am granted the opportunity to dig and excavate valuable pieces from history, to evaluate the past and its connection with this juncture in time.

And as a therapist, a professional who studies relationships, I have the privilege of witnessing just how powerfully we, as social beings, are impacted by the intricate details and perplexing behaviors of those who have come before us, those whose lives—their cultures, values, thoughts, and beliefs—have shaped and impacted our own.

Apparently, I have always been curious about that space inside where truth resides, where words are not manufactured to manipulate, blame, or impress others. Where what is spoken comes from a sacred place in which honesty, wonder, and imperfection boldly trump our insecurities, and where we are free to search for what is true without fear, shame, or condemnation.

There is no plot more real, no story told with more integrity, than those that unfold in therapy, where valuable clues are pieced together. Attention is paid to missed and twisted turns, hazy recollections, and troublesome behaviors. Insights gathered in this secret place are rarely communicated beyond the four walls of the office, yet treasures are packed in each travelogue of the explorers who have come, willing to share what they have experienced and discovered on their journeys. Within our weathered exteriors are gifts that only our deepest fractures expose. Amid gritty tribulations and darkened memories are blessings to enlighten us, pearls of wisdom awaiting the courage of an internal glance, a soulful dig, and the illuminating light of awareness. As with an oyster or a geode, it is only by opening our defensive shells that we will find a private cache of spiritual riches.

As humans, we are not alone in our wanderings. We are each, story by story, offered gems, grace, and serenity to direct us toward a more compassionate and abundant way of living. Like the surprise of sun-drenched daffodils appearing from winter's rock-hard, barren ground, triumphs emerge, in their season, from the seeds and tears of tragedies buried long ago. As we share our lives and priceless discoveries, we gain clarity to right and revise our stories, and to create the happy endings that are waiting to be written.

1.10 | HEALING THE PAIN

Too often we underestimate the power of a touch, a smile,
a kind word, a listening ear . . . or the smallest act of caring,
all of which have the potential to turn a life around.
—LEO BUSCAGLIA

People wound people with their words and deeds, and people bring healing. We learn by example in childhood and carry on what we saw and accepted during our earliest, formative years. But so much of what we learned about ourselves as children was gleaned without conscious awareness, with the simple logic of a young, inexperienced mind.

Unless we are willing to open childhood boxes and examine their contents, we are likely to perpetuate our childish beliefs. Self-examination and insight are necessary to fully understand our histories in a way that brings health to us and to others. Ironically, both the emotional injuries we sustained in our attempts to grow up and the *healing* of those old, painful lesions happen in relationship to one another.

Healing happens in relationship!

From my office come the brave stories of those who have shared their lives with me. Connected by fate and a struggle to set ourselves free, we unite here in endearing kinships that begin with a phone call. Grown children come to recount secrets and sadnesses, long hidden away. Psychic infection oozes within the safety of a quiet, sunlit room equipped for personal journeys through anxiety, depression, compulsive behaviors, phobias, and addictions.

Irritating remnants are sloughed off, debrided layer by layer, and cleansed in a salve of empathy. With encouragement, inflamed traces of shame, night terrors, and self-doubt get left behind, bit by bit, in a quest for relief and understanding. Eventually released from the constraints of old, debilitating residue, freedom grows and finds its way to the surface with a vitality that generates healthy new skin.

The names of those whose lives have touched my own in this place are protected by confidentiality. But, with permission or alterations to safeguard identities, I share these accounts to remind us that the actions of a single person can significantly affect the life of another. We all play a part in the messages, chapters, and lives of those around us. We depend on one another to become our best, most enlightened selves as we invest in the days and pages that fill our interwoven biographies.

Each of us has the ability to make the world a more loving and compassionate place, and we start by taking responsibility to tend our own story, seeking truth that restores, transforms, and sets us free. As a young girl who absorbed and tucked sorrow away in a box, and as a therapist who is opening the lid, I release the words and narratives that have shaped who I am and am choosing to become.

As caretakers in an interdependent world, we have the potential to inspire and help ourselves and others grow, as well as the capability to clip developing wings, putting ourselves or others in bondage with thoughtless words or acts of cruelty. We all hold tremendous power. By sharing our stories, and the stories within them, we help one another recognize a greater wisdom to value ourselves, right our lives, and find the glorious freedom we all seek.

1.11 | SITTING IN THE CHAIR

Where we are wounded, we are gifted.

—CARL JUNG

It is no secret that a therapist's chair is commonly occupied by a wounded child, and mine is certainly no exception. While the woman sitting here today is grateful for redemption, it has taken a while to get to this place. Being a wounded healer means that I, too, have had to gain clarity about my own mistaken notions and have struggled to find self-acceptance and freedom. And, like most transformational stories, mine includes awakening and validating the impressionable child inside who still remembers . . .

Climbing three cement steps to the landing, I breathlessly open the screen door and knock. "Mommy, it's me," I shout in my loudest voice. But no answer. I ran the whole way home from kindergarten, speeding ahead of other kids to make it to the bathroom. I've waited all day because I need help; I couldn't get out of my new overalls and was too uncomfortable to tell my teacher about my predicament.

By now I am dancing about, pounding on the locked door, and yanking on the puzzling hooks that have imprisoned me inside the denim jumpsuit I was so eager to wear to school, but they still refuse to budge. So I restlessly wait for my mother to answer as I continue knocking and yanking on the brass clasps, hoping that the contraptions holding me in their clutches will spring open and grant my release, and that I will make it upstairs to the toilet in the nick of time.

For a five-year-old, this is quite a dilemma; no one seems to be home, and I don't know what to do. I can taste the salt in my throat as tears begin to topple, despite my best effort to hold them at bay. I have run out of options, and panic is setting in, when the next door of the redbrick row house flies open, and there stand my neighbor Mrs. Lincoln and my mother. "What are you crying about?" my mother snaps in an annoyed tone, as she and Mrs. Lincoln watch me dance a purposeful jig on the front porch we share.

"I can't get my strap . . ." I begin, and my mother and Mrs. Lincoln burst into a duet of laughter. They howl as they watch me jiggling about, and with precious moments ticking away and a last-ditch effort at self-control, I feel a burning flush of embarrassment as I wet my pants. Right there on the stoop, a heated trickle makes its way down each leg, warming my jeans and my socks, and finally saturating my sneakers. Right in front of all the kids passing by, there I am, soaking wet, with a humiliating yellow puddle widening around my feet.

Now, plenty of kids wet their pants, and it's not the end of the world to be laughed at. Compared with being maimed or tortured, it's really nothing. And rarely does one random incident shape how we eventually end up feeling about ourselves. Rather, it is from an accumulation of happenings in our young lives that we develop our self-esteem. As children, it is our collection of deductions that forms the private logic and beliefs that we ultimately accept as true.

On the front porch, my pants soggy, I feel embarrassed and exposed, as I often do—feelings that are accompanied by a familiar sense of inadequacy and shame. It seems that I am not able to care for myself or ever get it quite right, and I feel unprotected in a hostile world in which I am apt to be punished or belittled. I remember feeling these things as a toddler when my mother would abruptly betray me, pinching my cheeks until my lips quivered and I eventually cried, more in shock than in pain. And then she would cackle with delight, as though my tears were a kind of sadistic entertainment for her.

I remember spilling my milk, being slapped, and feeling those feelings as I was pushed away from the table with curses and mutterings about how much work I was, and how my mother wanted me out of her sight. I remember a continuous sense of dread, a fear of making a mistake and contributing to my mother's misery. And I never knew if or when or how I might cause trouble, so I tried my best to be ever so careful.

Once, while I was selling Girl Scout cookies, a giant dog chased me for what seemed like a mile. At one point in this race for my life, I fell, skinned my knee, and dropped some of the money I had collected. Eventually, the dog heeded a whistle and ran for home, and I caught my breath. But by then it had grown too dark to retrace my steps, so I gathered what I could and left the rest behind.

As much as I had been terrified of that dog, I was equally terrified about going home. My mother would be furious with me; I had bloodied my knee, torn my tights, and lost some of the money that had to be turned in at the Brownie meeting the next day. I slunk in the unlocked door, tiptoed to my room, and quietly dumped everything on the bed. Frantically I calculated, as well as an eight-year-old Scout can, how many boxes I'd sold, how much money I should have collected, and what was missing.

With a pounding heart and the desperation of an embezzler, I broke into my piggy bank to manipulate accounts and cover my error in quarters, dimes, and nickels. I felt horrible, ashamed, and deceitful, like I was committing an illicit act of fraud. Bad. I always seemed to feel bad, no matter how things turned out. It was the default setting I had grown accustomed to.

For whatever reason, on this particular day, my mother came to my room and casually wanted to know what I was doing. The money had been replaced and the ripped tights were hidden in the bottom of the trash can. Vulnerability, in my house, was dangerous; it usually ended up with my crying and being hit or laughed at by a mother who didn't have much of a protective nature.

I certainly didn't feel free to be myself, to goof up or learn from childish mistakes. My feelings were inconsequential, or, actually, more like fodder for ridicule. Mostly, I felt bad. Just plain bad. "So, let's count the money," my mother said. And I wanted to tell her everything: how I got chased, fell, tore my tights . . . and lost the money. I wanted to cry, to tell her I was scared and sorry.

"What happened to your knee?" she asked, and with hesitation and heat rising up, like a panicked criminal facing interrogation, I answered cautiously, "I got chased by a dog." And then she said something I never expected: "Oh, that must have been scary. Let's go clean up your knee." I couldn't believe it! No cursing. No yelling. No anger. Just kindness.

It had all worked out somehow, or so it seemed, and I was relieved. I was getting in my pajamas and had nearly made it into bed, when she decided she wanted to check the cookie orders and count the money. I could barely contain myself. I felt physically ill. I wanted to confess, to feel safe enough to tell her what I'd done, but I just wasn't sure about what would happen. So I kept it to myself.

She looked at the order, counted and recounted, and then announced, "Something's not right." Oh no. I must have added wrong. *"There's too much money here," she said, and I knew the jig was up. I'd goofed, and I was in big trouble. So, with trepidation, I broke down, came clean . . . and braced for the anger. But, funny thing, my mother didn't even seem to be upset. She smiled and said that I had tried my best and "shouldn't worry about it."*

That night, I went to bed feeling ecstatic, like a weight had been lifted, like the whole world was good and everything was just fine. My mother had shown mercy, hadn't gotten mad or anything. Maybe she'd felt sorry for me because she was petrified of animals, or maybe she was going to be nice from now on. I was confused by this turn of events, which left me feeling understood and protected. I am sure I was smiling as I fell asleep, relinquished from all guilt and shame. It is still a cherished memory, one of the few in which I was granted a brief reprieve from feeling like an unacceptable, bad little girl.

Today, though that child is a valued part of me, the truth about me has expanded. I have worked to change the internal dialogue in my head and am no longer routinely burdened by feelings of disgrace, but I still come face-to-face with plenty of toxic shame in the stories I hear. As a therapist, I understand and relate to those who come seeking release from the dreadful strongholds that years of condemnation have rigorously erected.

From this seat, I listen intently to heartbreaking narratives and depressing secrets. And, sometimes, as I lean in to extend the hand of empathy, a collective ocean of tears rises up in a groundswell so powerful and triggering that it drags me under and nearly sucks the life right out of me.

But, after years of quiet and debilitating sorrow, I am learning to get out of the turbulence from time to time, to play and relax on the shore amid rays of splendor sent to warm and resuscitate weary, drowning spirits.

My obsession with grief has taken me to dark and sinister places, and I have needed balance from the deluge. And so, after an assortment of chairs, decades, and sad stories, I am being renewed by beauty and tranquility, finally taking time to notice and bask in the overlooked pleasures and goodness that provide repose and have been here all along, patiently awaiting my arrival.

The search for freedom has taken me from childhood through many seasons, floods, and sordid tales, and finally to a place of grace where unquenchable desires are at last satiated, where contributing to the emotional well-being of yesterday's children, today's grown-ups, and my own life and private logic has been an adventure to satisfy my deepest yearnings. My story and your story are our gifts to one another, reminders that we each have a destiny to fulfill and a quest to find contentment, regardless of our anguish or beginnings.

Our narratives help us find the way out of stifling boxes built of our own construction. Through challenges and victories, joys and sorrows, we enlighten one another about what it means to be more fully and respectfully human. It is in the sharing of our experiences that we offer hope and direction to each other, opening doors to a better life for ourselves and for those whose lives our own will forever touch.

* We are social beings, shaped by our upbringing and relational experiences.

* Wounds from childhood are carried into adulthood; they do not simply go away.

* Dysfunctional rules and crazymakers cause damage that keeps us stuck and needs treatment.

* Telling our stories is how we begin to overcome early misconceptions, heal emotional injuries, and gain psycho-clarity.

* Therapy is not about casting blame. It is about our mistaken ideas, toxic shame, and personal journeys to freedom.

1.12 | YOUR STORY

It's your turn to tell your story. Imagine you're the client.
Get comfortable. Breathe deeply. Use the following prompts to make
discoveries and gain clarity on your way to personal freedom.
Use a journal to capture any thoughts, feelings, or images that come
to mind or talk into a recorder. Welcome to your session ...

What are *your* beginnings?

What do you know about your birth and early years?

What was it like inside *your* house?

Were you cared for? Did you feel protected? Loved?

How would you describe the atmosphere there?

Was it warm? Cold? Dark and gloomy?

Were there sunny days? Scattered showers?

Dark clouds? Changing seasons?

Did you experience the frequent storms of:

Addiction? Rage? Abandonment? Mental illness? Abuse?
Neglect?

How were you disciplined as a child?

Which dysfunctional family rules or messages remind you
most of home?

How so? How have they impacted your life?

Were you affected by a crazymaker? Who?

How did his or her behavior influence or inhibit your
growth?

TWO

Welcome to Therapy

2.1 | SEEKING HELP

The only way for us to help ourselves is to help others and
to listen to each other's stories.

—ELIE WIESEL

All of us get mixed up from time to time. We lose our way, get confused or sidetracked, become fearful and discouraged. We doubt our abilities when challenges overwhelm us, leaving us feeling off-balance, anxious, or depressed, and suspect that *something* is wrong. But when we can't seem to regain our footing, when we isolate or feel ashamed of who we have become or what we are doing, we wonder if this something is within the range of normal and hope that it isn't an indication that we have somehow stepped into the realm of *crazy*.

But what *is* crazy, exactly, and when it comes to mental illness, who decides? To those who watch the news, travel on airplanes, or interact in a world full of strangers, sanity has become an important issue. Crazy, irrational behaviors certainly have gained the attention of all of us who share the planet, and are of special interest to those of us who study psychology and those who come to see me here, behind the door.

If we are having panic attacks or bouts of depression or are drugging ourselves for relief that does not come, it is often a worried relative, friend, or voice of inner wisdom that emphatically says, "*You need help*." We despise these words, as though they indicate failure, as though life is a giant test and we are cheating if we ask for guidance or clarification along the way. And the thought of having a "mental illness" is so distasteful and unsettling that most people will suffer a long time before they ever call for an appointment, or will never call at all.

But until we are willing to wave the white flag of surrender and admit that we are struggling or missing a few pieces in a confounding puzzle, we are unlikely to free ourselves from ruminating, losing sleep, or repeating destructive behaviors in an endless loop of our own spinning. Few people ever reach out for help, though one in four of us will suffer from a mental illness at some point in our stress-filled days. And, simply put, crazy people do not show up for therapy.

Interestingly, only the strong ever make the call. Seeking help is awkward and embarrassing—it takes humility, a lot of effort, and usually a referral from "someone who knows someone else who *got help*." And it carries a dreaded stigma: *Crazy* people go to therapy. But it is *not* the crazy ones who seek freedom from their distress.

Crazy people do not show up for therapy.

Truly crazy people do not believe they are crazy; they believe that something is wrong with the *rest* of the world. It is not "crazies" who show up for therapy. Those who call and schedule an appointment are stuck—their compass is off, and they are willing to admit it. They want to get to a healthier place in life but simply do not know how to get there. And with a few tools and a change in perspective, they will be on their way.

No change yields no change.

If we could figure out how to make our lives better, we

would. Most mental illness is simply a *thought* disorder. Something in our *thinking* is standing in the way, but we do not know what it is. It takes a humble spirit to admit that something is just not working. Confessing that we do not have it all together is an assault to the ego, which is set in place to shield us from any trace of shame or failure and to help us appear as though we *do* have it all together.

Only the most courageous seek therapy.

Only those ready and willing to peel away pride and pretense in order to consider new ways of thinking and being will ever show up here. Rather than a place that cures illness, the therapy room is a place of exploration where hearts and minds are unbound to discover perspectives and practices that bring healing and health—physically, spiritually, and mentally.

A psychotherapist is someone who helps people get unstuck. My job is not to be a "shrink" as therapists are sometimes called, but to be an *expander*, someone who enlarges the realm of possibilities with insights that open awareness and lead to truths that set us free.

2.2 | REACHING OUT

*The way to figure out how to get back on course is through
the exploration process—reaching out through self-help books,
workshops, friends, support groups, therapy . . . As long as
you are open to reaching out, help will be there.*

—SUSAN JEFFERS, PHD
AUTHOR OF *FEEL THE FEAR AND DO IT ANYWAY*

Even after all these years, my anxiety looms when I
hear the voice of a complete stranger who is reaching out. Something is wrong, and you are calling *me*. I
battle fears and lack of confidence by reminding myself that
you are nervous, too, and that it has taken an act of courage
to call my number and leave a message. I hear it in your
voice. You sound vulnerable, childlike, as you tell me your
name and information. Sometimes you cry or have a hard
time getting the words out.

None of this was ever part of your plan. I am aware of a
sense of injustice here, an underlying protest in every inquiry made in secret, often without the knowledge of
friends, coworkers, or even your spouse. Your life has been
disrupted, overwhelmed by a disorienting gloom. It is not
fair. You may be devastated, outraged, or embarrassed, but
you are hoping that I have something to offer, maybe the
right words or advice.

Though I feel inadequate, I have a deep reverence for
this juncture in time and the power of a healing partner-

ship. I know that my return phone call affords me just a few minutes to communicate that there is a way out of this debilitating fog. I want my words to be convincing, fully aware that as I offer hope and understanding, I am also selling my wares.

It is difficult for any of us to reach out and admit to being stuck. This is a most important first step, and I want to reward the valiant effort it takes by letting you know that you are brave. Though rarely embarked upon with the enthusiasm surrounding a cruise, a trip has already begun with this phone call, one that can turn out to be a fascinating, eye-opening experience.

You'll want to feel better right away and will need time and attention, but you really won't want to pay for something akin to renting a friend. The greater the wound, the more likely you are to want my services and sympathies for free. But there is a cost for this journey, and it is not one that most people want to pay. If I agree to guide our expedition, we will become a team, you and I, impacting each other in ways we cannot yet anticipate. And it will take time, dedication, and a fee.

What you may not know is that this can be a life-changing passage—an opportunity to discover deeply buried treasure. This moment in time is not simply about injustice or bad luck. Somehow, *today*, I must use this single phone call to encourage you to buy a ticket and get onboard; there is an adventure to be had.

You are at this junction because of a story that needs tending. Others have involved you, mistreated you, and abandoned you. You are likely in this predicament because of someone *else*, but you are required to pay with *your* time and money. It often adds insult to injury, seems unfair. But all of our stories involve other people, and we need to edit and revise them in a way that gets us back on track toward long-lost joy.

I dial your number and hear a receptive voice. You tell me how you got my name from another sojourner, and we exchange pleasantries. Then I listen. I hear the tears, the betrayal, even intimate secrets that friends haven't heard. I don't want to lose you to your embarrassment, fear, or unwillingness to see a benefit worth paying for, but I have no tangible product to sell, no quick fix or painkillers to prescribe. So I choose my words carefully, knowing that this is a delicate encounter. A door has opened briefly, and you have invited me inside.

With the urgency of a salesperson, in a role that makes me uncomfortable, I communicate that there is hope. Strangely, unexpected gifts and enlightenment come from walking through pain. Somehow, as I listen, I must also communicate that the inward journey directs us to the light of healing and freedom. My challenge with this, and every phone inquiry, is to convey the value of this process, my abilities and passion. With empathy and only a few minutes, I face the task of convincing you that this excursion is well worth your time and money.

There are no photos or souvenirs from previous passengers. There will be no statements made by satisfied customers, no slick marketing strategies, no written guarantees; they are all hidden behind an ethical veil of confidentiality. I can sell only myself, a quiet room, and time together. My voice and words are the essence of what I have to offer you, the stranger on the other end of the line. I hope you will trust me enough, during this one phone call, to schedule our first session and set sail.

2.3 | SHOWING UP

True change occurs only in the context of relationships.

—MARY PIPHER

The chimes jingle softly on the outer door, announcing your arrival. You're here! I feel a sense of relief knowing that you have made it. Except for our brief phone conversation, we are complete strangers to each other. With the excitement and curiosity of a blind date, I look forward to meeting you as I gather a folder and legal pad and you complete the intake forms in the reception area.

I wonder what you look like out there beyond my office door, what you are thinking and how difficult it may have been for you to come today. You are likely anticipating what I'll be like and what you will say in our time together, as you case the unfamiliar rectangle in which you have taken a seat, looking for clues from book titles and furnishings, magazines and wall art.

In this reserved space, behind the door, our words will not be heard by another soul. On this side of the hidden realm, our visit takes place in secret, unnoticed by the outside world. Only you and I have the privilege of being here. Within these bounds, no one is granted access without your permission. These cloistered walls do not have a real window, just a skylight, so no one can even take a peek without your invitation.

But something will happen here that is mysterious and transformational. As with the refuge of a chrysalis, a phenomenon occurs with uncanny regularity, as this plain, quiet space becomes a haven, a respite, *time*. From twisted thoughts, disclosures, and memories, history mixes with reality as we cultivate fresh perspectives and both grow in the process.

The small button to the left of my desk begins to pulse with the fiery red glow of a beacon, announcing that our time has come. With anticipation, I open the door, walk down the hall, and see you there, nestled bravely in the corner of the couch with clipboard and completed paperwork on your lap. I extend my hand, smile, and introduce myself, delighted that you are here. I want you to feel welcomed.

I recognize that the mightiest of steps has already taken place in this struggle to seek therapy, where truths and fears and secrets will be extracted like painful splinters begging for release. From experience, I realize that this is not a trip sought by the weak, but you have no way to know that yet.

"I'm glad you have come today," I say, with affinity for a fellow sojourner. You are just the kind of valiant adventurer I admire, but you don't know that yet, either.

You extend your hand and smile back. "It's nice to meet you, too," you add.

Our paths have intersected, and it won't be long before we will cease being strangers. Courage has brought you here, and a numinous journey has begun, one from which you will eventually take your freedom flight.

As I close the door, you wonder what treasures might be hidden within these walls, awaiting discovery. Your eyes continue to roam as I take a seat in the therapist's chair, the one most directly in front of you. From the sofa, you are sizing me up, studying me for clues and deciding whether you like me so far, hoping all the while that I might have something to offer you but wondering what it could possibly be.

I look at your face, smile, and can only imagine who you are behind those pensive eyes. After required procedures that include information about the therapeutic process, bounds of confidentiality, and office policies, there comes a moment of hesitation—a stillness—as you acknowledge that you understand and give your consent to begin treatment. And then, with your signature in place, with a sense of reverence for honesty and boundaries and this newly established partnership, we agree to embark on our joint venture.

You grab a pillow, exhale, and shift as you settle more deeply into the cushions. An important story is just about to unfold, but first we will undoubtedly deal with the beguiling topic of *crazy* . . .

2.4 | VISITING CRAZY

*Insanity: doing the same thing over and over again and
expecting different results.*

—ALBERT EINSTEIN

With consistency beyond coincidence, crazy will be mentioned in some way or another at the beginning of therapy. Within the protective boundaries of this refuge, after forms and formalities, it often finds its way into an opening line, a common lead-in to an uncommon, and uncomfortable, situation: "You'll probably think this is *crazy* . . ."

Sometimes, after we've discussed why you've come, or after you've shared a bit of disturbing family history, it will be posed in the form of a question, followed by a nervous laugh: "Is this *crazy* or what?" or "Is that the craziest thing you've ever heard?" Admitting to neurotic thoughts or troubling behaviors gives rise to fear about what is normal, how you'll be perceived, and whether or not you may have slipped over the edge.

Opening yourself is a courageous act that can activate apprehension and embarrassment and often expresses itself in a reality check, an inquiry in search of reassurance. After breaking codes and unlocking doors, you may wonder whether you have shown me too much or said more than you should have. What if I've written a diagnosis in your chart that questions your sanity? You study my face for reactions and a final verdict, fearing that I may be judge and jury: *Does she think I am crazy? And what happens if she does?*

But crazy, in one form or another, is what I will hear about behind the door. Time travel, like a conduit, links emotional energy to dark nights with secrets and confused children. Psychiatric hospitals. Blackouts. Dysfunctional families. I know it well. And for those who have lived with it, crazy's peculiar charge pulses with memories that can put a teary lump in your throat or prickles over your skin.

Jaycee Dugard was only eleven years old when she came face-to-face with crazy. Kidnapped by a stranger, she was locked away in a dark shed, handcuffed, and raped regularly. While still a child herself, she gave birth to two daughters in a backyard shanty, where she loved and educated them and never tried to escape from the clutches of that crazed pedophile. When rescued by the police after eighteen years in captivity, she asked them with uncertainty, "Is he crazy, or am I?"

There is something about crazy's pull that captures and immobilizes bewildered victims. It manipulates with an unrelenting magnetism that draws us together, here, in this place. Those who have experienced its power have been dragged through much of life like helpless shards, seized in an ominous grip from which we struggle to liberate ourselves. But just the word *crazy*, spoken with unusual concern or a sense of dread, offers a clue to a disturbing story that I'm about to hear, one that's likely never been told.

2.5 | MARIE'S STORY

Before sunlight can shine through a window,
the blinds must be raised.
—AMERICAN PROVERB

Marie lived with crazy and still feels its unsettling tug. She doubts her abilities. Feels out of balance. And she wonders whether she is having a "nervous breakdown" or is permanently damaged. "I hope I'm not mental," she says with a look of uncertainty. Recently, she lost her job because of anxiety and panic attacks, and she hasn't been able to get a new one, probably because she is an employer's nightmare: obese—close to three hundred pounds—with diabetes, bad knees, a bad back, and a history of depression. Mostly, she just sits around, watching TV and crying.

She is crying now, sobbing in the quiet of the office, wondering what she is going to do with her life. I listen as she talks about her constant sadness, her failed marriage to an alcoholic husband, and a desire for children that never came. And, in due time, I am introduced to the vibrant little girl who endured a foul, destructive life of crazy.

Marie never knew her dad; he was likely just one of the many men who came and went. She didn't recall any of them treating her kindly, though she welcomed their attention, hoping that one of them would stay and be her father. It was just her mother and her . . . and the men.

Most of her mother's boyfriends used Marie in some way,

sending her to the store for cigarettes, paying her to stay outside, or abusing her sexually. Though she tucked away these shady memories, she recalls the photos, threesomes, and fear. And though she tried to tell years ago, in the way that children do, it only ever got her in trouble, so she stopped. Until today, that is.

Opening up, she begins telling me what she has carefully hidden away. And she is embarrassed, second-guessing her need to share a story that is nearly forty years old. We start with her earliest memory: her very first day of school. She was in kindergarten, and the teacher asked the class to draw a picture of their family. And so she did. She drew herself, wearing her favorite yellow sundress; her mother, with her jet-black hair, crimson nails, and bright red lipstick; and an unidentified man holding a beer can, sitting in a chair with his fly down and his penis hanging out for all the world to see.

The teacher was horrified, and she marched Marie to the principal's office, where they reprimanded her and called her mother. Clearly, the educators were uneducated about the behavior of sexually abused children, who often act out disturbing stories in ways that upset or offend unsuspecting adults. They were aghast, and, rather than offer her sanctuary and protection, they shamed her, telling her that she was a very bad girl and that her despicable behavior would not be tolerated. And when she got home, her mother beat her with a belt, convincing her to think twice before ever doing anything stupid like that again.

At school, she was known as the girl who drew the dirty picture, and through the years she acquired additional labels, like "bad seed" and "slut." She remembers being caught masturbating in first grade, and by second, she was pulling her pants down to show the neighbor boys what a girl looks like "down there." She had recurring bladder infections, tried running away from home repeatedly, and gave birth to a stillborn child at age thirteen.

Still, no one ever considered that she was a victim who needed help.

The real tragedy of this and of all stories involving crazy is that even the victims come to believe that they were somehow in the wrong: flawed, dirty, and deserving of their misfortune. Because of their childish involvement, they often blame themselves for participating in the shameful activities that haunt their dreams and have condemned them to a life of critical looks and whispers telling them that they are a disgrace and should have known better.

After trying to tell or escape, hide in a closet, or tiptoe over quicksand covered in eggshells, crazy's children, by necessity, become skilled detectives. Because something in their lives felt threatening and precarious, they learned to scan for clues and danger, and they continue to do so long after they've left home. They find it difficult to relax because a life of crazy has left them with an uneasy sense of dis-ease, but they don't know why or how to fix it, or whether a cure is even a possibility.

Compelled to a vigilant state of arousal, many of crazy's children suffer in adulthood from anxiety disorders, depression, perfectionism, obsessive-compulsive symptoms, food issues, or addictions. And, no, they are *not* crazy. Those who come to therapy willing to courageously unlock their stories are closer to freedom than they realize.

Though clients like Marie arrive in despair—discouraged by hopelessness, fear, or overwhelm—with understanding and support, their courage will return.

*The antidote to dis-*courage-*ment is en-*courage-*ment.*

So, in order for therapy to be successful, I must make an empathic connection during this first session. As I listen, here and now, I imagine what it feels like to be you, appreciating your strengths and inherent gifts and extending a warm shoulder in a cold world. With a glimmer of hope cast into the darkness, I encourage you to trust the healing power of this new relationship, your own inner wisdom, and the spirit of truth to guide us. Then, together, united as "co-therapists," we will connect past and present, gain new perspectives and resources, and be directed to a place of personal freedom and abundance.

*The meeting of two personalities is like
the contact of two chemical substances;
if there is any reaction, both are transformed.*
—CARL JUNG

During this first encounter, I will ask why you've come. The answer will be predictable: something in your life is not working; it has gone terribly wrong or is different from what you expected. Somehow, a pattern has set itself in motion, and, even with determination, you can't seem to find a way out of the mess. It's not that you haven't tried—it's that you are stuck.

Each "presenting problem" is a crucial puzzle piece from a life that has gotten out of whack. As with a brain-teaser that has become more scrambled through the years, valuable information is buried in the repeated attempts and thwarted efforts to find a solution. Things are mixed up, but unlike a Rubik's Cube, there is no arrangement or color coding, no simple formula to get it back in order.

Maybe it's depression, or insomnia, or lack of appetite. Sometimes it's an addiction to pills or alcohol or the Internet. Perhaps you suffer from panic, a phobia, or an annoying compulsion. But, always, the turmoil began in a relationship and is ultimately played out in one, and therein lies much suffering. The conundrum involves a disappointed parent, a misunderstood teen, a mystified spouse, grieving children, rejected lovers, the wounded and abused.

When asked what you hope to accomplish in our time together, you will again offer a predictable answer:

"I just want to be happy."

You say it as though it is such a simple thing, happiness. You *just* want to be happy. Interesting. But what does it mean to actually *be happy*?

"What would happy look like to you?" I ask.

"I don't know," you tell me, with tears that rise up suddenly and are let loose in the first of several tissues, "but I don't want to feel like this anymore."

You want to feel good, and you know that *something* needs to change to make that happen. Your happiness seems to be shackled by habits and messes that feel unmanageable, beyond your understanding. What inevitably unfolds during your intake is that you feel *bad*: depressed, anxious, irritable, abused, ashamed, furious . . . Or, sometimes, you feel nothing at all—completely dead inside. Something has become bound in a relationship that has taken a wrong turn and become a source of sorrow.

You are burdened, no longer carefree, in skin that is barely holding you together. While happiness is the goal, the message I hear in every intake, in words unspoken, is, *I am stuck, and I want to be free.* You want to find a way out of the self-defeating design that is trapping you in a sticky web of your own spinning. Your neurosis, new affair, or drug of choice is a misguided effort to find a way to the freedom that eludes you.

We seek truth for its claim that it will set us free, and we make our way to therapy in hopes that our rigorous honesty might loosen troublesome patterns and attitudes that are holding us hostage. At the heart of our nature is the desire for autonomy. So important is our independence that, in a democracy, our freedoms are considered inalienable rights, safeguarded by men and women who have died to protect them.

Enslaving human beings and taking away their free will is considered a reprehensible act of malice, a punishment, because at the core of our happiness and its pursuit lies freedom. But somehow, even in the land of the free and the home of the brave, internal programs have the power to baffle and constrain us.

"Why do I do that which I do not want to do?" Saint Paul laments, along with the rest of us. It is a human dilemma that holds us in bondage. In this most common of struggles, how do we break free from the traps, mistaken beliefs, and confusing patterns that are beyond our awareness?

It seems simple enough to "just say no"—to drugs, to anxiety, to pornography. Stop the bad behavior. Get rid of anger. Refuse to be depressed. Quit obsessing. As the song suggests, "Don't worry, be happy."

Why isn't it *just* that simple?

2.7 | EXAMINING SYMPTOMS

Half the beds in our hospitals are filled with people who
worried themselves into them.
—DR. CHARLES MAYO

Neuroses are our attempts to calm anxiety and feel okay. They are our trademark way of dealing with uncertainty and powerlessness, and they grow into symptoms that can create concerns about our mental health. Some of us get depressed and go to bed for days, while others hit the mall for a massive dose of retail therapy or the pantry for an entire bag of cookies.

We each have a unique way of distracting ourselves from troubling feelings. We may gamble, watch porn, drink to excess, or, perhaps, at the other extreme, grab at control by eliminating every fat gram, pleasure, or creature comfort with disciplined, oppressive conviction. Sometimes we do a combination of these things, all in an effort to help ourselves feel better.

Our particular neurosis is what we bring to therapy as our "presenting problem." It is what we do to mask inner turmoil when life feels too big and out of control. When we *don't know what else to do*, and we don't want to feel the apprehension that comes when we fear the worst, our obsessions (thoughts) or compulsions (behaviors) are the misguided means we use to gain mastery over *something* in the present moment.

Not all neurotic behaviors are bad. Jogging or cleaning, for example, can be beneficial—*unless* it becomes so excessive that it consumes too much time, interferes with relationships, or detracts from everyday functioning. While neuroses are the troubling patterns that bring people to therapy, they aren't the core problem. Eliminating them requires us to gain awareness about their origin and duration, and what triggers them, and then free ourselves from the *fear* and *discouragement* that keep the obsessions and compulsions flourishing.

The challenge of therapy is to uncover the crisis point— the time of lost courage and sense of inadequacy that contribute to a neurosis—and gain hope and tools to better handle anxiety, improve self-esteem, and make positive lifestyle changes. Our crazy symptoms aren't crazy at all. They serve to soothe our fears and discouragement with ritualized, preoccupying (dis)comfort zones that attempt to shield us from *feeling* flawed and imperfect, dissatisfied and ashamed.

The neuroses that bring people to therapy include eating disorders, substance abuse, hoarding, gambling, obsessive-compulsive disorders, perfectionism, hypochondria, trichotillomania, kleptomania, cutting, phobias, fetishes . . . and nearly anything *excessively* imbalanced: sex, video gaming, Internet surfing, shopping, collecting, exercising, dieting, etc., etc., etc. . . .

Psychoses are different than neuroses. Sufferers of a psychosis have episodes in which they are out of touch with the real world. They are alone in a world in which they may see or hear things that don't exist, and they are convinced that their thoughts and experiences are rational. In these altered states, psychotic individuals often become paranoid that other people are conspiring against them and are usually noncompliant about getting treatment for their symptoms.

While neuroses can be successfully alleviated in therapy (or, in some cases, with a combination of therapy and medication), therapy alone is ineffective in dealing with a psychosis. Psychotics require medical intervention, often with the involvement of family or the courts, and psychotropic medications to balance brain chemistry.

So, when it comes to diagnosis and treatment, neurotics recognize that they have a problem, and they can benefit from the psycho-clarity process of therapy. The psychotic, on the other hand, has a physiological mental disorder, an imbalance, marked by a debilitating break from reality and the need to be under the medical care of a psychiatrist before therapy is even considered.

Neuroses are our attempts at managing life. Compulsive, troubling behaviors follow overwhelming thoughts and feelings about things being out of control: unsafe, dirty, intolerable, or in need of better organization. And, like OCD (obsessive-compulsive disorder), every neurosis comes with apprehension and a strong, compelling drive to *do*—or *avoid doing*—something *now*.

OCD

Oh, dear me!
Fixate.
Ruminate.
Get into a tizzy.
Do something.
Anything.

Just stay busy.
Clean.
Straighten.
Vacuum all the rugs.
Launder every sheet.
Spray for nasty bugs.
Wash your hands.
Dry the sink.
Wipe your dirty feet.
Erase all signs of human life.
Check carefully.
Repeat.
Arrange.
Organize.
Double-check the locks.
Sanitize . . .
The whole wide world.
Put it in a box.
Lock it up.
Dust the lid.
Hide the only key.
But where?
And what if I forget?
Oh, dear . . .
A-n-x-i-e-t-y.
Fixate.
Ruminate.
Get into a tizzy.
Do something.
Anything.
Better get busy . . .

The world is full of suffering. It is also full of overcoming it.
—HELEN KELLER

Hannah was a successful insurance broker who drove a Mercedes and lived in a six-bedroom home with a pool—until her husband left after twenty years of marriage. He just up and walked out, and her life changed forever. She never saw it coming and never imagined that her best friend would end up being the reason why.

It blew her circuits, but she continued working, supporting herself and two teenage children. When he took her to court to claim bankruptcy, sell the house, and cut off alimony, she just worked harder. She'd learned to be self-sufficient as a young girl: a Jane-of-all-trades who grew up in a single-parent household where she cared for her grandmother while her mother worked. Her dad left when she was just a baby, so she was used to a life of women supporting women.

The hoarding didn't start until later. Growing up, she cooked and cleaned and got A's in school, but she never seemed able to please her perfectionist mother. She even learned how to handle a hammer and power tools and was the "man" of the house whenever they needed one. Her mother didn't seem to notice her abilities, nor did she give her much credit, and so Hannah never expected any. Though she tended the house and children, entertained clients, and put plenty of money in the bank for over *two decades, her husband never seemed to appreciate her efforts, either.*

When her eighteen-year-old daughter was killed in an auto accident, Hannah wished it had been her. She found a way to go on after the funeral, cooking and cleaning, fixing things around the townhouse she'd moved into during the divorce, and showing up at the office on days when she could pull herself out of her pajamas and get dressed. She closed her daughter's bedroom door, left everything intact. Saw her son off to college the following year. Even after she'd moved her aging mother into assisted living, the hoarding still wasn't an issue.

It wasn't until her mother died in 2014 that Hannah inherited crates full of papers and dishes, clothing, years' worth of junk and fabulous treasures. She stored them in the garage, along with her own accumulation of boxes and furniture that needed her attention. Occasionally, in the still of the night, she'd wedge herself into the garage, peek into a box or two, and handle the contents, reading through legal papers and taking a walk down memory lane. And that's when the hoarding took a devious turn.

Maybe it was the photos or the baby clothes. Perhaps it was the box of dolls, the yellowed valentine from her father, or her daughter's graduation tassel. It all felt so valuable, and so comforting. When she was lost in loneliness, when the nights felt long and empty, she would drag a box into the house and inspect the objects inside.

She welcomed every precious memory, one at a time, like old friends that had come to visit, seating them at the dining room table, on shelves and mantels, on countertops or on the living room floor. They kept her company all around the house, in every nook and cranny, chronicling her life, sharing the good times and resurrecting the dead.

It wasn't long until Hannah was buried in stuff that occupied her time and energy. Procrastination and emotional overwhelm became a way of life that made it difficult to show up at work, make decisions, or even perform daily household functions. The piles and trinkets obscured her grief, perhaps, but what was cleverly stashed beneath the rubble was the organic root from which Hannah's neurosis—and all neuroses—flourish: intolerable feelings of loss, anxiety, and quiet desperation.

2.9 | BREAKING BONDS

Every intake and presenting problem is fascinating. We meet clandestinely, as two strangers, and with unusual focus you will spill intimate details about your life. Accompanied by anxiety, depression, addiction, a phobia, or a compulsion, your story slowly unfolds with tears and significant secrets. I'll pay attention to your words, body language, inconsistencies, and hidden messages, and by the end of the session I'll be drained. A wad of tissues will likely have accumulated, and you will rise to deposit it in the wastebasket, an ending ritual of sorts.

Before you leave, I will ask how you feel about having disclosed information that you may have been guarding for years. You may say "fine," or some version of "okay," and may even seem lighthearted and relieved. You'll tell me that you are glad you've come as you get to the business of writing a check, and though we have become fast friends who have shared a gamut of emotions, I'll offer a warning about what may come after this first meeting.

Though we've made an empathic connection and might even hug like old pals before you go, you may have a sudden change of heart as you exit the building and drive away. After this initial transference, something happens with regularity, so I'll bring it to your attention before you open the door: The childhood guilt that keeps secrets secure has been tampered with, and, like a blackout curtain that has been parted, it may attempt to close with a vengeance, blocking the light and engulfing you in that dank shroud of dread that effectively darkens moods and silences victims.

Disclosures you made easily moments ago during the intake can twist themselves into shameful pangs of treachery. And by the time you hit the road, replaying the dialogue of our session, remorse may wash over you in a sickening, feverish wave that accompanies mistakes that seem too big ever to be undone.

With the compunction of a reluctant informant, you may feel regret heat up into a fiery ball that churns deep in your stomach or high in your chest: *Why did I say that? What was the point? She probably thinks I'm really screwed up . . . This is not good... I should never have talked about it.* There in the car, you may begin to feel as if the whole emotional experience is foolish and threatening.

Fear-based judgments spin into self-doubt, draping you in the same cold, claustrophobic sweat that happens just before the panic attack, binge, compulsion, or crisis of confidence. Breaking through this suffocating sheath of denial is a battle for freedom, yet it can feel all wrong, like a dangerous act of betrayal. *What was I thinking?* You may want to press a "delete" button in an effort to free yourself from this membrane of anxiety and escape from the whole upsetting experience.

You have violated several of the key rules learned in a family with secrets: "Don't talk. Don't feel. And certainly *do not tell.*" Getting untangled from this agreement feels like infidelity, dangerous even to those of us who have grown beyond childhood. You may question your memory, wonder if you made up the whole thing or deviously altered the truth. You will feel the futility of having opened yourself up to a complete stranger. It may seem confusing or counterintuitive or even like a perverse act of treason. And you will spend the next few days debating whether to ever return to therapy.

Hopefully you will remember the consent form you signed at the beginning of our session, noting that therapy may bring up uncomfortable, disturbing emotions, along with the warning to watch for this oddly familiar covering of disgrace to be activated. Staying present to notice what happens *after* our first session continues the process of breaking through—and becoming aware of the struggle that takes place when we attempt to free ourselves from old, unspoken contracts.

The only way through pain is *through*. There is no shortcut, no magic pill, no behavior to obliterate the memories or feelings that cause us distress. The only way to shed this casing that keeps us constricted and suppresses our pain is to detect it and *feel* it—and, when we do, to know that we are headed in the right direction.

As we tell our stories, our recollections spill sorrows never before shared freely. They were tucked away long ago because it was not safe to tell them or to be sad. And now we are dredging them up. We may have learned to hold in our pain because a frustrated parent made it clear that no crying was allowed; grief often activates uncomfortable feelings in the people around us, and so it is quickly shut down.

Many adults simply do not know how to deal with their

own disappointments, yet alone those of an upset child. Instead of being empathic, some adults become irritated, even punitive. Without a clue or model to handle grief, children's tears or sorrow can be taken personally, misunderstood by an adult who perceives even a hint of sadness in the eyes of a child to be a reflection of his or her own failure or inadequate parenting. Adults want children to be happy, contented. Sometimes parents even expect their children to bring them happiness, as if they are owed a kind of thank-you for giving them the gift of life. An *unhappy* child, on the other hand, is needy, a drain of time and precious resources to an already-busy adult. Sadness can easily be misconstrued and scorned as nothing more than attention seeking or a hindrance to optimism, and its expression is often "proof" that a child is ungrateful, inappropriate, or just plain difficult.

Sometimes our tears were interpreted as a sign that we needed to be taught a lesson to toughen us up. A child with emotional issues can be an additional burden to a parent already struggling to cope or provide. Whether the significant adults in our life were negligent, abusive, or doing the very best they could, the sadness beneath our tears often needed to be stuffed away because it was neither understood nor welcomed.

We conditioned ourselves to hide sorrows that were dangerous to talk about. There seemed no point in revealing them, so we swallowed our tears and found ways to preoccupy or numb ourselves. What we didn't allow ourselves to feel *then* is still here *now*, however, and we can become small and vulnerable when these feelings are triggered. Though we do our best to keep them undercover, our grief gets activated in certain situations and will not dissipate until it is recognized and acknowledged. The sadness that returns to us brings with it the story of a little child who has carried it for all these years.

There is a war going on inside each of us, a mixture of thoughts and feelings—a courageous wanting to tell, wanting the world to hear the story, secrets and all. A sense of empowerment has risen up from a place that contains no fear, that wants to write the truth on a banner, share the experience with a witness, and shout with unrestrained freedom; *See,* this *is my life's story in all its complexity. Now you know what it's* really *like to be me.*

But the bravado quickly wanes as guilt reappears, and, like Adam feeling ashamed in the garden, we feel a sense of panic set in: *Hide yourself. What have you done? It's taken a long time to push these feelings down so deep that you don't feel them anymore. It's over now. This is stupid. The memories and sadness of long ago have been buried and nearly forgotten. What's the point of dredging them up now?*

The simplest solution is just to maintain the status quo, forget the whole thing. And if we could, we would. The problem, however, is that we have tried that for years, and it just *does not work.* Grief accumulates. It builds upon itself, layer upon layer, and when stuffed away, it causes depression. Troubling feelings, with or without their memories, will return again and again as a profound sadness that contributes to mental and physical illnesses, until they overwhelm us with their need to be acknowledged and released.

As they say in twelve-step programs, "We are only as sick as our secrets." We are infected with pain-soaked memories that need to be flushed from our system. They have sickened us and keep us from optimum health. Like a fever helping us to burn away an infection, tears rid toxins from our bodies, and so we cry in an effort to purify our minds and hearts, and will likely feel worse before we feel better.

2.10 | LINDA'S STORY

> *Heavy thoughts bring on physical maladies;*
> *when the soul is oppressed, so is the body.*
> —MARTIN LUTHER

Linda was rushed to the hospital a couple of weeks before she came to see me. "My heart was pounding so hard, I couldn't catch my breath," she explained with wide-eyed apprehension.

"I couldn't breathe," she continued, raising one hand to her chest and gulping a mouthful of air. "It felt like I was in a vise. I really thought I was dying."

After a night's stay at the hospital, with monitors and little sleep, Linda was told that she could leave. "They found absolutely nothing wrong with my heart. Made it sound like it was all in my head. According to the doctor, I had a panic attack. It was all really embarrassing."

Even though panic attacks are common and are a symptom of underlying anxiety, Linda was humiliated. Sent home with a prescription for Valium and a suggestion to "relax and see someone," she was convinced that the doctor was politely telling her she was crazy, as her husband often did.

"It's been hard for me since Ashley left for college, but I don't actually think I'm psycho," she said, with the usual reference to crazy and concern about my evaluation.

A recent empty nester just turning forty-two, Linda admits that she is at a loss for what to do next with her life. She lists her occupation as "homemaker," though she has earned several degrees and enjoyed varied successes in other areas as well. She describes her greatest accomplishment as "raising two wonderful children who are the loves of my life."

She seems apologetic as she confesses, "I don't know what has gotten into me since Ashley left. I have gained over thirty pounds, am nervous all the time, and don't have any energy. My husband is upset with me and tells me I should appreciate my blessings, but nothing seems to matter. I've tried diets but can't seem to lose weight."

"How are you feeling right now, here, in this room?" I ask.

Without digging, most clients will say something vague and socially appropriate, like "okay" or "fine," or sometimes will respond with a more honest "not so good." We simply are not used to being asked about what we feel. It is not something we discuss, except in the cordial-greeting sort of way. Most of us have learned that if we don't want someone to glaze over mid-sentence, the correct response to "How do you feel?" is to smile pleasantly and simply reply, "Fine, thank you," even if we are dying inside.

But here in the office, the rules are different. Feelings provide valuable insights, clues into details about a deeper, usually hidden, part of ourselves. While the question about feelings is often answered with a statement like "I feel as though my life is a mess," or "I feel like my daughter is driving me crazy," they are about thoughts or beliefs. Even though a sentence may start with "I feel," it may be about our reasoning, not actually about feelings at all.

"I feel like the tranquilizers are helping, but they make me sleep too much. I feel okay, I guess, but I don't feel like anything is getting better, either. . . . My husband has to drive me every-

where now, like I'm an old lady, because the pills make me sleepy. The doctor warned me that this medicine can be habit-forming, which makes me nervous."

"It sounds as though you are feeling drowsy and nervous most of the time."

"Pretty much, and fat and ugly, too."

"And how about sad—any sadness?"

Now, this is a no-brainer. Sadness is all over Linda's shoulders, on her forehead, in those round, ebony spheres that dominate her small, olive face. At the mention of sadness, after a moment of silence, tears appear like precious water pooling in darkened, dry wells.

Bubbling up from an underground source, sorrow begins flowing for children grown and gone, for a brokenhearted little girl, for identities lost, snatched away without consent. Her eyes pull me in, until I find myself, like Alice in the looking glass, toppling through space and time into a disorienting story.

Linda was born somewhere in Greece as the youngest of five children. When she was very young, her mother died tragically. Perhaps well-intentioned, or perhaps not, her father decided that as the baby and only girl of the family, she needed a mother, and he set out to find one for her.

And so, at age four, Linda was given, or sold, to a wealthy American family who happened to be visiting the island. She did not speak English, and they, a man, woman, and twelve-year-old boy, did not speak Greek. "I'm not sure of the details, because my parents changed the story every time I asked to hear it."

"I was crying as I left the house, holding a doll. I remember clinging to it, which is the most vivid part of the memory. The rest is sketchy." Linda knew something big was going on but couldn't really grasp it. "I don't think I had any idea that I was being taken away from my family forever."

The trip was a blur of airports and cars and strangers, and a world far beyond the familiar walls of her village. And as if that weren't enough, after they landed in America, during a stopover in Washington, DC, Linda was hit by a car as she stepped off a curb. For three months she lived in a hospital, enduring painful surgeries to mend a crushed pelvis and multiple broken bones.

As she tells the story, I wonder how anyone could give a little girl away to complete strangers, and how panicked and helpless she must have felt in that strange new world. I want to say I am sorry, or to hold this forty-two-year-old child in my arms as she sobs, but I act the part of a professional, extending empathy in nods and the gentle, breathy sounds of an interested listener. It seems like the least I can do as she reaches for yet another tissue.

She speaks about the hospital as a real-life nightmare in which she felt utterly lost, with no control, no way to communicate, no way to find her way home. "I was afraid and in pain and couldn't even tell anyone," she says. "I didn't understand what was happening to me." I can only imagine how terrified she must have felt.

Eventually, she arrived at her new house, where she had a pink room and plenty of toys. She remembers balloons and a party and wonders now if it might have been her birthday. "It wasn't long before everything in my suitcase disappeared." Even the beloved rag doll she adored was replaced with a cleaner, brand-new model made of plastic, with its own wardrobe and accessories.

Gradually, she learned enough English to go to school. "My name was officially changed, and overnight I became Linda." With plenty of girlie clothes, toys, and good food, she was reminded regularly that she was very lucky. "If I was caught crying, Mother would remind me that I was not acting like a grateful little girl."

It wasn't long until tears were not tolerated at all, and so she learned to weep quietly, all alone in the night, no matter what nightmare or grief visited her. Adding to her burden was her new brother, who, within years of her arrival, was molesting her in the sanctity of her canopy bed. There was no safety for Linda inside this picture-perfect American home.

Riddled with secrets that she couldn't mention; even her name betrayed the truth of her identity. The family ate ice cream every night after dinner, but it was not a happy home, and she continued to miss a family she could barely even remember. There were food issues, and diets, and rejection by her peers. "And then there was the surgery to change my nose." Concerned that Linda looked "too ethnic," her mother bleached her hair to match her own and continued finding ways to help her "look more like the rest of the family."

"I couldn't wait to get out of there." And so, with little hesitation, Linda did exactly that as soon as she graduated from high school and found a man who professed his love for her. But he, too, was unable to understand or tolerate her tears and just wanted her to be happy. But "just be happy" wasn't working.

So, how do we ever get to a place of joy with a grieving heart? When we are plagued with depression as adults, it is often because of a lifetime of tears and sadnesses that we have stuffed away. When our buckets are filled to the brim and we suffer yet another loss, difficulty, or transition—an empty nest, divorce, retirement, death, disappointment, health issue, or financial setback—we hit a tipping point, lose our enthusiasm for living, and feel as though we're drowning in the accumulated sorrows we've swallowed through the years.

IMPRESSION – EXPRESSION = DEPRESSION

Like a simple formula, impression minus expression equals depression. The images and experiences we draw in through our senses form our feelings and reality. When they are tainted by secrets, shame, or unbearable pain, they get pressed down, hidden from consciousness with psychic energy that finds its way into obsessions, compulsions, addictions, and dreams. And if never expressed, never brought to the light, these powerful impressions live on in flashes and emotions that overburden the system with anxiety and posttraumatic stress that cause dis-ease, a lack of vitality, and the hopelessness that we call depression.

After years of clinical research, James Pennebaker, PhD, a professor at the University of Texas, was able to demonstrate how inhibition is physical work that can overwhelm our biological defenses and result in stress-related illnesses. In *Opening Up: The Healing Power of Expressing Emotions*, he writes that "any kind of trauma may result in long-term health problems if the victim cannot talk about it." Expressing our deepest thoughts and feelings is *healthy*.

When Linda's daughter left home, the painful, all-too-familiar emotions of losing what was beloved and familiar were reactivated, and Linda's delicate identity was assaulted once again by loss and another unwelcome transition. So, what's the next step to finding relief? In therapy, we simply offer a safe place to be, to *express* thoughts and feelings without judgment, and to initiate the invaluable emptying process that lightens laden nervous systems and provides a space to take a deep breath and renew. And what better way to begin a story than to start at the beginning—by revisiting childhood.

* Only the courageous reach out and show up to therapy.
* Neurotic symptoms are our individualized attempts at handling discouragement and anxiety.
* Psycho-clarity begins with the awareness that something is not working and needs to change.
* "Don't talk, don't feel, and don't tell" makes breaking through denial feel like a dangerous act of betrayal.
* Therapy examines the connection between past and present to alleviate pain and gain the insights necessary for healing.

2.11 | YOUR STORY

It's your turn to tell your story. Imagine you're the client.
Get comfortable. Breathe deeply. Use the following prompts to make
discoveries and gain clarity on your way to personal freedom.
Use a journal to capture any thoughts, feelings, or images that come
to mind or talk into a recorder. Welcome to your session ...

What needs to change in your life?

When you are afraid or overwhelmed, what do you do?

Do you feel helpless? Angry? Driven? Paralyzed?

At an intake, how would your describe your symptoms?

Are you anxious or depressed? Do you struggle with a compulsion?

Rage? Addiction? Self-loathing? Food issues?

Perfectionism? Workaholism? Obsessive thoughts?

When you are upset, do you have trouble calming down?

Are you more likely to withhold comfort or overindulge yourself?

How do you handle doubt and fear?

What are you likely to say to yourself when you are feeling stuck?

Growing up, what were you told, or shown, about success?

When you made a mistake as a child, what happened?

Who have been your biggest cheerleaders? How have they encouraged you along the way?

What words of encouragement would you most like to hear right now?

THREE

Tell Me About It

3.1 | GRIEF

Give sorrow words; the grief that does not speak knits up
the o'er-wrought heart and bids it break.

—WILLIAM SHAKESPEARE, *MACBETH*

People come to therapy because something has happened that was not anticipated, not welcome, not in keeping with the way they imagined life was supposed to be. Along with the sorrow that comes from a freshly emptied nest or widowhood, financial setbacks or a tragic accident, the grief that shows up in my office often results from relationships in which there was injustice, lack of resolution or restitution, and an untreated case of lingering heartache.

All of therapy is about grief in some form or another. Whether loss comes from the natural order and transitions of life or from the specific actions of another person, clients come to me because their distress needs to find a way out. And grief, like all wounds, requires its own time and space to heal—a season to be mourned.

When those closest to us are the ones who have hurt us or let us down, our grief is intensified. Not only have those we love betrayed or abandoned us, but the faith we gave them has been squandered. Our innocence has been exploited, our trust eroded. When our parents, spouses, partners, siblings, and best friends hurt us, we are wounded in ways that shake our deepest belief in goodness and shatter our confidence in humankind.

Pangs of anguish, when swallowed and ingested, grow into tendrils of anxiety that make it difficult to breathe. And when there is no outlet for our pain—no one with whom we can share our weighty, suffocating burden—our sleep and appetite are affected and we are slowly sickened by a discouragement we feel unable to soothe or remedy.

In an effort to handle the injustices we didn't deserve and couldn't prevent, some of us sling around anger and bitterness; others live with self-loathing, posttraumatic stress disorder, or throbbing regrets that beg for a stiff shot of pain relief. As grief accumulates through the years, it grows heavier and more cumbersome.

Over time, we become exhausted by the lingering shock of our misfortune and a voracious dread that we can never trust life, happiness, or anyone else ever again. Vines of deadly depression grow dense, depleting our energy, our convictions, and the tiny bit of hope that we have managed to hang onto—or they twist themselves into brambles of frenetic activity that is driven by an apprehension that we don't fully understand.

Grief needs to be *grieved*, or it takes on a life of its own. While we may believe we should mourn when no one is watching, burdens that are shared are lessened.

Healing begins when we allow another person to help bear the pain we carry. Grief accumulates, its bucket growing heavier and fusty, until its contents are dumped out and the tainted sediment clinging to the bottom is shaken loose and washed away. By opening up, telling our stories, and baring our souls, we find relief.

Mourning requires a *season*, not a lifetime. But if grief has nowhere to go—if it is shoved below the surface to fester—its season lengthens and becomes polluted with sickening loneliness, self-pity, and despair. All grief has its blueprint and personal phases, and an essential need for time and expression, if it is ever to morph and transition into an acceptance of life in all of its complexity.

In 1980, Elisabeth Kübler-Ross wrote a landmark book, *On Death and Dying*, in which she made a lifetime contribution to our understanding of the grieving process. From her observations, she identified the five stages of grief that are commonly experienced when we attempt to deal with death, or the many tragic losses and injustices of life.

THE FIVE STAGES OF GRIEF

Denial

The first stage of grief is usually denial, when the world seems unfair and senseless and our pain totally overwhelming, Denial, like shock, provides numbing relief and a blurring of time that allows us to passively deal with our loss and basic survival. When we are filled with thoughts and feelings we're not yet ready or able to handle, denial provides us with a way to deal with our pain and loss in small, hazy increments.

Anger

When anger appears, it is a sign that our emotions are coming back online and our pain is surfacing. It may be uncomfortable, and upsetting to others, but it is necessary for healing, providing us with the energy we need to move out of the void. Though it feels awkward to be mad at the world, other people, and even God, it is far more harmful to suppress this burly stallion of fury that is seeking release and safety in unfamiliar territory. From underneath the anger will eventually come other feelings waiting their turn. But first, this startled dark horse needs time to run unbridled before it can settle down.

Bargaining

After losing loved ones or a cherished way of life, we try changing what has happened through wishful thinking. We attempt to take control with promises or what-ifs, or we beat ourselves up with guilt-ridden messages about what we could have or should have done differently. We may blame ourselves mercilessly as we strive to bring back the past, redoing the situation in our minds with: *If only I had been there or said something different; had been kinder, more attentive; hadn't been driving so fast; had prayed harder. . . .* And, of course, we hope that if we are exceedingly *good*—or sacrificial—maybe we can strike a bargain with God or the universe and miraculously alter the circumstances.

Depression

When denial and anger lift and bargaining hasn't worked, the realization sets in that life will never be the same again. Sadness hits with full force, along with a lack of desire to get out of bed and face this new way of life. With loss comes *suffering* that permeates mind and body, manifesting in sleep and eating disorders and distraught inquiries about the meaning of life. Under the weight of this heavy cloud, it is a struggle to associate with people who want to see us happy, because we're not. Though depression is a normal part of the grieving process, pushing through it by coming out of isolation and *sharing our sorrow* is a balm that helps us heal.

Acceptance

Change begins with an ending—and resistance. And so it takes time and a lot of travel to get to a place of acceptance. The trip there can't be rushed and involves passages through the previous four stages. We don't arrive there all at once; maybe we start with just one good hour, and then a good day here and there, and a recognition that we will never return to our old life but we *are* living a new one. And then it happens: We *enjoy* something—a sunset, a bird on the windowsill, a shared laugh with a friend. We feel a change in the air and begin to let go a little bit as we slowly start to live again. Though we can never replace what was lost, we allow ourselves to move forward—to grow and slowly accept a few new moments—and then, eventually, the next season of life.

While these five stages of grief are universal, the stages are not linear, and each individual handles them differently. They don't have to be done in any particular order, nor for any specific length of time—and most people cycle and recycle through them, as needed, while navigating the complicated grieving process. According to Kübler-Ross, the most valuable principle we can take away from this five-stage template is to allow *time* for grief to be processed, and, above all, regardless of the stage, to be willing to simply *listen.*

Not all grief looks like bereavement. While losing a loved one is sure to cause sorrow, grief comes from a variety of life events in an assortment of packages. Depending on its stage and intensity, it can present as a sluggish depression after a painful breakup, a rebellious act of irresponsible behavior after a disappointment, or a nagging compulsion that is attempting to remedy a hurtful, lost childhood. When it comes to grief and recovery, there is no "normal" and no truth to the notion that time alone heals all wounds.

You never really understand a person until you consider
things from his point of view . . . Until you climb inside
of his skin and walk around in it.
—HARPER LEE, *TO KILL A MOCKINGBIRD*

After the customary greeting in the waiting room, a walk down the hallway, and a look through completed forms and questionnaires, Carlos gives his consent to begin treatment. But treatment is tricky business. Not only does it require a graduate degree in psychology, internship hours, and licensing exams, but here, behind the door, it requires, above all, intuition that enjoys sniffing about a mystery like a bloodhound on a dedicated mission.

In our introductory meeting, I block off one and a half hours to collect a family history, make a connection with you, address your presenting problem, and gather enough information to formulate a diagnosis, collaborate on our goals, and collect my fee. I find this task quite a challenge, even after doing it hundreds of times, and can't help wondering how any therapist pulls off a "fifty-minute hour," especially for this first session. It baffles me.

In Carlos's case, his story and diagnosis begins with our hello in the reception area. While some disorders need to be pieced together or coaxed out of hiding, his missing eyelashes and eyebrows are obvious clues. It is no surprise to learn that Carlos is suffering from anxiety and a recurrence of trichotillomania, an impulse-driven compulsion that results in pulling out one's own hair.

It has taken a mighty effort for Carlos to overcome family and cultural rules about talking outside the family, and especially for him to be sitting here, all alone in the room with me, a female with no Hispanic roots or Spanish fluency. He has a hard time looking me in the eye, and I feel his discomfort as he tells me about his upset over a recent job loss.

I know it is imperative to create safety, and so I must factor in anything that might stand in the way of our ability to trust each other. We talk about our differences, bringing the obvious into the room, and Carlos admits that crossing cultural and gender barriers feels awkward. But he seems relieved to speak about it, communicates well, and is determined to get to the root of his problem. So we agree to move forward, acknowledging that we are both gaining a valuable learning opportunity.

Though he now seems more at ease, I must be careful not to delve too quickly or deeply into the shaft of pain that is feeding Carlos's presenting problem. Always willing to explore grief and the perplexing behaviors it generates, I've grown to understand over the years that moving too quickly in this direction can cause further stress and anxiety, not relief.

So the next order of business—one that wasn't modeled in graduate school or during my internships—is to spend plenty of time determining what is right about Carlos's life: what he enjoys, what he does well, and whom or what he turns to for support. Without resourcing the goodness and strength in a client's life, anyone can easily lose footing and be swept away by embarrassment, or retraumatized and disoriented by remembering what he or she has spent years trying to forget.

Therapy isn't all about harrowing memories and presenting problems; ultimately, it's about resiliency, wisdom, and our innate capacity to heal and grow. So, after your signature and the mention of "crazy," I'll spend time quieting your anxiety with deep breaths and pleasantries that may seem like small talk. But in order for you to open up, there must be a strong enough connection between the two of us for you to feel secure, lower your defenses . . . and grieve.

"I started pulling out my hair in middle school," Carlos says, "and I was so embarrassed. But I kept doing it."

Even with bald spots, downy patches, and missing eyelashes and eyebrows, Carlos says he was unable to stop his strange behavior. He had no idea, at the time, that this malady that fetched stares and ridicule actually had a name. What Carlos was doing to himself in secret is listed in the Diagnostic and Statistical Manual of Mental Disorders as an obsessive-compulsive disorder known as trichotillomania (hair-pulling disorder), in a category that includes other impetuous compulsions like hoarding and excoriation (skin-picking).

Though his appearance often made Carlos the victim of malicious jokes throughout junior and senior high school, his trichotillomania was never diagnosed or directly acknowledged. No one, not even teachers or other adults, ever seriously asked him about his hairless patches or missing brows and lashes. Eventually, after he graduated from high school and moved in with a cousin, Carlos's urge to pull out his hair subsided. But now it's back with a vengeance.

"Growing up was hard. My dad would leave us sometimes, and we never knew when he would show up again—drunk."

Carlos tells me that his mother worked two jobs to support them, and that while she was gone, his brother, Sal, who was six years older, would be left in charge as his babysitter.

"There was, like, something wrong with Sal. But we didn't know it then. He would get real mad and chase me around, hit me and stuff."

Even when his mother was home, she was unable to stop Sal

from taking out his frustrations on Carlos. And nights were the worst; when Sal got agitated and couldn't sleep, he would burst into Carlos's room in a fit of rage to yell, throw things, and pound on his defenseless little brother.

"I was always afraid to go to sleep. I tried to barricade the door, but he would get in. If Dad came home drunk, there would be a lot of fighting and yelling. He would beat up on my mom. And Sal would freak out and curse at him, punch holes in the wall, or cry . . . then turn on me later."

Carlos felt trapped and riddled with anxiety. He slept with one eye open, or not at all. He was helpless, and he couldn't imagine how to gain control. As a child in a dysfunctional family, he knew reaching out was not an option. And so, in an effort to get relief, he engaged in something he could do. His trichotillomania gave him a focus and diversion, a means of alleviating tension when it seemed intolerable.

Trichotillomania—like hoarding, cutting, skin picking, exercising, cleaning, or any other compulsive behavior—is an individualized attempt at combating emotional overwhelm in the moment. But if the code isn't unlocked, if an individual doesn't figure out when or why the unmanageable feelings originated, and what is triggering them now, impulsive reactions are sure to grow more habitual and more impossible to resist—adding additional weight to an unwieldy burden of grief.

After Carlos tells me his story, I thank him for being so candid. I let him know that I respect him for his willingness to share his pain and seek help. The secret that he has silently carried—the one he wears on his face—has found its voice and so has already begun losing some of its mystifying power.

3.3 | SECRETS

We are only as sick as our secrets.

—ALCOHOLICS ANONYMOUS

Our secrets can actually make us sick. The thoughts and feelings that are too troublesome to acknowledge and articulate get shoved from our awareness—but they don't go away. Instead, they become stuck and are recycled through our nervous system with an anxious energy that churns itself into somatic disorders, depression, addiction, and other neurotic behaviors.

In our ignorance, we have mistakenly believed for too long that retelling a tale can cause more pain than holding it inside. For years, we accepted the age-old notion that talking about something makes it worse and *not* talking about it allows it to go away. But painful impressions that are not given the opportunity to be expressed often result in debilitating depression that cannot simply and solely be healed by the dutiful hands of time.

Burdens of life that cannot be shared build up steam like children full of restless energy. In untamed feelings that need to be expended, often in words that can be wild or rough around the edges, they push to be set loose on the playground to run amok until something shifts or settles down. This ruckus isn't easy to listen to; it can be unnerving, raw, and tiresome. And it brings up the desire to fix what might not be fixable.

When we witness firsthand that bad things really do happen to good people, that life is not always fair, and that we don't have all the answers, we are tempted to push suffering away. Seeing and hearing others' grief and difficulties threaten our own sense of competency and control, and can activate both an unsettling sense of helplessness and a chivalrous desire to eradicate all that is troublesome with not-so-helpful advice.

In our insecurity and discomfort, we offer bumper-sticker fixes that admonish grieving loved ones to "'forget about it," "stop crying," or "get over it." And amid simple solutions like "get a hobby," "date online," or "have another child," sorrows and pain-laden memories get buried alive, creating environments in which dis-ease flourishes and manifests as headaches, panic attacks, high blood pressure, ulcers, and other maladies.

Somewhere in the grieving process, well-meaning friends and family often send the message that our time is up—that no more tears are allowed. Grief reaches an expiration date, a time when others cannot stand to witness another day of our despair. So we stuff away our reality and accompanying feelings, and depression, anxiety, and other mental and physical illnesses begin brewing. The longer grief incubates in solitary confinement, the greater its potential to cause serious damage.

People readily shut down when others suggest they should quit whining about the past and get on with life. Banned by those who have difficulty listening, we hide away our disturbing truths as feelings and secrets that we cannot share. Because of embarrassment, humiliation, fear of rejection—or, in some cases, retaliation—these admissions become too psychologically painful to bring up again, and so we keep them at bay, shelved in darkened stacks of forbidden topics, where they gather dust but are never too far out of reach.

In cases of incest or sexual abuse, it is noteworthy that what has been fearfully stored and *nearly* forgotten for years makes a surprising resurgence when there is enough time and distance for the victim to feel a level of safety. In my experience, secretive memories of childhood sexual abuse resurface most commonly when victims have children of their own or hit their thirties, or when troublesome thoughts and feelings get stirred up and blended with a fresh batch of life's disappointments and losses.

Disclosure has always had its place in religious traditions and self-help groups, where the act of telling is seen as a way to unburden oneself and be set free. Sharing one's story, confessing what is true, requires an act of humility that has healing potential—for our bodies, minds, and spirits —in a world where it's unsettling, *but perfectly normal*, to be imperfect, and where it's really no secret that *everyone* has a closet full of doubts, and fears, and transgressions begging for release.

3.4 | WINNIE'S STORY

Suffering is a sign that you're out of touch with the truth . . .
Suffering points out that there is falsehood somewhere.
—ANTHONY DE MELLO

Winnie is a tiny, vibrant woman with a pleasant voice and an inviting smile. Her intake form reveals that she is seventy-five years old, which greatly surprises me. She conceals her age, not because she is cosmetically altered or lacking in wrinkles, but because of her youthful exuberance and vitality.

"I'm not sure why I'm here," Winnie tells me. "I have a really good life, but lately I have found myself crying for no reason."

She laughs when I mention her colorful polka dot socks and eagerly tells me that they were a birthday gift from her teenage granddaughter, along with an assortment of other polka dot items, including a scarf, a hat, and even underwear. She names her husband as her "best friend" and talks about having gotten married later in life, having adopted a son and daughter, and enjoying two granddaughters, who live in another state.

"Oh, don't get the idea I'm lonely. I'm not. My life is really full. I'm an elder at my church and spend a lot of my time working with the young mothers there. I guess you could say I'm a mentor. I love it. My husband and I teach a class together on marriage. It keeps us involved; plus, we have to read the books and communicate."

My usual hypothesis is being challenged here. When someone shows up to therapy in his or her senior years, it's often because of loneliness or a loss of purpose. Generativity, the final devel-

opmental task of life, requires that we reflect on our experiences in our golden years and find fulfillment by passing along our unique gifts and wisdom to the next generation. And Winnie seems to be doing just that.

Maybe this has more to do with early childhood issues and a crazy family system, or perhaps with a recent loss, illness, or transition. But I soon learn that nothing out of the ordinary has happened recently. So why is she here now?

"I'm just not happy like I used to be. I can't quite put my finger on it. Not sure what the problem is. The doctor says I have high blood pressure and some anxiety, though I seem to be healthy. I have been wondering if I might be depressed."

"Any idea what you might be depressed about?" I ask, hoping she can shed some light on this unusual turn of events. But she just shakes her head, shrugs, and offers an apologetic look.

"I was really sad when my mother died, but that was over ten years ago, and Daddy died two years before that. They both lived long lives, and I wouldn't have wanted them to live beyond their years. I'm okay with it."

We search for residual grief, for trauma, or for that crazy family system with its critical messages, but she has little to report. And though she talks of being depressed, she admits that she doesn't actually feel sad, but rather feels out of sorts, unable to feel much of anything, good or bad. And so we start at the beginning, looking to stumble upon something that might be at the root of the problem.

"I was an only child and had a great family. My mom and dad were good parents, kind and loving, and I lived with them until I met my husband. I worked as a kindergarten teacher and didn't leave home until I was nearly thirty-five. I also spent a lot of time with my grandparents, who adored me."

I ask the usual questions about the atmosphere in her home,

about abuse, drugs and alcohol, and other forms of craziness, but nothing surfaces. She loved school as a child and was close to her aunts, uncles, and cousins, who all lived nearby and spent a lot of time together. I learn about her relationship with her mother, her father, and extended family members. No crazymakers seem to be lurking in the shadows as Winnie recalls a life of encouraging role models and plenty of joy.

And so we move on. We talk about her marriage, which she reports has grown deeper over the past forty years. She tells me about her children and grandchildren, and how she enjoys being a mentor to the young moms at her church. And then, in a quiet admission, she offers a hint into a darker, sadder part of her life:

"I'm not proud of the mother that I was. I was young. And I drank."

Winnie spills some tears as she talks about her regrets, the amends she has made over time, and her twenty-five years of sobriety. And after she talks about her children and her mothering, I ask about her decision to adopt.

"I couldn't have children. I just couldn't."

There is something about Winnie's tone that carries shame, something connected with sorrow and remorse. She is holding a heavy secret, one that she has been carrying since she was a girl of only fifteen, one she has tried to obliterate for nearly sixty years—one that is finally making its way to the surface.

"When I was fifteen, I had a boyfriend. I guess I was pretty naive, and, without really knowing what happened to me, I was pregnant. I know it sounds stupid, but no one talked about sex. I wasn't even sure how you got pregnant back then."

She reaches for one tissue, and then another, and buries her face as she cries quietly. Then she pauses and takes a breath and looks straight into my eyes, pondering whether this is the right moment, the right place, the right person.

"I've never told anyone this before," she says in a confessional whisper. *And with a decision to move forward, Winnie takes another deep, cleansing breath and boldly continues.* *"My boyfriend found me a doctor, and after we got some money together, I had an abortion. The doctor—if he even was a doctor—told me to put it out of my mind and never think about or mention it ever again. He told me to just get on with my life and forget about it."*

And so it was never mentioned, and no one ever found out about Winnie's pregnancy or her illegal, back-alley abortion. The boy moved away not long afterward, and her parents never knew what had happened to their daughter—they knew only that she struggled for years with unexplained infections, gynecological problems, and a damaged uterus that made having children an impossibility.

"To this day, even my own husband has no idea why I couldn't get pregnant."

Strangely, secrets never really die. For Winnie, as for each of us, they hide the truth of our experience and cause us to suffer all alone, with guilt and shame that beg to be brought to light, shared, and shown mercy. Secrets take their toll.

3.5 | PTSD

Trauma causes the body to be frozen in a state of fear,
terror, and hypervigilance.
—BESSEL A. VAN DER KOLK, MD

Posttraumatic stress disorder is also linked with secrets and is always connected to the past. It is a diagnosis that first appeared after the Vietnam War and, prior to the mid-1970s, may have been known as a nervous breakdown or shell shock. Once considered a severe anxiety disorder, PTSD is better understood as a mind-body response to having experienced or witnessed a shocking, life-threatening event that stuns the nervous system. While war is an obvious trauma, sated with injury and death, there are many other situations in which intense fear, horror, or helplessness results in the massive overwhelm coined PTSD.

The internal stress generated by a traumatic incident is a *natural physiological response*—not really a *disorder*. It is a reaction that is automatic, coded into our human survival instinct. But if the nervous system stays revved up with intense sensations that cannot be shut down, this neurological activation can result in arousal symptoms like flashbacks, hypervigilance, nightmares, anger, crying binges, dissociation, numbing, sleep disturbances, agitation, or difficulty concentrating.

Our physiology is designed to detect danger and take on the task of protecting us from harm. Our "primitive" brain (also called the "reptilian" brain), which is located at the brain stem, governs our instincts and reflexes. It is designed to keep us alive, and if we are in jeopardy (or someone else is), it sends data with astounding speed to the limbic system (the "midbrain")—an SOS that instantaneously activates our stress hormones and muscles, preparing us for aggressive fight or rapid flight.

Programmed to save valuable time in threatening situations, our brain processes from the bottom up. Messages from the primitive layer at the base of the brain are immediately received by the limbic, midbrain circuits that handle the nonverbal emotions and drives that set us in motion. The neocortex (the "thinking" or upper brain), which governs reasoning and language, is the last to be involved in the fight-or-flight reaction: We react first, then feel, then think.

What happens, however, when we are involved in a terrorizing situation in which we have no ability to *actively* participate—to run, hide, save ourselves (or other victims), or stop the predator—is that our mobilized system stays aroused. We are flooded with terrorizing feelings and sensations, and our body is galvanized by a lifesaving energy that makes it difficult for us to unwind and recover a sense of safety. Highly stimulated with bound energy that recirculates the shadowy threat of annihilation, a traumatized nervous system is constantly triggered, unable to either utilize the aggressive response or reset itself.

According to the *Diagnostic and Statistical Manual of Mental Disorders (DSM-5™)* published by the American Psychiatric Association, PTSD is a trauma and stress-related disorder that stems from an external event. A trauma survivor has been exposed to "actual or threatened: death, serious injury, or sexual violence" with accompanying feelings of fear, helplessness, or horror. An encounter that activates PTSD can stem from direct personal experience, from witnessing a tragedy, or even from indirect exposure —hearing about or confronting a traumatizing situation that is impacting a close friend or family member.

While war is an obvious threat, upsetting to any nervous system, plenty of other situations result in post-traumatic stress disorder, as well, and not every soldier suffers from this phenomenon. Why? After decades of study, we realize that the inability to cooperate with and complete the survival instinct of fight or flight creates an immobility response that is highly charged. We are learn-ing that it is not just about the intensity or the actual situation that causes trauma, but it is largely about the experience of having had no sense of control—no ability to *do something* to protect one's life or the life of another—that is at the core of posttraumatic stress disorder.

The murky experiences that happen in the torrents, shadows, and highways of life can be so upsetting and difficult to process that we push them into the deepest caverns of our minds and bodies. In wordless sensations and a frozen state of helplessness, we bury alive these untold horrors, fears, and shame far away from light, with a hope that they will go away. But what is hidden underground does not rest quietly nor vanish. Instead, what we attempt to suppress and hold captive often gains a powerful hold over us.

While we start out as warden, effectively keeping these disturbing happenings under lock and key, we often end up as bewildered hostages, bound by feelings and flashbacks beyond our control. Stored pain and secrets inevitably find their way out of confinement, escaping into dreams, compulsions, inflamed cells, and panic attacks. Unless the energy from unwelcomed memories and traumatic events finds release, it can continue to rev up the system, cause internal suffering, and get relived, over and over again. According to Peter Levine, the author of *Healing Trauma* and founder of Somatic Experiencing®, "[t]raumatic symptoms are not caused by the event itself. They arise when residual energy from the experience is not discharged from the body. This energy remains trapped in the nervous system, where it can wreak havoc on our bodies and minds." Sadly, victims continue to be revictimized by this stored energy until it is recognized, connected to its source, and set free.

PTSD is the human story of how our brain and body deal with life when it overwhelms us. The tragedies endured by a Vietnam vet, a sexually abused child, or a Holocaust survivor are not stories that can be held in darkness. They carry too much pain for any one person to bear. Their energy becomes a torment that needs to be released. When disturbing memories are unlocked and brought to the light to be thawed and acknowledged, the burden lightens and something begins to happen. With validation and empathy, a tortured soul finds an outlet to begin the healing process.

During times of adversity, our human spirit is more likely to triumph when we have the support of others. A helping hand, a warm meal, a listening ear, or a hug can help to balance the world of shadow with the light of goodness. And though suppression seems to make common sense—hide struggles and pain until they go away—it does not work in reality. Although people may silently endure in the aftermath of trauma and expect to move on, people actually *need other people in order to heal.*

Often, *people* have caused our greatest suffering, and it will be *people* who will facilitate our healing. *Healing comes in relationship.* Our stories need to come out of darkness, to be unbound and shared with those who can cheer us on when we feel too broken or discouraged to pick ourselves up. As Ecclesiastes (4:9–10) reminds us, "[t]wo are better than one. . . . If one falls down, his friend can help him up. But pity the man who falls and has no one to help him up!" We are not meant to go it alone.

When something happens that shatters our world—something so unfathomable that it can be neither acknowledged nor put into words—it recycles through our mind and body like an unfinished task needing resolution. Experiences that get cast into the deepest recesses of our beings are frozen there, held in captivity, along with a valuable piece of us. Plenty of addiction springs from the horrific events that cause PTSD, and it's possible that a dysregulated neurological system may play a significant role in bipolar and other mental disorders, as well as immune deficiencies and physical illnesses.

With PTSD comes a horrific story and its tears. But when we are given the freedom to speak our sadness, anger, shock, rage, fear, or shame, the consuming experience and its overwhelming thoughts and feelings begin losing some of their intensity as energy is released in the telling. Additional methods of dealing with tormenting sensations, images, and nightmares include mind-body applications like Eye Movement Desensitization and Reprocessing (EMDR), Somatic Experiencing® (SE™), Thought Field Therapy (TFT), and Emotional Freedom Technique (EFT), used by therapists who are specially trained and certified in these procedures.

Naturally, none of us really want to hear about the suffering of others; knowing that a priest has molested a young boy or that a serial killer has murdered yet another college coed tarnishes our idealism and corrupts our innocence. But only by acknowledging what is true, including the pain that victims and their families have had to endure, can we become more honest about the human condition. For some, it's a "downer" to do so, but the truth is that we live among sinners and saints here on the planet and are affected by both. Light and dark are balanced only when we neglect neither good nor evil in our assessment of reality and are willing to shine a beacon into the shadows.

We are all learning how to help the victims among us, and we will construct a more sensitive humanity when we recognize that, in order to heal our wounds, we need other people to listen to our stories. Until the recurring nightmares give way to a decent night's sleep, the voice of a victim is not ready to be silenced. Tears are evidence that the body has more work to do. And, regardless of *our* timetable or expectations, healing—like a scab—is not finished until its repair work is done.

Emotional pain does not simply go away. It is a part of life for all of us yet is uncomfortable for most to speak about. And in this success-driven world, it's to our advantage to stay on the sunny side of the street. Our natural tendency is to avoid what we do not want to acknowledge, and unresolved emotional pain is one of those things. Dealing with tragedy and its aftermath begins by reaching out and embracing those who are still suffering.

Listening patiently to the struggle of society's victims—

our veterans, our children, our traumatized, our abandoned, our widowed, our divorced, and our disenfranchised—takes time, and it often leaves us feeling powerless. But this simple act of empathy is a balm that offers relief to the wounded and creates a more open, mentally healthy, and humane world for all of us.

3.6 | MAUREEN'S STORY

Your neighbor is your other self dwelling behind a wall.
In understanding, all walls fall down.
—KAHLIL GIBRAN

Maureen has called again. Though she is nearly fifty years old, the voice mail she left sounds eerily like that of a little girl. She is crying and wants me to hear the poem she just wrote. Maureen's mother passed away years ago, and she takes comfort in thinking of me as a mother, her mother, though I am only a few years older than she is.

It's common for clients to want a secure attachment to a warm, nurturing mother who finds them fascinating, or to a partner willing to hang on their every word. I become a surrogate mother, friend, or respectful spouse for many, and because of my own need to be needed, these connections can become a dangerous source of flattery, especially if I am not careful to check in with a colleague or my own wiser self on a regular basis.

As a therapist, I need to set serious boundaries in order to keep these relationships, and my own head, from getting muddled. I have a private life with an actual husband and real children who want a wife and mother, too. I seem to continuously struggle with the delicate balance between my life and the needs of others, often feeling overly responsible for those in my care, like I'm a frazzled Mother Goose in an enmeshed, overgrown family.

Maureen's poem, left on my phone, is about the aftermath of incest and her struggle to feel safe. She tells me that she had been watching a TV show about Charles Schulz, the creator of Peanuts. Apparently, the cartoonist had difficulty communicating in his everyday life, so his comic strip became the voice he used to express himself to the world. Maureen identified with his loneliness and isolation and was inspired to find a way to open up her own voice in a poem:

> *He is dead.*
> *Gone from the world,*
> *But not from my being.*
> *Uncle Walter won't hurt us anymore.*
> *Maureen will keep you safe,*
> *Frightened little ones.*
> *I will protect you*
> *And listen to what you have to say.*
> *I promise.*
> *After so many years of being scared,*
> *I agree to play with you.*
> *And on a really good day,*
> *We can pretend that*
> *Everything is okay.*

Sadness and fear have dominated Maureen's life for as long as she can remember. She tells me that she can't sleep and needed to make a connection with someone. And through sobs, she whispers in a tiny voice, "Thank you for listening." Then she hangs up.

Maureen is one of five women in my Thursday-evening group, where all of the participants have experienced cruelty and mistreatment early in their lives—childhood abuse—which, unfortunately, is a common theme for many who see me here. Within every account of exploitation beats the bruised heart of a frightened child, and despite all that I have heard behind the door, I am stunned by just how badly these five innocents have been terrorized.

Each woman is here because she is struggling with debilitating depression that has impacted her daily life. By necessity, their stories were hidden away in darkness years ago, usually after their families discounted or rejected them. Though a few secrets may have spilled here and there, during stints in mental hospitals or therapists' offices, each group member longs to find freedom from the haunting memories that float to the surface at the most inopportune times.

All five of these women have come here hoping to find release from the experiences and visions that cruelly replay in their heads, dragging them back to another place and time over and over again. Here, they are willing to share, listen, and not run away. Here, tonight, as trust develops, vaults and closets are unlocked and traumatized babies, little girls, and teenagers emerge, hoping to be rescued from traumatic situations in which help never came.

With a red crayon in one hand, Maureen drops from the couch to the floor, her unfinished drawing clutched to her chest. As she folds into a fetal position before my eyes, no one flinches or even seems to find the situation unnerving. As in a preschool classroom, the others continue about their business with the faces and ease of unaware children, as I suddenly find myself the only adult in the room, the only one present to deal with the crisis at hand.

Instinctively, I grab a blanket, kneel down, and make a lap for Maureen to rest her head. I cover her gently as she whimpers softly, and, with the soothing sounds of a seasoned mother, I rock and stroke her back as if she were a precious, beloved child. I know that I am being a compassionate human being but wonder if holding a grown woman who has curled up on the carpet of my office is an okay thing to do as a therapist.

Without skipping a beat, Judy, the woman in the next seat, eagerly begins sharing her drawing as if she's a child taking a turn at show-and-tell. She holds up her picture of stick figures and explains what is happening with the voice and emotions of an oblivious five-year-old.

Here I am, alone, late at night, in a candlelit room with five women who are all dissociating. I am in a precarious situation; every woman is regressing as memories dislodge and overwhelm fragile psyches. Perhaps this was not a good idea. What have I gotten myself into?

Recollections are being shaken loose from storage, and now what? Maybe this endeavor is too much for me, for them, for anyone. I am moving into uncharted territory here and don't know what I'll find. There was no guidebook years ago to treat the complicated cases of multiple personalities depicted in movies like Sybil *or* The Three Faces of Eve, *and there certainly isn't one for treating Maureen and the others here tonight.*

How, after all, can children make sense of terror and circumstances that are beyond their guileless comprehension? None of us has the ability in our earliest years to grapple with evil. As children, we are clueless about the manipulations used to satisfy the whims and compulsions of an adult, especially when that adult is one who purports to love us.

In 1994, multiple personality disorder was renamed dissociative identity disorder in the Diagnostic and Statistical Manual of Mental Disorders, *used by mental health professionals. Though there is a history of debate surrounding the cause and treatment of multiple personalities, DID offers a complex and fascinating window into the creativity that the human mind employs to manage suffering. In my experience,*

DID always involves a childhood story of trauma that is appalling to imagine—something that would be impossible for any child to handle.

Adults who sacrifice others for their own indulgences defile our ability to trust. Ultimately, if the women here tonight are to have faith in anything or anyone ever again, they must first relearn to trust themselves and to unearth the truths they've buried within layers of secrets and shame. Sadly, when judgments and choices seem to have betrayed us long ago, we can end up doubting and blaming ourselves, as children and victims often do.

Somehow, these five women, each with PTSD and DID, have found their way here in what seems to be a divine appointment. They needed help and had tried everything, including medications and hospitalizations. When all five finally met in my office and considered continuing together as a group, we knew it would be risky. Each participant read and signed the customary Informed Consent agreement, with the usual disclaimer that therapy offers no quick fixes and no guarantees, and that things may actually get worse before they get better. Harsh, but true.

Each of the women had already spent a considerable number of years in therapy, and all were on psychotropic medications. And, according to them, having "tried it all," they were willing to try something new. And so, with the understanding that therapy can be upsetting, and that I could offer no promises or cures, they agreed to go forward with this group experiment. Despite the guise of a medical office with psychological jargon and insurance codes, therapy is spiritual work at the core—a place where souls touch and refine one another through stories, shared and rewritten.

And so we remind ourselves that the only way to get to the other side of pain is to go through it. We know the path will likely be bumpy but hope to find gifts like freedom and serenity on the other side. I agree to travel alongside them as a Sherpa, providing direction and the security of a base camp equipped with candles and music and overstuffed couches. I am the designated grown-up, the person who will stay big and not abandon them in this process. And the rest will be about trust and courage, theirs and mine.

They will serve as witnesses to one another as I facilitate and hold to the light whatever comes up. Nothing has totally prepared me for this experience, however. What I have taken on is an experiment in trusting my intuition—which is what I will have to lean on as we topple into the realm of mental illness diagnoses, tortured children, and breaks from reality.

The willingness to hear another's truth and trust that it will somehow make a difference will mix with the healing power of compassion as these five women open up and share their pain. Together, we will journey into the unknown, looking for keys that unlock shady memories and set them free, making room for new, brighter ones. As pioneers, all we have as we move forward is the uncertain excitement of new beginnings and hope for a better life. We will bear one another's burdens during this adventure, knowing there will be twists and dangerous triggers along the way.

So what exactly do I do now that these grown women are reverting to babies and tiny girls before my eyes? I take a breath and find myself praying silently, being reassured with a sense of calm and a message that it is somehow okay, admirable, even, that here in this place where fear meets courage, they have stepped out of their closets to meet one another. We have embarked upon an important passage, and we are in this together, at least for the next twelve weeks.

Healing, after all, takes place in relationship. It is the antithesis of the wounds one human being inflicts upon another. Just as relationships are the basis of the kind of human suffering for which people come to see me, so are they the means by which each human being heals.

None of us could have predicted what would happen here, but we have one another for support, a quiet room, and a spirit of camaraderie. Perhaps, with understanding, we can effect healing just by sharing and lightening our crushing loads—loads that were never meant to be carried all alone, particularly by children.

Bits of memories are shared in words and crayon drawings as these five women grieve and cry together. And by the end of the two-hour session, Maureen is safely situated on the couch again, along with the others, all of whom have grown back into adults capable of reciting the Serenity Prayer, touching up their lipstick, and carefully driving their cars out of the parking lot.

Back at home, I eat my trusty bowl of cereal with a dazed look that my family recognizes. It bothers them. They know that I have encountered something at my office, in that secret space in which they are not invited to participate. It has drained my energy and drawn the color from my skin. I know it worries them, but, besides finding a new line of work, I am not exactly sure what to do about it.

This night, like many others, I cannot sleep. What I see and hear when I close my eyes haunts me. Little girls, torture, sex games, and ritual abuse. Betrayal. Negligence. Broken bones. And this is not a nightmare—it is real life. I have fallen into a shaft so deep that I have trouble finding my way back to the safety of my bed. Unable to see around a blind corner, I fear that I have lost my way in the darkness.

With humility and self-doubt, I pray for guidance, and sleep eventually comes. And with the light of day comes a hardy feeling of assurance that I am, somehow, heading in the right direction.

3.7 | EATING DISORDERS

The intellect has little to do on the road to discovery.
There comes a leap in consciousness, call it intuition or what
you will, and the solution comes to you and
you don't know how or why.

—ALBERT EINSTEIN

An eating disorder requires exploring below the surface, venturing into territory that is confounding and secretive. And, as with other psychological disorders, effective therapy requires listening to that inner voice of intuition to lead the way. While food is the drug of choice in an eating disorder, *food* is not the entire issue. So much attention is paid to diets, to fat grams and calories —consumption—but an eating disorder is about the *appetite* and how or why it has been seized by internal and external apprehension that makes eating problematic.

Those who struggle with an eating disorder have been figuratively kicked in the gut, are carrying a nauseating secret, or are literally starving for understanding and support. Their stomach has flipped and is out of sorts. They have lost their appetite, are so voracious they cannot be filled, or can no longer hold down what they've ingested. An eating disorder is the body's attempt to speak—from the gut—what words cannot.

The body has its own unique language. While some people routinely have tension headaches, others manifest stress in searing back pain, heart palpitations, or bouts of diarrhea. Alfred Adler, a holistic psychoanalyst who recognized the mind-body connection as early as 1900, coined the term *organ jargon* to explain how our physiology communicates in personalized, nonverbal—physical—ways.

Doctors today are aware that stress can be somaticized, causing real pain and illness in uniquely personal manifestations. But we still have much to learn about the mystery and complexity of how our own mind, body, and spirit are joined, and how they connect to the world at large and those with whom we share it.

In my experience, anorexia, bulimia, and obesity are never just about the body, but the body doesn't lie. It tells us about sadness that troubles the soul—that is so disturbing as to turn one's stomach or create a craving that cannot be satiated. It speaks to us about wanting relief to calm a restless hunger. Using food as its focus, the stomach sends messages about too much, not enough, what it should or shouldn't have. And in cooperation with mind and spirit, it strives to make sense of what is good and right, in a struggle to understand what one does or doesn't deserve.

3.8 | KATIE'S STORY

The opposite of love is not hate but indifference.
—ELIE WIESEL

Katie is one of my first clients. At our initial encounter, what I notice most are her beautiful aqua eyes, crystal clear as the birthstone I treasured as a child, and her frail, emaciated frame. An intern at the time, I get her name from the list kept in a dusty file cabinet near the clinic's front desk, and, according to the record, I learn that Katie has been referred by an anonymous "someone from her church." There are no further details about her, just a date indicating that she has been waiting for an appointment for nearly three months.

With supervisor approval, completed paperwork, and an authorization for social service funding, Katie becomes an official part of my life and mounting caseload. Though only fifteen, she acts considerably older than her years and is sweet and pretty in a no-frills, old-fashioned way that high school kids probably wouldn't notice. Her delicate features, flawless skin, and gemstone eyes are those of a cover girl, but she is clearly an overlooked beauty, a Cinderella in recycled clothes and a greasy ponytail.

Katie talks to me about her difficulties at school—how she was a good student until her only real friend, a girl from church, died from leukemia nearly a year ago. She does not cry; she stays articulate about her thoughts and feelings, though she often lowers her eyes to look down at the floor or the dirty white high-tops that she has graffitied with doodles and inked hearts. She seems eager to tell me about her tragic loss and how much she misses her friend. When I begin asking about her family, however, she becomes uncomfortably quiet, and so I back off . . . and reach for the paper and crayons.

Adolescents are notoriously the truth-sayers of their family. They spill what other members can't or won't. Often, they shout it with anger or act it out in behaviors that punish them or someone else. When teenagers make a fuss, withdraw into depression, or suffer from an obvious eating disorder, the shadow of the conflict stirring within them can lead us behind closed doors to a troubled family system in need of help.

I wonder what I am about to learn as Katie opens the Crayola box and, with sanguine ease, picks a crayon and begins to draw. "I love art," she tells me. This precious girl sitting in front of me looks so innocent, and yet I sense a despair holding her captive as she creates a picture—a house with a smiley-face sun and a rainbow—in a story that is not quite ready to be unlocked.

For several sessions, Katie's family remains cloaked in mystery, and so I am completely unprepared for the shock that comes when I finally meet Katie's dad, Samuel. He is huge— close to four hundred pounds—unkempt, and not at all what I expected. He is wearing a stained white T-shirt with holes in it, and his rolls start at the place where a chin should be, hiding any sign of a neck and spreading down from there. He breathes with difficulty, as though his lungs are being crushed under a mountain of flesh, as he squeezes into the chair directly across from mine.

A million thoughts compete for my attention. He is an anomaly; while Katie has the skin of a china doll, Samuel's is covered with skin tags—hundreds of them—and some obvious blackheads. He is her physical antithesis in every way. Gathering my wits, I edit my face as I remind myself that I have to play the role of a professional—there is work to be done here, and most definitely an interesting story to be uncovered.

I hear about Samuel's struggles in special education classes as a child, about how he never graduated from high school and hasn't been able to hold a job. I am told about his wife's jealous "fits," about his three sons and one daughter, and how the family has no money. I learn about his personal struggles "with the devil," about his shame, about how he steals, and about why he is too embarrassed to go to church.

By the end of our session, Samuel has poured out his heart and has become a real person to me, though he seems more of an overgrown boy than a man. Still, I cannot help but wonder if Katie, like Marilyn Munster, is living in a family in which she really just doesn't fit. For months, Samuel and Katie are the only members of the Quincy family who come to the clinic, where each of them shows up regularly for their individual appointments and seems to enjoy having someone to talk to.

Samuel touches often on his struggle "with Satan," and I know there is evil lurking around the corner, waiting for just the right time to make its sinister appearance. He never once wears a clean shirt to his appointments, nor one without holes, though he apparently has money enough to have a cell phone, always a super-sized soda in hand, and even a brand-new pickup truck. It doesn't take long to realize that he definitely does not like to part with the one dollar he agreed to pay the clinic as his contracted "fee" for counseling services.

With no sign of embarrassment, he nearly always offers a flimsy excuse, a tale of bad luck or forgetfulness, but no money. When it comes time to pay his nominal donation for the session, he dramatically digs into empty pockets or goes to his truck and returns with a handful of pennies or a hollow pledge to pay double next time. It is unsettling—a story within a story of boundaries being evaded and promises broken. The pieces are coming together, not in words, which can be used to deceive, but in behavior, as they always do.

What I come to learn about the Quincy family is even more shocking than the initial jolt of meeting Samuel. Unlocking this twisted tale of teenage anorexia ultimately involves sessions with Katie's mom and brothers, hospitalizations, and the involvement of Child Protective Services. Unwrapping menacing secrets at the root of Katie's anorexia takes well over a year and uncovers a brutal story of a wife and children held captive by rape, incest, and fear that breaks my heart—and breaks it still whenever I think of Katie and her family, even some twenty years later.

Perhaps the children and adolescents who make it to a therapist's office are the lucky ones. Someone has singled them out—maybe as the scapegoat of the family or as someone who is depressed, angry, or showing signs of an eating disorder. But someone has *noticed* and has taken the time to find a listening ear and place behind a closed door where there is care, where secrets are safe and insides matter.

For many of us, it was precarious to put our thoughts or feelings out when we were children. For whatever reason, our innermost self had to remain hidden. There had to be an air of nonchalance, a mask, an alter ego covering for us at all times. Even a facial expression or gesture could be a dangerous giveaway, fair game for ridicule, punishment, or abuse.

I am thankful for the anonymous caller that helped

Katie and her family. Not all children, however, find a sacred space to deposit their secrets, hopes, and dreams. It is a freedom that many never get to experience. Even a diary with a golden lock and key can be much too risky to be kept in some houses, where enemy hands are astute at foraging through drawers and closets and covert places, invading boundaries and looking for something to censure or someone to misuse.

It can be risky business to listen to the stories that children tell. There are sometimes disclosures and ethical considerations that require confidentiality to be breached and transgressions to be exposed. But even though it is always sticky to question or shatter the status quo, children like Katie and her siblings need our eyes and ears, *our attention*, in order to be granted a protective haven where they can be seen and heard, free from harm.

3.9 | ADDICTION

With toxic shame there's something wrong with you
and there's nothing you can do about it;
you are inadequate and defective.
—JOHN BRADSHAW

Buried within the heart of every addiction is un-reconciled shame. Whether the drug of choice is food, pornography, alcohol, prescription medications, an irresistible compulsion, or codependency (an addiction to pleasing and seeking the approval of other people), shame reminds us of our failures and regrets and nauseates us with feelings begging to be numbed or hidden away.

While shame tightly clutches the key to our healing, its retrieval and treatment are complicated. When it comes to shame, we partner in a cover-up masterminded by our ego. Events that evoke feelings of disgrace are often suppressed, discreetly concealed from our awareness. The stuff we don't want to see or believe, our private stash of remorse and im-perfections, is tucked securely away. To dredge up feelings of embarrassment and humiliation—to bring shame to the light—seems dangerous, counterintuitive to our sense of self.

Being caught with a hand in the cookie jar evokes the natural shame that comes with deceit and wrongdoing. A built-in mechanism—our conscience—rides our back, alert-ing us when we are not being honest or our best selves. Like a motivating teacher, it lets us know that we are off course and need to correct. Similarly, failing a test or losing a job stirs up personal insecurities and a sense of inadequacy. Shame sets about its task of nudging us, letting us know that something needs to change.

But when, in our comparisons and judgments, we determine that there is no way to measure up, redeem ourselves, or move forward, shame becomes toxic, a mix of guilt and self-loathing. We convince ourselves that we are "bad"—that we have blown it and *nothing* can make it right. If we mistakenly deduce that life is about outcomes, not about learning and growth, we are filled with the damning misconception that we are damaged goods unworthy of abundance, losers in the game of life.

On an exhaustive journey to find freedom from an addiction to alcohol and its pit of shame, Bill Wilson sought the help of the renowned psychiatrist Carl Jung. Announcing that there was nothing, medically, that he could do, Dr. Jung informed Bill that "without a spiritual awakening," he would surely die from his alcoholism.

With little more than a sincere prayer for help and the synchronicity that followed, Bill was directed to join forces with Dr. Bob Smith, another hopeless alcoholic, and the two became teammates in a grand experiment. There in Akron, Ohio, in 1935, their commitment to each other—to rigorous honesty and to abstinence from alcohol—became the beginning of a model of recovery that has saved and enriched millions of lives.

Today, with over two million members, Alcoholics Anonymous is the largest self-help organization in the world, and a testament to the power of people helping one another by sharing their stories out loud. Unable to defeat the sinister demons of shame and alcoholism *alone*, two men found healing by reaching out to each other and to a Power greater than themselves.

Camaraderie with a fellow struggler increases the strength of both people. In AA, sponsors pass along the support they received at some point in their own lives, and whether a story is told by a newcomer or a veteran, something happens when people join together to seek and speak truth for a common good. Though the encounter fortifies both helper and helpee, something bigger takes place as well—something exponential that has the power to pay it forward and touch multiple lives.

The story of Bill and Bob is the story of how we heal. All of our stories of renovation are about seeking the support of another human being, about digging past the ego, clearing away deceit and denial, and being courageous enough to share the humble truth about who we are when nobody is looking.

Shame and ego fight hard to keep our embarrassing stories of fear and failure from being revealed, but if restoration is to begin, so must a searching and fearless personal inventory. If we are to learn anything from AA, it is that transformation requires a willingness to boldly investigate and earnestly share our lives with at least one other person and the God of our understanding.

The story of Adam and Eve is the universal account of shame and its cover-up. Our human tendency is to listen to the voice of shame and push it away until we lose conscious touch with its nagging message or do what is necessary to *change what needs changing*. When we hide our shame, we inter it in the darkest recesses of our interior, live with unresolved guilt, and create diversions to quiet the unsettling emotions it stirs within us.

We attempt to deny its existence by medicating ourselves with food, sex, alcohol, or behaviors that keep us busy. When we do this—when we become self-destructive, numb, or completely distracted—we are trying to lose connection with the *source* of our addictions and the pesky feelings that beg to be acknowledged. But when the cause of our discomfort is hidden away, it remains very much alive, eating at us like a virus and vying for our attention.

In the rooms of twelve-step meetings, it is said that "some people spend a lifetime trying to avoid a five-minute feeling." Shame, above all, is the feeling we attempt most to evade. It causes us dis-ease—a sense of imbalance and doubt about our worth. It is uncomfortable. Yet, paradoxically, to get to a place of self-acceptance, shame must be felt and investigated.

The more successful we have been at burying our disgrace in remote inner spaces, the greater is our need to dig deeply to uncover it. Freedom depends upon exhuming every trace of shame and bringing it to the light, which is tricky business, because the map to locate its source is often just out of reach. By design, we deny shame by concealing it in secret places, often beyond awareness. And we are about as motivated to recover it as we are to testify against ourselves in a court of law.

Unless we are seeking growth, we have little interest in finding how dusty old traces of shame may be stunting our lives and relationships. All attempts to unearth it will alert the ego, which is dedicated to directing us *away* from the shadows within our interior. It watches out for us like a militant guardian, protecting our self-image by shielding us from critical assessment.

The ego has been on duty since our birth, pushing us to

have a sense of worth so that we can handle life and exist in a competitive world. Its full-time job is to remind us that we are capable, a miraculous, one-of-a-kind, magnificent human being. It has walked with us through each of our developmental stages like an overbearing stage mother, motivating us and pointing us in the direction of our ego-centric interests.

Ironically, it is our ego that can also pinpoint shame's obscure hiding places. While it does everything in its power to divert us from feeling ashamed, it unwittingly provides valuable clues to areas in which those feelings have been stifled. Follow the ego as it attempts to cover up insecurity, embarrassment, or a sense of guilt, and you will find the precise spots where shame is being harbored.

In its tireless work to help us survive and look good, our ego alerts us to anything that casts us in a negative light or leaves us feeling deficient or slighted. It goes to bat for us and, when offended, will engage in a battle to defend us and win. Its role is not to get to the whole truth of a matter but to *be right*, which is why uncensored egos escort us into adversarial relationships.

Feeling ashamed or misunderstood signals the ego, and, once involved, it attempts to help us out of our trouble with a number of defense mechanisms. If we notice what we vehemently defend against, chances are we will uncover baggage from the past: old wounds, disappointments, survival issues . . . and shame.

With curiosity, we can become observers of our complicated selves. This will not happen easily, of course, because the ego is persistent and protective. But in order for growth to occur and addictions to be treated, we must recognize that the defensiveness we use to cover our anxiety is a clue to deeply sensitive areas where damaging pieces of shame have been stuffed away without resolve.

By examining defense mechanisms and noticing how our ego uses them to protect us from a truth that is difficult to face, we can uncover shame and bring it out of the shadows. Breaking through bonds of denial may involve a tug-of-war with a pushy ego, but it is a prerequisite for healing. Humbly facing the truth, even when it means feeling ashamed and powerless, is a necessary first step in overcoming any addiction.

Breaking through bonds of denial is a prerequisite for healing.

Defense mechanisms are protective devices that operate unconsciously and can *distort reality*. If the view we hold about ourselves or the world is jeopardized, or if we are overwhelmed by thoughts and feelings that seem out of our control, the ego will attempt to help us cope by disguising any truths that feel harsh and unwelcome. In an effort to protect us from feelings of anxiety, contempt, or despair, these common ego mechanisms come to our defense to soften the blow but often keep us locked in denial:

Repression

The pushing away of anxiety-producing memories, desires, or thoughts until they are out of awareness and "forgotten." Memories of childhood sexual abuse are often repressed for years, until a time in adulthood when it feels safe enough to "remember" them. Initially, when these memories surface, they come with overwhelming, unsettling feelings.

Suppression

A more deliberate form of forgetting, a conscious avoidance of particular memories, desires, or thoughts. It is a state of mind that refuses to admit that something exists. In homes where addiction was present, family members often learn to "not notice," to not feel or talk about upsetting circumstances. Denial, in AA terms, is a form of suppression that attempts to overlook, minimize, or forget what is troublesome.

Projection

When an undesirable urge, memory, or thought is attributed to someone else because it causes us too much anxiety to own it ourselves (e.g., "My daughter-in-law hates me because she's jealous of my relationship with my son"). Projecting negative feelings onto another makes that person the "bad" one and lessens shame by altering the painful truth (e.g., "I dislike my daughter-in-law because she took my son away from me").

Reaction Formation

When someone keeps a repressed wish at bay by engaging in an opposite behavior (e.g., a sister who resents her new baby brother secretly wishes he was never born, but she showers him with gifts and affection so no one will detect the truth).

Rationalization

When inappropriate behavior or thoughts are justified by socially acceptable explanations. Rather than taking full responsibility for our actions as creators of our destinies, we attempt to minimize shame by becoming victims of circumstances (e.g., "I would never have gotten involved, but I didn't know he was married—he wasn't wearing a wedding band"). It is common to overlook red flags as a rationale to avoid knowing the truth—a convenient way to remain blameless.

Regression

What happens when a person reverts to an earlier stage of development after a difficulty or traumatic event (e.g., following her parents' divorce, a twelve-year-old starts sucking her thumb again, or after the untimely death of a friend, a formerly dependable adult begins acting like an irresponsible, risk-taking adolescent).

Sublimation

When unacceptable urges are transformed into socially acceptable behaviors (e.g., a couple whose marriage suffers from no intimacy and years of resentment appear to be a picture-perfect pair, hosting lavish parties and charitable events; or someone who feels deep sadness becomes a comedian surrounded by laughter). Impressive accomplishments or an appearance of "happiness" can be attempts to compensate for disappointment and shame generated by a sense of personal insufficiency or failure.

Displacement

When overwhelming feelings (often hostility) get discharged onto objects or people in place of the objects or people who actually caused the feelings. Whoever is *there* often gets the fallout (e.g., a mother is the recipient of her teenager's angst or toddler's tantrum, or adult frustrations over work or finances are taken out on an innocent spouse, child, employee, pet, wall, door, tennis racket, pillow, etc.).

Overcoming addiction requires a personal inventory and willingness to break through denial. When we acknowledge our private struggles, mistakes, and critical inner dialogue, shame is coaxed out of hiding. By getting honest with ourselves, another person, and the God of our understanding, we release the ego-driven illusion that we are, or anyone else is, without flaws. Only then are we free to let go of our defensive cover-ups, imperfections, and shame—and let God restore our true identity and self-worth on a path to recovery.

* Grief needs to be grieved, or it takes on a life of its own; denial, anger, bargaining, depression, and acceptance are the five stages of the grieving process.

* The recurring symptoms of posttraumatic stress disorder are linked to intense fear, helplessness, or horror that we have buried inside us.

* Transformation requires a willingness to boldly investigate and earnestly share our lives with at least one other person and the God of our understanding.

* Our ego, and its defense mechanisms—though intending to cover up our shame and imperfections —keeps us locked in denial.

* To overcome an addiction and get to a place of self-acceptance, we must be willing to feel and rigorously examine shame.

3.10 | YOUR STORY

It's your turn to tell your story. Imagine you're the client. Get comfortable. Breathe deeply. Use the following prompts to make discoveries and gain clarity on your way to personal freedom. Use a journal to capture any thoughts, feelings, or images that come to mind or talk into a recorder. Welcome to your session ...

Are you experiencing grief from:

The loss of a relationship? Old emotional wounds? A health issue? An injustice? A life transition?

Which stage best describes where you are in the grieving process? With whom have you shared your pain?

Are you carrying a secret that needs to be released?

Do you ever experience the arousal symptoms of PTSD?

What situations trigger you? Do you know the source of your fear?

Are you struggling with a substance or behavior that causes you to feel out of control? What is it?

Do you carry shame that is manifested in an addiction to:

Drugs? Alcohol? Gambling? Food? Perfectionism? Spending? Approval seeking? Cutting? Stealing? Porn? Anything else?

Have you ever reached out for help? To whom?

What unresolved grief, fears, secrets, or shame might still be impacting your life?

What, if anything, is holding you back from rigorous honesty?

How might your ego be keeping you locked in denial?

Are you willing to share your whole story with at least one other person, and with the God of your understanding?

FOUR

Examining the Facts

4.1 | PRIVATE LOGIC

If you would be a real seeker after truth, it is necessary
that at least once in your life you doubt, as far as
possible, all things.

—DESCARTES

The story that we tell ourself has the power to keep us stuck, not only because it is commanding, but because it plays in our head *out of awareness* and is often full of distortions. This narrative program that runs our life has a powerful hold on us, with hidden agendas that affect our thoughts and direct our movements.

Our stories begin before our conscious memories do. With our birth and formative years comes an unfolding, a determination of who we are and what we will become. In our lifetime, we attempt to answer all the big questions about being human and live out our solutions with a unique brand of private logic directing the story.

Our earliest conclusions make up our private logic. Without realizing it, we figure out what life is about and how we will find our meaning in it—all by the time we enter elementary school! And today, unless we have updated our assumptions, we will continue to remind ourselves of our philosophy in every thought we think and move we make, processing information and countless choices through this screen of early reasoning set in place years ago.

Unless we update our earliest assumptions, our private logic will be based upon those conclusions.

Private logic is just that—private. It reflects the limited view of the world that we gathered through the subjective lens of our mind's eye. From our unique vantage as children, we took in images through a distinctive filter of deductions that colored everything we saw and experienced. Making their way through the shutter of our feelings and senses, our impressions were stored away, intact, along with the suppositions we believed to be true.

What we saw, felt, and *reasoned* about those experiences is compiled in a memory album that we use to recount the story of our lives. Recollections pulled from these photo journals are considered untouched snapshots, but the observations stored away on the negatives were not made through the impartial lens of a simple point-and-shoot camera.

What we gathered through our viewfinders was tinted and manipulated before it ever reached the film. The collections of pictures we recall as our stories are digitalized renderings that reveal the perspective, artistry, and convictions of each photographer. The photos we remember from yesterday have been creatively altered—processed and interpreted through a discriminating, uniquely personal haze of private logic.

Though it masquerades as Truth with a capital T, private logic isn't objective reality. It is the sum total of our belief system, sifted from early experiences and biased by our primitive understanding of the world. It is *our* truth, our certainty, and our conclusions about how things were and are and should be *today*. But private logic is flawed from its humble beginnings; it's the truth that was gathered with limited life experience and insufficient tools.

The simple interpretations and misinterpretations made by a wide-eyed, inexperienced child, teen, or even young adult must be reevaluated if we are ever to get closer to the honest truth about ourselves, others, and the world in which we live. As the Chinese proverb reminds us, "There are three truths: my truth, your truth, and the truth."

Our perspective is limited, and getting to *the truth* calls for a hard look at what we have seen and come to believe. This is not an easy process, because it assaults our growing-up presuppositions, challenges our reality, and shakes up the comfort of tradition. It asks us to look once more with eyes of wonder, from another time and space, from a different vantage point, and with a maturity that values objectivity in its search for facts.

Developmentally, we are called to this task in its most obvious form during our adolescent years, when we attempt to differentiate from our parents. With growth toward adulthood came decisions about what we would accept and hold as *our* values, and what we would let go of, as Dad's or Mom's or someone else's *opinion.* An appropriate and necessary part of individuation, this assignment to reevaluate and search for authenticity is a task that continues throughout our life span.

Left undone in one season, this quest for congruency and purpose will command our attention, showing up in another as debilitating dis-ease, a midlife crises, or a sense of imbalance. While our private logic may seem like truth, it can be harsh, erroneous, and depreciating. However, by examining our private logic with an inquisitive flashlight and sense of adventure, we open the door to finding bona fide truth, the truth that sets us free with hope and grace, correcting misconceptions, restoring mind and body, mending broken relationships and fractured spirits.

4.2 | GREG'S STORY

In every movement of the body, in every expression and symptom, we can see the stamp of the mind's purpose.
—ALFRED ADLER

Greg and Susan are here to work on their ten-year marriage. Susan has made the call and tells me that she's not happy, though she's willing to see if there's a way to breathe new life into their anemic relationship. Greg agrees that he really doesn't want a divorce. They have two young children and hope to figure out how to stay together.

"He never wants to go anywhere or do anything," Susan says with folded arms and a locked jaw.

I ask them about their early relationship models, about possible dysfunctional patterns and crazymakers, and about what they saw that convinced each of them that the other had something special to offer—that special moment called a FECK (first encounter of the close kind), when the heart suddenly beats with the excitement and surprise of newfound love.

Greg first met Susan at the hospital. She was a technician, and he was there for a chest X-ray. They connected right away. He lit up as he talked about how sweet and pretty she was at the time, and how he wanted to ask for her phone number but felt too awkward.

"And then, about a year later, I went to a buddy's Super Bowl party," he said with a smile. "Apparently, we had a mutual friend but didn't know it, and there she was! When I saw her, that was my moment."

"Actually, my moment was right there in the hospital," Susan said, as she leaned forward and uncrossed her arms, glancing at her husband. *"He was such a gentleman, and handsome, too. I even peeked in his chart to see if he was married, but didn't feel right about stalking him. But I never did get him out of my mind!"*

Though we start with this initial attraction and the highlights of their life together, we quickly piece together a pattern of disappointments, illnesses, and hospitalizations for Greg that showed up early on, one that was in plain sight from their very first meeting.

"It seems like I have spent every holiday and vacation alone," Susan reports, *"or with the boys. Greg always ends up with a cold, upset stomach, or headache. We tried going on a cruise once, but he ended up in the hospital with chest pains and we didn't go."*

I hear a story of missed work, too many sick days, and years of tests and visits to doctors' offices. And, amid shelves full of pill bottles and vitamins, their two sons have watched and worried about the health of their father, who has spent most of their young lives avoiding crowds, excitement, and even their sporting events.

"I know I get sick a lot," Greg remarks, with a look of dismay, *"but I can't really help it. I feel bad about missing so much as a father and husband, but I can only do my best."*

I learn that Greg has had asthma since childhood. He gets B_{12} shots and frequent headaches. He has had panic attacks, eats mostly vegetarian, and avoids sugar and gluten. And he has a history of inconclusive medical tests, years of excessive worry about assorted health issues, and, likely, a case of hypochondriasis.

The mind always strives to protect our ego from failure and will, if need be, create a diversion to protect our self-esteem. The problem is that it can outsmart us, leaving us clueless and confused by our own behavior. Hypochondriacs, obsessed with physical sensations, illness, and fears, are not usually aware of the underlying emotional issues that may be feeding them.

Hypochondriasis is a prolonged preoccupation with bodily concerns and illnesses—with or without an actual medical condition. It is psychosomatic, meaning that both mind and body are involved. Hypochondriacs are not faking; they are physically distressed or ill, significantly impaired by a handicapping ailment or ailments that keep them from boldly overcoming doubts and fears that hold them back from participating in the game of life.

All neurotic symptoms are subconscious *reasons* to be given a pass. In a somatoform disorder like hypochondriasis, the problem is actually the ego's *solution*, manifested *in the body*. The mind finds a way—and the body cooperates—to grant us special permission to sit out and avoid the challenges that feel too daunting or dangerous. We are spared from the race because of our disability, without which—we tell ourselves—we would surely be victorious.

Like all neuroses, hypochondria serves a protective purpose and is best handled with sensitivity and respect. Premature confrontation only raises the risk of denial and an abrupt end to therapy. Because the mind and ego can be mischievous and deceitful in their effort to keep our shame under wraps, it is no surprise that there is resistance when self-doubt, fears, and failings get aroused.

And so, suspecting hypochondriasis, I will ask if Greg is willing to meet individually for our next session, to gather more history and pieces from this cryptic story attempting to be unlocked. With time and safety, perhaps he will more readily acknowledge his struggles, becoming a seeker of truth courageous enough to look through the mind's eye into the bleeding ulcer that is draining him and depleting his marriage of its vitality.

My hope is that eventually Greg will be curious about the patterns that have become habitual, the private logic that is at their core, and the *purpose* of the enduring behaviors and persistent maladies that have become a debilitating way of life. But time will tell.

4.3 | LIFESTYLE

The unexamined life is not worth living.

—SOCRATES

Like Greg, everyone comes to therapy as a whole package: a mind, body, and spirit that cannot be separated. And by design, when it comes to our behavior, the mind is always in the driver's seat, influencing the body —determining exactly when it should blink, fight, or run, or release more stomach acid, insulin, or laughter. So, if we want to understand our *behavior*, we must pay attention to our *thinking*.

Though our actions reveal what we believe to be true, and we attempt to make sense of our life and movements, we are often clueless about why we do certain things. Whether or not we are aware of it, we formulate what we believe, and then, based on those beliefs and private logic, we develop habits and traits that become a personal way of life—our unique lifestyle.

To understand our behavior, we must pay attention to our thinking.

The meaning we ascribe to life, and the way we approach underlying goals (that are primarily out of our awareness), are all determined in childhood. Our personalities and attitudes are typically set within our *first five to seven years of life*. Imagine that! All of our thoughts and behaviors cooperate with our earliest interpretations, and so it's likely that the deductions we've made about the meaning of life and how best to live it originated years ago, when we were children with little knowledge or expertise.

Unless we are willing to revaluate our attitudes for possible misinterpretations and faulty logic, we function with the conclusions of a very young child, possibly a preschooler. And those simple beliefs do not automatically change as we grow. Without examination, the thoughts and meanings we adopted in childhood become stored "facts" that continue informing and motivating us as adults.

Our simple beliefs do not automatically change as we grow.

Finding meaning and purpose is often an unfinished task, for the very reason that life can go on, as is, without examination. The stages of life become thwarted when effort isn't made to continue developing throughout the life span. Today, we have the good fortune and tools to move beyond survival, to reevaluate old values and beliefs, and reformulate them in a way that leads us to greater wisdom and fulfillment.

Perhaps this explains the appeal and unrivaled success of *The Purpose Driven Life*, by Rick Warren, which topped the best-seller lists of *The New York Times*, *The Wall Street Journal*, *Publishers Weekly*, and *USA Today* in 2002, selling over thirty million copies and continuing to generate sales for one of the longest-running periods in history. At the same time that we are seeing sickening violence and worldwide corruption, we are also witnessing a surge toward greater integrity, contentment, and spiritual growth by seekers of all ages and nationalities.

Each of us must determine whether or not the attitudes we acquired as children serve us and the planet, or whether they need to be modified. In an effort to find fulfillment, we can free ourselves from faulty, self-defeating notions, but *only* if we are willing to revisit and inspect the thinking of the little child who thought them. If we do not invest-igate our premature reasoning, our beliefs and attitudes remain the same as the decisions we made in the very earl-iest years of our lives.

Correctly or incorrectly, every movement we make is determined by our mind to be the most advantageous action for that moment. In the case of mental illness, while there is sometimes a chemical imbalance, more often it is simply the result of disordered *thinking*; the direction chosen by the mind—the one that seemed most advantageous—was actually a mistake. What was decided and how the body responded ended in confusion, disorientation, and physical and/or emotional upset.

When symptoms arise, the body is speaking, telling us that our compass for living is out of whack. Neuroses, for example, are misguided choices, made by the mind, to find behaviors that will *momentarily* mask a sense of overwhelm. The more we learn about the mind-body connection and our own private logic, the more fascinating it is to recog-nize that every movement of the body is a hint into the mind's purpose.

Even the smallest bodily movement, a deep breath, a clenched jaw, or dilation of the pupils gives information about internal messages being received. According to Alfred Adler, MD, the task of therapy is to "discover the wrong assumption the person has made in choosing her life style, the way her mind has interpreted her experiences, [and] the meaning she has ascribed to life."

By exploring the lifestyle of an individual, looking at

the direction that has been taken in an effort to find meaning, we can bring to light and examine the subconscious goals that we have tucked away. So, after the initial session, with its presenting problem, intake forms, consent, and history taking, we join together as a trusty team, "cotherapists" who set intentions for the remainder of our time together and move forward with curiosity for the fascinating dig known as a lifestyle assessment.

4.4 | LIFESTYLE ASSESSMENT

Like our dreams, every neurosis is a story being told in code. By assessing the lifestyle, we can gain insight about what it is that we have come to believe, what we are continuing to tell ourself, and *why* it makes perfect sense that we would be doing what we are doing. And through the assessment, our private logic—the code's secret language—becomes evident, ultimately clarifying how and why our particular style of living came into being.

But it takes a certain amount of discomfort and *willingness* to unwrap the convictions we have held about ourself, others, and the world, and to allow ourselves to see what actually *was* and *is*, not necessarily what we have *believed* it to be. And it will take a collaborative effort to decipher the information we discover. It's not about assaulting the ego—cracking open defense mechanisms or breaking through denial—and it isn't about an expert, top-down interpretation that gets us unstuck.

Successful therapy, from the very beginning, is dependent upon you and I aligning ourselves with mutual respect and agreed-upon goals. Anytime I have all the "answers" or press for change that is not in keeping with *your* intentions, resistance and conflict are sure to take therapy in the wrong direction, or to a frustrating, grinding halt.

Change is difficult, an inside job that even external consequences, rehab, or prison might not affect. Good therapists are not authorities setting out to *change* their clients. The only time people actually change is when *they* want to do so. The goal of therapy is not change, per se, but is—simply and powerfully—to clarify with the client what he or she is in fact *doing*. Then it is up to the client to decide when—or if—to change, what, and how.

Psycho-clarity is the ultimate goal of the lifestyle-assessment phase of therapy. The client is invited to help in a psychological investigation that involves collecting significant data; looking into thoughts, feelings, and actions; and identifying the effects they have had on relationships, past and present. From this process come surprising discoveries that shed light on a client's thinking, choices, and unconscious goals.

True change comes from *knowing* our mind. We cannot change our mind without knowing it; and without language to share and evaluate our thoughts, we will not *know* our mind. Speech mines our private logic, putting into words what has been hidden from us, helping us to examine our mind and internal dialogue by speaking what has previously been unacknowledged—and, by doing so, eliminating certain behaviors that no longer seem necessary.

We must know *our mind in order to change it.*

So, after the initial forms and explanations, we establish therapeutic goals and a sense of camaraderie, ready to move forward as seekers of truth. We discuss what it is that we want to accomplish here, how we will know when or if progress is being made, and when therapy should come to an end. The major goal, of course, is that you will feel good, or at least better, and the relationship—with yourself and/or others—will improve. But until we agree on what that means, we may have different expectations. So we get in alignment by writing down our objectives as a kind of itinerary for our journey together.

Therapeutic goals are related to the presenting problem(s). You may decide, for example, that you want to:

"Stop obsessing about my ex-boyfriend."

"Lose five pounds."

"Sleep through the night without nightmares."

"Go through a day without crawling back into bed."

"Express myself without shouting."

"Quit smoking . . . bingeing . . . compulsively spending."

Stated as behavioral objectives that can be evaluated with regular check-ins, our mutually determined goals become the markers that will indicate whether something is, or isn't, shifting. But the overarching goal, expressed in a variety of ways, is a desire to comprehend your nature and choices. You may, for example, want to:

"Understand why I do what I do."

"Gain insight into my patterns."

"Figure out why I keep doing the same thing over and over."

"Know why I keep sabotaging myself."

"Get clear about how I end up in the same destructive relationships."

And so, with willingness, and a stated desire to *better understand*, we begin the psycho-clarity process as early as the intake, with facts about your relationships and history, including a description of the family atmosphere in which you were raised. Then, in subsequent sessions, we continue gathering additional pieces of information about your development, decisions, and personal attempts at finding meaning and fulfillment.

The following questions and topics thoroughly examine the environment in which you grew up, taking a comprehensive overview of the territory in which private logic got rooted, where troublesome patterns may have been cultivated and gained momentum. The Lifestyle Assessment Guide is an effective, time-saving overview that can be used to revive memories, reveal significant experiences, and unearth major lifestyle themes in the therapeutic process.

LIFESTYLE ASSESSMENT GUIDE

Family Atmosphere

What was the climate like in your home when you were growing up (in meteorological terms)? Sunny? Foggy? Frigid? Stormy? . . .

Family Milieu

Where did your family live? Socioeconomic status? Ethnicity?Religious/cultural characteristics? Rituals/celebrations? Can you draw a map of the interior of your house? Bedroom?

Family Constellation

Birth order: firstborn? Second, or . . . ? Baby? Middle? Only?
Description of siblings, oldest to youngest . . .
Sibling relationships/interactions/coalitions . . .
I was the child who . . .

My sibling/s was/were the child/ren who . . .
Childhood fears? Illnesses? Accidents?
Birth-order vantage (benefits/disadvantages)?
Role in the home? Expectations for you/others?
Family values? Motto? Secrets?
Relationship with your mother? Her favorite child?
What kind of woman was your mother?
Relationship with your father? His favorite child?
What kind of man was your father?
Parenting style: mother's? Father's? Teamwork?
Relational image: the nature of Mom and Dad's relationship?
Masculine/feminine guiding lines?
How are you just like your mother? Your father?
How do you feel about that?

Big Numbers

Age when you become an "official" woman/man?
Significant deaths—ages and circumstances?
Age when you are likely going to die? Why?

Other Significant/Influential People

Who was the most influential person in your life? How?

Life in the Neighborhood

How did you feel about your neighbors and surroundings?
How did you relate? Fit in?

Life at School

Difficulties? Favorite/least favorite subjects? Successes?
Peers? Teachers? Popularity/social life? Opposite sex?

Bodily Development

Appearance? How did you feel about your looks?

Sexual Development

How/when did you learn about sex? Experiences and initiation?

Puberty

How did you feel about/handle it?

Adolescent Experiences

Challenges/difficulties? Family's response?

Chronology of Significant Life Events

Recall a timeline version of significant milestones/events.

Repetitive Dreams

What is happening? Who is in the dream? What feelings are evoked in the dream/upon waking? When have you felt these feelings recently/in the past? What dilemma is the dream attempting to solve? Possible solutions . . .

Early Recollections

How far back can you remember? Recall your earliest memory first, with as many details, feelings, and thoughts as you can remember . . .

In Greg's case, information is gathered with ease and budding curiosity in our first individual session. Being willing to work individually for a time allows Greg to gain personal clarity before engaging in the complicated relational issues that arise in couples' therapy. Among Greg's personal goals, he says that he wants "to figure out how to feel better [lower his anxiety and blood pressure], talk to my wife [openly express his thoughts and feelings], and be a better dad [be regularly involved in his kids' activities]."

I always find it incredibly exciting when the ego relaxes, shedding its protective ways long enough to open the door to honest inquiry and reflection. For Greg, after just two sessions he is on board, earnestly digging for clues and making significant connections, starting with an interesting look at a "big number" and "early recollections":

"One of my big numbers is definitely thirty-five," Greg announces with certainty. "That's how old my dad was when he died."

Greg discloses that he was just five years old when he learned of his father's death, and that he didn't want his own children ever to have to suffer the loss of a dad like he did. And, yes, he believed that he would die at about the same age, of a heart attack, just like Dad.

"It was all so sudden. He went off to work one day, and next thing I knew, I didn't have a father anymore."

Greg's fears are obvious to both of us. And so is his grief. He clears his throat repeatedly, as if to swallow away the tears that have been stockpiling for a very long time. He has already outlived his father by four years and feels each year of borrowed time pushing him closer to the inevitable end of his life.

4.5 | EARLY RECOLLECTIONS

Change your thoughts and you change your world.
—NORMAN VINCENT PEALE

Using paper and crayons, Greg takes a visit back in time, recollecting his very first memory. He uses his nondominant hand to capture this pivotal moment in time with brilliant clarity, crafting a snapshot into a childlike drawing of stick figures in a room with a couch, a table full of food, and a little boy with an obvious crescent-shaped frown and cobalt blue tears.

"I'm five years old, and I remember this room. It was the living room of our first house, and we had a brown sofa . . . and something was happening on this day; neighbors were coming over, bringing food and stuff. I was told that my dad died, and then people kept coming to the house. This is me, right here."

In the picture, I see a child sitting by himself on the couch while four adults stand nearby. The one he identifies as his mother wears tears and a frown, too, and the other three are faceless neighbors who have come to help. Though Greg is unable to remember exactly who they are, he recalls that one of them gave him the stuffed animal he is holding on his lap, the toy dog he named Buddy and slept with for years.

As we look at the face of Greg's younger self, streaked with colored teardrops and a sorrowful frown, I ask about the details and, more specifically, how he felt in that moment as a little five-year-old:

"Oh, I was so sad. And confused. I remember people talking to my mother, then looking at me. My mother was crying a lot, and I was, too. And people would pat me on the head. Sometimes they would say things."

"And how do you feel here, now, as you look at that scene and into the eyes of that heartbroken, bewildered little boy?"

We take plenty of time to dip into the grief of this five-year-old child, as Greg feels sensations and sorrow and is able to acknowledge and extend compassion to the little child who still resides within this man of thirty-nine. Imagining how small and helpless he must have felt, Greg recalls the sadness and fear, and how perplexed he was by all that was happening; he had no real understanding about death or why Dad wasn't coming back home, and certainly didn't know what to do to comfort either himself or his mother.

"What kinds of things might they be saying here?" I ask, in response to Greg's earlier statement about the neighbors' comments.

"Well, I remember things like 'It will be okay' and 'Your dad is in heaven now' and stuff like that, but I think what sticks in my head most is 'You are the man of the house now,' and that I should 'be a big boy and quit crying.'"

The statements that echo most loudly in Greg's memory come with a forcible wallop, making it difficult for him to say them aloud. They catch in his throat on their way out, reverberating and bringing with them a flood of emotion. It's apparent that these admonitions hold significance for Greg and need further investigation. Resounding, emotionally charged messages are often rudimentary edicts that have been embedded in private logic and are feeding the lifestyle.

"And what might that little boy have decided at that time?" I ask.

"That I am . . . well, supposed to be the man of the house. Only I didn't even know what that meant. Every time my mom cried, I felt like I was letting her down. I knew that it was my job, but I didn't know how to do it."

Early recollections, like this one of Greg's, are powerful. They hold within them our earliest deductions in memories that we have placed in storage because they are noteworthy incidents that have shaped, *and explain*, our private logic. We cannot change our mind until we *know* it, and an early recollection is a vivid way to *witness* the mind's philosophy gathered from a significant experience and subsequent decisions. And, interestingly, we have only a limited number of these valuable and instructive early recollections—typically fewer than ten!

Early recollections reveal our childhood philosophy.

Naturally, Greg and I will explore the directives for him to be a big boy, quit crying, and somehow grow up and take charge. Together, we will wonder just how a five-year-old might go about filling a man's shoes, finding a way to take away his mother's pain, and, in the process of our assessment, gain psycho-clarity about how Greg's style of life got entrenched when he was a young boy who was trying his best in an overwhelming situation.

When I ask Greg to look at his picture, to imagine and speculate about what he, as a five-year-old, might have decided, I ask him to complete the following prompts as I write down his words verbatim:

"I am . . .

. . . alone."

. . . keeping Mommy from crying."

. . . maybe going to die, too, if I leave the house."

. . . not going to let anyone see me cry."

. . . bad."

"*Other people [Dad, Mom, and/or neighbors] are* . . .

. . . upset."

. . . never coming home. Dead."

. . . expecting me to figure it out and not be sad."

. . . trying to help but can't make it better."

"*My world is* . . .

. . . lonely."

. . . scary."

. . . unpredictable."

. . . never going to be the same."

. . . tragic."

And when I ask what his picture would be titled if it were hung in an art museum, Greg replies without hesitation: "The Day a Life Was Shattered."

Early recollections are rich. They take us back in time, giving us a panoramic view through the mind's eye, helping us to see overlooked details and early programs that have elapsed our awareness. With the benefit of *today's* experiences and vantage, our original decisions are brought into sharper focus, helping us see our own thoughts—what we have come to believe—and why, based upon those particular conclusions, our lifestyle patterns have made uncommon sense.

Greg's second recollection is as informative and powerful as the first. Again, I ask Greg to recall a memory—the very next one that comes to mind—and to use his nondominant hand to draw what he remembers, in as many details as possible (a picture truly is worth a thousand words). I note his verbiage and reactions, writing them down as he speaks:

"*I am six years old, and I remember having tonsillitis. It wasn't too long after my dad died. And it seemed like I was always sick after that—mostly with colds or respiratory things. I ended up missing a lot of school and was diagnosed with asthma . . . I think by the time I was in third grade.*"

In this second memory, Greg is tucked in his bed, propped up with several pillows. His mother is seated at the footboard, holding a book in her hand, and Greg is looking at her with a glint of a smile. There is a window with red curtains that match the bedspread, books and picture frames on a shelf, a plate of cookies on the stand next to the bed, and his stuffed dog, Buddy, resting close beside him.

Greg explains that whenever he stayed home, his mom was always there. The two of them would spend time together, and it felt good. His mother would read stories, or they'd watch TV and play cards. They had each other, and when he was sick, his mother would spend the night in the other twin bed in his room. "Sick days" came with treats like cookies, pudding, or cocoa and cinnamon toast.

It is no surprise that Greg developed a long history of illnesses or that he accumulated plenty of absences from school and attention from his mother. Sick days and illnesses became a successful means of keeping his mom involved and away from her pain. While, as a six-year-old, Greg couldn't figure out how to be a man, keeping his mother involved was something that he could do. And by focusing on his health, playing it safe as life went on, Greg could perhaps prevent the cycle from happening again in this generation.

Amazingly—and just beyond our awareness—the body will always cooperate with the mind's plan. When our mind detects a dilemma, our body and ego get involved in devising a "perfect"—albeit completely unconscious—*solution*. And Greg will come to see how this has been the case in his own lifestyle pattern, as we examine the information gathered —and deductions made—from these two early recollections.

4.6 | DOLORES'S STORY

Intelligence will be used in the service of the neurosis.
—SIGMUND FREUD

Dolores has had a hard time showing up for her appointment. Her husband called to reschedule three times. But she is finally here, perched erectly on the edge of the couch in the waiting room, with her purse and paperwork cradled in her lap.

She is wearing a gray dress, stockings and heels, and a light purple cardigan, which is a spot-on match with her lilac lipstick and nail polish. Her husband reaches out his hand, introduces Dolores and himself to me, and then pats her leg, as if to say, Honey, you're okay. I'll be waiting right here. *And with that, Dolores stands, glances at her husband for a last bit of reassurance, as she and I head back to the office together.*

Taking a seat on the sofa, she seems nervous and stiff, clutching the strap of her handbag like a frightened child, eyes darting about and breath catching high, barely making its way into her chest. The first order of business for Dolores is to slip through the anxiety of what's to come, into the safety and ease of the here and now.

So I invite her to get comfortable: grab a pillow, lie down, change seats, or do whatever she'd like to do. And with encouragement, she takes time to look around the room, check out her surroundings, and take in a fuller breath or two. She comments about a favorite book she has spotted on the bookshelf, as she scoots back into the sofa and relinquishes her purse to the floor.

"I like the way your nails and lipstick match your sweater,"
I mention, as she relaxes more deeply into the cushions.

"I have always liked to do that," she tells me, "ever since I
was a teenager."

We spend time talking about nail polish and lipstick, and I
wonder aloud about the logistics of coordinating outfits and
polish changes, as she informs me how wearing a lot of purple is
a way to keep it simple.

We talk about her children, her fifty-year marriage, and
how she enjoys cooking.

And, eventually, our conversation makes its way to the
forms: confidentiality, informed consent, crazy . . . and her pre-
senting problem.

"I just don't want to leave the house," she tells me. "I like it
at home, but when I have to go out, I get really nervous. I don't
even want to go to the store or drive anymore."

She tells me about a few of her many fears: How she might
get in an accident or pass out, not be able to find a parking space
or get lost on her way back home. Or what if there is a tornado
or she is exposed to the latest flu virus? She has stopped watch-
ing the news, and if she reads the newspaper or thinks about the
world, with all of its problems, she feels riddled with anxiety.

It wasn't always like this for Dolores. She spent over two
decades as an executive secretary, a job that she loved, and
enjoyed tennis and being involved in her children's school
activities for years. She was a Girl Scout leader and an officer in
the PTA and often went out by herself with her friends or her
husband.

But after she retired, something shifted. Dolores began
spending more time at home, and when she would go out, she'd
suddenly feel as though she was in terrible danger of something

happening or doing something dreadfully embarrassing. Once, while waiting in line at a crowded department store, she began to feel dizzy and panicky, couldn't catch her breath, and has been afraid to go anywhere ever since. For nearly two years now, she hasn't wanted to leave the house.

"Life feels out of control. It really has gotten dangerous out there; people are getting shot in movie theaters and bombed on the streets. You just never know what might happen anymore. And I don't want to have a panic attack somewhere or get stuck on the freeway . . . so I just feel better if I stay at home."

Agoraphobia is an anxiety disorder that typically leads to an avoidance of certain situations. Often, someone with agoraphobia has had a panic attack and develops a fear of having another attack in a similar situation. Apprehension may center on crowds; travel by air, car, or bus; doing something embarrassing; getting stuck on a bridge or in an elevator; or being unable to escape from circumstances fraught with potential danger. Accompanied with panic-like symptoms that stem from one or multiple phobias, agoraphobia is characterized by fear-based *avoidance*.

The ultimate goal of every mind is survival, and the drive toward security is intrinsic in our private logic and lifestyle choices. We are programmed to find a means to provide ourself with a feeling of safety and success. And so, in the case of agoraphobia, the resolution to any sense of vulnerability and defenselessness is simply to find protection in the fortress of home.

In Dolores's case, home is the very place she currently feels most successful; she has a beautiful new kitchen with cookbooks and recipes that she's neglected for years, and she even has the attention of a husband who is willing to do errands and grocery shopping. What Dolores doesn't have, however, in this shaky new territory of aging and retirement, is a sense of purpose or any vision for a meaningful future. The world has become scary, and her place in it meaningless.

The most basic of human goals is to survive and feel *secure.*

When the mind concludes that there is no way to be secure or successful, neurotic symptoms can serve as a way —*a solution*—to avoid a sense of failure or harm. If need be, the mind will use misguided ego-protective *excuses* to provide us with a sense of security—the most basic of our human goals and strivings. Agoraphobia, like all neuroses, is an attempt to be sheltered within a comfort zone of purposive, albeit confounding, behaviors that "help" to divert our personal disappointments, vulnerability, and feelings of insecurity.

Most people get exactly what they want—only they don't
know that they want it.

—RUDOLF DREIKURS

Both Dolores's and Greg's stories give us a look at
how fear can impact behavior and how resourceful
the ego is at finding ways to keep our pride intact by
excusing us from trying—and possibly failing or looking
foolishly inept. When tasks of life create an overbearing
sense of insecurity, the mind and body team with a cunning
ego to protect our vulnerability and self-image in a brilliant
plan of self-preservation.

Most of us opt to shield ourselves from being exposed,
protecting the egotistical false self that never makes
mistakes, fails, or loses control. When issues of significance
and success force us to hide, to disown our doubts and fears
—pieces of ourself—we become a carrier of secrets, separated from truth. Shame whispers that we don't measure up,
that we need to keep up appearances, and we begin denying our imperfections *and* our individuality.

Disconnected, we lose the ability to be completely
honest with ourselves (and others) and live in a fog of
denial that dims our enthusiasm. We are surprised by our
own behaviors and can't seem to access what is motivating
them or why we feel so driven. And to find out, to investigate what has been obscured from our awareness, is a
threat to our dutiful, image-enhancing ego.

The ego is not all bad, however. It is the seat of our desires, and it propels us to realize our destiny and stay *alive*. It is built into us as part of a program that does a stunning job of looking out for "number one," motivating us to strive for our wants and dreams. But it is best stabilized with help from the spirit within us, another part of our program, that is set in place to direct us to what is right and good for us.

The spirit is the character piece that balances our self-centered behaviors with wisdom, discerning not only what is best for *us* but what is also good for others and the planet. The fountainhead of love, the spirit has a heart for creatures, creation, and creativity . . . and the Source of them all. And while it affirms that we are precious and need to care for ourselves, it also reminds us that we are not the center of the universe, that we have gifts to share and are part of a much bigger story and community.

Narcissists are people with ego problems who want the world to revolve around them—and it seems as if it does. In our narcissistic culture, narcissists win prizes, elevate themselves, and are constantly feeding a me-first, entitled ego. What they get and how they appear on the outside are much more important to them than who they are deep down when no one is watching.

And while they may be talented and successful at what they *do*, narcissists neglect the gentle nudging of the spirit, subduing their inner wisdom for accolades and applause. But the problem is that joy, peace, and love come from spiritual development, and are rewards that the ego—even with all of its trappings—cannot provide on its own.

Coming clean, purging pretenses, and dredging up judgments and self-doubt is a responsibility many shirk, because to understand ourself, to truly *know* our mind, is not for the deluded, weak, or arrogant; it's the very reason why narcissists don't readily participate in the therapeutic process. Our ego must humbly step aside long enough for compassionate self-acceptance and truth to be brought to light. And for that to happen, we must be willing to speculate about potential errors in our own reasoning, and the ways in which our faulty notions and misconceptions might be keeping us stuck.

It takes integrity and courage—and a sense of humor—to peer beyond our pride into our deeper beliefs, desires, and agendas with rigorous honesty. We have to tolerate shame and embarrassment in order to acknowledge—even chuckle at—our foibles and human condition. And, by knowing our thoughts, making sense of our behaviors, and uniting with inner wisdom, we can own our imperfections, understand why we are doing what we are doing, and gain a fresh perspective about past, and future, lifestyle choices.

A successful therapeutic dig explains why life has been difficult for us and illuminates the behaviors and excuses that have arisen from our attempts at coping with these difficulties. Though we gain clarity and self-compassion by connecting past and present, if therapy concludes here—in the investigational phase (as it all too often does)—it can end with blame, a sense of injustice or entitlement, and no sense of resolution. While it is essential to the therapeutic process to uncover facts and recognize how our history has influenced us, there is more to healthy development and good therapy.

In order for real transformation to ensue, the information we gather needs to be thoroughly unlocked to inspect not just *what* happened and how it impacted us, but *why* it is of such importance to our lifestyle today. The ultimate goal of therapy is not just to know about our experiences, but to discover how we have *interpreted* them, and how our private logic is continuing to affect our life and current relationships.

The ultimate goal of therapy is to determine how we have interpreted our experiences and how our private logic is impacting us today.

All behaviors are purposive, meaning that they serve us in some way. Actions—even hypochondriasis and agoraphobia—are attempts at accomplishing *something* on our behalf. The mind and body will always cooperate, directing our movements toward a sense of security and success. Troublesome patterns arise when we've deduced that we are falling short and are overcome by self-doubt and anxiety. The issues that bring us to therapy, like all behaviors, are goal-directed movements: individualized (subconscious) efforts to help us feel protected, evade fear, and escape from overbearing feelings of failure.

"Neurosis," according to Rudolf Dreikurs, MD, "is a statement of bankruptcy. It is an expression of defeat." For some, this giving up becomes a neurotic flight from life and overwhelm that looks like agoraphobia. For others, it's a withdrawal into the fetal position of depression or the adrenalized whirlwind of fast cars and liquid courage. But, somehow, we find our own diversions—comfort zones that come with a concealed "benefit" that the ego devises to shelter our insecurities.

Without a strong alliance, therapy is unlikely to get this far. Only the boldest bare their souls, take off their masks to "guess" about unconscious goals and mistaken notions buried within their thinking and patterns. Without humility, it's impossible to analyze this data objectively, to take responsibility for the errors of our ways and consider new ones. Hopefully, we will be united in our intention to clarify what is really happening, *why* it is going on, what it is going on *for* . . . and what it is ultimately costing us to keep these behaviors going.

4.8 | SECONDARY GAIN

All neurotic patients exclude every aspect of life in which
they do not feel strong enough to achieve dominance.

—ALFRED ADLER

The only way to understand how our behaviors have
had purpose is to spotlight what we might be getting from them: to become aware of the secondary gain
they may be providing. When body, mind, and spirit unite
to manage pride and unlock the truth, we are able to acknowledge our doubts and apprehension and untangle the
reasons why we may be doing what we are doing. But this
requires that we push our ego aside long enough to uncover
the faulty assumptions and unconscious goals that have, without our awareness, been directing our thoughts and actions.

The way we go about this process is by remembering
when we became discouraged, taking a look at what was happening when we began having misgivings about our ability
to meet a particular challenge or to protect ourselves, and how
our ego—in its uniquely brilliant way—has been helping us
save face and evade the reactions and fears associated with
failure: *stress, rejection, humiliation, and meaninglessness.*

Dolores recognizes that after retirement, she felt disoriented, and
easily pinpoints when life took a discouraging turn, stirring up
self-doubt with feelings of loss and panic. After years of
working, and with nothing new set in place to occupy her time,
she found that the "golden years" of retirement quickly became a

lonely and dark time in which she lost confidence and courage.

"I didn't know what to do with myself; I no longer had a daily schedule, a regular paycheck, or even a reason to get up in the morning."

The distance between her and her husband became magnified, as did the unresolved hurt of a little girl abandoned by her father, and a wife rejected by her husband's previous affair with a neighbor and current one with late-night porn.

"I never said anything to Charlie about his affair or what I found on the Internet. I'm sure he doesn't think I know anything about it."

Amid secrets, betrayals, and an unsatisfying transition, Dolores began isolating, grasping for control. She noticed tragedies in the news, felt rootless and unbalanced. When she'd go out, she'd feel afraid and panic would set in. She wondered if she had dementia or some version of "growing old and worthless" and was stressed and humiliated by the changes in her behavior and her inability to get a grip.

Dolores takes a look at what she's been trying to avoid, as well as what her hidden priorities have been. The comfort of home provides a means to alleviate her stress, and by controlling her life—and Charlie's—she minimizes the risk of being humiliated by simply staying inside the house (in the kitchen, where she feels most competent), with a newly devoted husband by her side.

When our hidden priority is to eliminate *stress*, we will find our own brand of *comfort*, and when we attempt to avoid *humiliation*, we will do whatever we can to *control* the situation. It makes sense, not because we have dementia or are old or crazy, but because it's the way we are wired. Our difficulties and insecurities will push us toward one or more "solutions": *comfort*, *control*, *pleasing*, and/or *superiority*.

If Your Priority Is:	You Want to Avoid:
Comfort	Stress
Control	Humiliation
Pleasing	Rejection
Superiority	Meaninglessness

Comfort is what many seek to avoid the stress of life's challenges and uncertainties. *Control* is an effort to circumvent humiliation when we doubt our capabilities, fear failure, or are afraid of being exposed and embarrassed. *Pleasing* is a way to pacify potential critics and eliminate rejection by being overly kind and helpful. And *superiority*—elevating ourself to gain recognition and status—is often a cover-up for feelings of insignificance and a disheartening sense of meaninglessness.

Dolores considers what she may be trying to gain and avoid; and begins speculating, guessing good-naturedly, about the powerful "reasoning" that has been out of her awareness. And by making valuable connections about her priorities and the price she may be paying for them, she is getting closer to setting new—conscious—goals that can give her greater purpose and satisfaction in this season of life.

By recognizing our unconscious intentions, we often discover —with a degree of astonishment—that our behaviors have been serving us without our awareness. While Dolores's agoraphobia appears to limit her, it also keeps her *stress* at bay in the safety and comfort of home and, at the same time, is a way for her to gain *control* over her domain—her kitchen, her fears, and even her husband—all without ever having to confront them.

Greg, too, found a way to unconsciously deal with his stress and apprehension. Within the "comfort zone" of medical tests and diagnoses, he was excused from insecurities and challenges that overwhelmed him. His illnesses provided the "solution": the disability label needed to mask and control deep sorrow, fear of death, and shameful feelings of inadequacy that had plagued him since childhood yet had never been addressed.

All behavior is purposive and often driven by unconscious goals.

All of our behaviors are purposive, so when our actions and choices seem to make little sense, secondary gain is likely a concealed goal, hidden even from our own self. By examining when our difficulties began, interpreting *why* they may have been set in place and how they may be helping us evade anxiety and distress, we can gain the psychoclarity necessary to discover what our behaviors may be *costing* us. And only then will we be ready to allow our mind to *consciously* choose a more advantageous action plan.

If Your Priority Is:	You Want to Avoid:	The Cost to You:
Comfort	Stress	Reduced productivity
Control	Humiliation	Lack of spontaneity and/ or intimacy
Pleasing	Rejection	Stunted growth
Superiority	Meaninglessness	Overly responsible and/ or burdened

When we seek *comfort*, rather than overcoming our challenges and fears, we are likely to end up feeling unsatisfied and unproductive. In the same way, if *control* is our default setting to avoid feelings of failure, we can become protective and inflexible, quelling a sense of adventure and intimacy in the process.

While *pleasing* is an effort to avoid criticism and rejection, it stunts our growth and development by focusing primarily on other people's opinions and happiness while ignoring our own. And *superiority*, the effort to earn praise and attention—to rise above others to "be somebody"—is an attempt to confirm our worth. But this ambitious drive for esteem often leaves us feeling burdened, overly responsible, and burned out.

The greatest cost, of course, is that when we hold on to our insecurities, regrets, grief, or fear, we *suffer*. Unacknowledged, self-doubt and shame can quietly take us hostage, locking us away in pain and depression, isolating us from others, and preventing us from accepting and freely exploring—*fully living*—the remainder of our lives and unique destinies.

In an attempt to unmask the "good" that the ego has been doing on our behalf, we must ask ourselves a simple but straightforward question:

How would my life be different if I didn't have this problem?

Once we identify what we are getting from our behaviors, what we have been trying to avoid, and what this way of living may be costing us, secondary gain is tarnished enough to lose its appeal. Change becomes a more attractive possibility with clearer vision, but altering default settings takes both insight and courage; we must recognize what we are holding on to, then be willing to reconsider, take a deep breath . . . and let go.

4.9 | LETTING GO

All suffering comes from attachment.

—BUDDHA

When our losses feel insurmountable or success no longer seems possible, we can lose our courage. Defeated by our disappointments and misfortunes, we convince ourself that there is no way out, and suffering can become a way of life—a lifestyle that evolves from sorrow. When we continually replay what happened to us and hold on to it with aching devotion, moving on ceases to be an option. And letting go, rather than being a way to be set free from torment, threatens to erase our experience or, worse, releases someone or something we might not want to set free.

Even misery can have its secondary gain. Strangely, it can become a sad comfort zone of blankets and blackout curtains that allows us to withdraw. We relive the way it *was*, dwelling on the past and keeping our memories alive. Our physical and mental agony attests to our pain, is worthy of sympathy, and provides a legitimate excuse to avoid the challenges (and pleasures) of day-to-day life. Naturally, we all need time to move through the grieving process—to drop out, heal, and regroup. But for some, misery will become an extended flight from daily *living*, a dedicated victim stance and lasting lifestyle.

Maureen, from my evening women's group, was so young that she cannot recall when her retired aunt and uncle first began babysitting her in their home. What she does remember is the garage, the stench of alcohol on his breath, and the image of two little black patent leather shoes on the ends of her tiny feet.

What happened to her in that place cost her plenty: loss of innocence, years of blackout drinking, psychiatric care, hospitals, and dissociation. And with the sexual abuse came threats and fears, PTSD, and the aid of multiple personalities that shared the secrets she kept tucked inside for most of her life.

Medical procedures, over a span of twenty years, never did find the source of her debilitating abdominal pain, so she eventually had a full hysterectomy. But even after "taking care of the problem" that would leave her unable to bear children, she continued experiencing the searing body sensations that took her breath away and, like the phantom pain of an excised limb, reminded her of earlier days and a precious child still needing protection.

There is a strange uncertainty, a nagging reservation that if we let go, leave the past behind, or forgive the unforgivable, it might somehow all be forgotten, obliterated, as if it never happened or existed. And so the ache of grief keeps tragedies alive in an ever-present sorrow reminding us that our story, and every experience within it, is *real* and will never be wasted or forgotten.

MISERY

Held tenderly
In its arms,
She wears her misery

Like an old sweater.
Knit with heartache
That's frayed and worn,
She is embraced by a relic
She cannot discard.
Clothed in fibers
That are spun of tragedy,
She discreetly travels
Through time.
In fabric and memories
Smelling of mothballs,
She resides in an heirloom
That validates her sorrow.

Suffering can be a way of holding on to the past, a tribute to what was painfully snatched away from us. After Anna's son died in a drowning accident, she immediately withdrew. She stopped playing tennis, stopped attending church or maintaining friendships. She barely went outside; she let her garden and marriage wither and was sucked into a debilitating depression for years.

The thought of ever enjoying life again was distasteful to Anna. For her to experience pleasure seemed like a betrayal. Until she recognized that the amount of pain we bear is in no way equivalent to the amount of love we hold, she was unwilling to let go. Anna needed to know that releasing her pain was not the same as relinquishing her love or the cherished memories of her son.

Letting go does not mean forgetting or not caring. It doesn't require that we discount the past; it has shaped us into the people we are today and has been our grandest teacher. And it certainly doesn't mean that what happened didn't forever alter our life or was just, or that perpetrators should be given a pass. But it does require an act of courage to move through our grief—relinquishing pain, regrets, or thoughts of revenge—to give up a root-bound attachment to what happened to us and find a reason to ground ourselves in the pleasures and beauty that *today* has to offer.

With wisdom, we can learn to accept not just the pain, death, and sadness that come with time and loss, but the *love*—extended to ourselves and others—that puts our memories in their rightful place, heals our wounded hearts, and inspires us to open up again to *living*: to goodness, friends, and loved ones. Happiness is seeded in present moments, enjoyed in ephemeral instances that can incrementally—one tiny, daring step at a time—develop into contentment, regardless of our current circumstances or history.

Are you willing to let go?

Our attachment to the pain of the past keeps us suffering. We must ask ourselves if we are ready and willing to detach and . . . *let it go*. Depression and sorrow can be seductive, a tale of woe that rejects any prospect of a happy ending. Moving beyond misery takes a commitment to resisting its captivating allure, glancing back only once in a while into the tragedy but keeping our story headed in the right direction. During dismal times, it takes resolve—and courage—to get out of bed, to put our face toward the sunshine, and to accept the warmth of a new day and hopeful promise of seasons to come.

* Our attitude and personality are set in the first five to seven years of life.

* Private logic comes from our earliest deductions and does not automatically change as we grow.

* To make changes, we must know our mind: examine our lifestyle choices and unconscious goals.

* The lifestyle assessment, including valuable early recollections, is a tool used to reveal our earliest perspective and private logic.

* By understanding what is motivating our behavior, we can let go of secondary gain and suffering, reevaluate, and change our lives.

4.10 | YOUR STORY

It's your turn to tell your story. Imagine you're the client. Get comfortable. Breathe deeply. Use the following prompts to make discoveries and gain clarity on your way to personal freedom. Use a journal to capture any thoughts, feelings, or images that come to mind or talk into a recorder. Welcome to your session ...

Use the Lifestyle Assessment Guide to connect with your history and private logic:

Describe yourself as a child.

What did you decide was your role in the family? Notice any topics that grab your attention.

Examine the assumptions/decisions you may have made then or any emotions that have come up now.

Recall/draw your very first memory and tell the story:

What is happening? Who is there? Capture the details and notice what you may have decided at that time:

I am . . . _____.

Other people (in the memory) are . . . _____.

My world/life (then) is . . . _____.

Recall a few more early recollections and complete the sentences.

What have you discovered about your early decisions and private logic? How does it apply to your life today?

What current behavior(s) would you most like to change?

When did this behavior(s) begin? What was happening?

How might your ego be using this behavior(s) to "help" you avoid stress, humiliation, rejection, or meaninglessness?

How would your life be different if you didn't have this problem?

Are you willing to detach from suffering? What will you let go of?

FIVE

Righting and Revising

5.1 | CHANGE

Everyone likes progress but resists change.

—MARY PIPHER

One of my favorite books, *The Road Less Traveled*, grabbed my attention years ago with its succinct opening line: "Life is difficult." I remember how that sentence roused me and how, instantly, I loved and hated it. The author, M. Scott Peck, a psychiatrist, was announcing that life and difficulties go together as a matter of fact, like soap and water.

Dr. Peck declared in a concise, nonjudgmental stance that life is problematic—though not because you and I are doing anything particularly wrong, and not necessarily because we are incapable, negative, or missing what everyone else has already figured out. Life is difficult because it's the *way life is*. And I hated the message because it popped the bubble of a flimsy, juvenile wish-dream; I wanted life to be simple, different than it was, and yet I knew it was absolutely *true*—life is just not that easy, not that fair, not that painless.

Life was never going to be the continuous tropical breeze or cheery bowl of cherries I was hoping for and mistakenly thought it *should* be. Apparently, I had adopted a simplistic formula along the way, *believing* that if it were done right, life could be trouble-free: Good things happen to good people, and bad things happen to bad. And if we

try our best, are kind and *perfect*, we can avoid life's difficulties. However, as with most beliefs, I had no awareness
that I was operating on this outlandish principle from
childhood, or was even thinking it at all.

Life is not necessarily easy, fair, or painless.

Clearly, my philosophy never added up, and while I
was drawn to sad stories that consumed and baffled me, I
couldn't make sense of why difficulties and tragedies seemed
so random, cruel, and unnecessary—not at all in sync with
the bad-stuff-happens-to-bad-people theory. I couldn't
deny that plenty of problems and crises have nothing to do
with getting it wrong or being punished. Life is difficult.
Period. And accepting that concept makes it less so. As
Peck says, "Once we truly know that life is difficult—once
we truly understand and accept it—then life is no longer
difficult. Because once it is accepted, the fact that life is
difficult no longer matters."

In my head, I had always wanted good to win, justice
to prevail, and people never to be wounded. I tried to make
sense of suffering and decided early on that if you did it
right and if I did it right, then life wouldn't be all that hard.
Admitting that life is difficult—like it or not—required a
shift in my magical thinking, a reconfiguration of ideals
about control, trying harder, and getting what we deserve.
And with that admission came a sense of ease, a release
from outmoded logic and codependent responsibilities, as I
surrendered to life on life's terms, wondering anew what it
is that makes life so difficult for so many of us.

Perhaps life would be a cinch, or at least a lot easier, if
it weren't *constantly* changing. It's not so much that *life* is
difficult; life is pretty awesome, full of mystery and beauty.
But it seems that about the time we get settled in, com-

fortable in one stage or season, relationship or routine, it all changes—a husband leaves after years of marriage, an infant becomes a toddler who says, "No," then a teenager who says, "I hate you!" Widowers lose wives. Parents lose control. Children lose innocence. It all seems so unnerving at the time, so utterly confusing and painfully unfair.

Life is wrought with challenges and losses, and our dreams don't always come true. As the first of Four Noble Truths, Buddha taught that "life is suffering"; heartaches and difficulties are part of life and cannot be avoided. And yet if we are to live, really *live*, we must learn how to tolerate, accept, and overcome adversity, instead of getting bitter, giving in to despair, or dropping out altogether. Maybe the changes and burdens that seem so unfair are the struggles that help us grow and develop to our fullest potential, like the process of cutting teeth or growing wings.

We must learn how to tolerate and overcome adversity.

Living well requires that we accept transitions and navigate the changes life is sure to bring. If there is one guarantee in life, it is that no matter what is happening at this time, it is sure to change. And therein lies a lesson for enjoying the distressing unpredictability of life that causes us to suffer: The best way to brace for change and the difficulties that come with it is to learn how to embrace the present moment, knowing full well that it is precious and fleeting and will surely not last forever—but it's here for *now*.

A dear friend reminds me regularly that "crisis is change trying to take place." Even after a diagnosis of ovarian cancer, multiple surgeries, and nauseating treatments, she is still reminding me of that quote, courageously focusing on love and silver linings in an unexpected alteration of life that neither she, nor any of us, would choose.

Crisis is change trying to take place.

Growing through life's many transitions—even those we do not want and never planned on—allows us to live life to the fullest. Change can engender expansion in us if we will let it; it can become a story of emotional maturation and spiritual awakening. Knowing that life will have its hardships is precisely what allows us to accept and transcend them by being open to discovery and willing to see things in new ways, gathering wisdom from lessons we could never have learned any other way.

5.2 | DEVELOPMENT

Those things that hurt, instruct.

—BENJAMIN FRANKLIN

Our lives evolve through many stages that require us to make discoveries and renew ourselves from our birth until our death. A psychoanalyst known for his ideas about human development and identity formation, Erik H. Erikson theorized that each phase in the life cycle brings with it a crisis, a specific challenge demanding our attention. The author of seven books, and a professor at Harvard, Yale, and Berkeley, Erikson taught that if we are to reach our full potential, we must resolve the conflict presented in each of the eight stages of psychosocial development.

Transitional steps that shape our identity and sense of individuality, these universal stages provide an overview of the skills and virtues we confront in our lifetime. And here, in therapy, they provide a guide to help us understand the process of social and emotional growth, where we may have gotten stuck in our own development, and how our personality formation has been impacted by certain crises—some that may still be in need of our attention.

Our identity is shaped by confronting a series of developmental challenges.

Failure to resolve the challenge of a specific stage creates instability, an *identify crisis* that we carry with us throughout our life span unless we revisit particular conflicts and revive the virtues meant to be birthed during that stage. In order to overcome current difficulties, we investigate what may have been left undeveloped in earlier stages, make needed repairs, and strengthen qualities that engender a healthier sense of self and purpose.

THE EIGHT STAGES OF HUMAN DEVELOPMENT

Stage 1: Infancy (0-1 Years)–Hope

Trust versus mistrust. This stage sets the foundation for all the stages and depends primarily on our maternal relationship. If we had a dependable caregiver (usually our mother), we likely developed a sense of hope that comes from being able to trust that our needs will be met. If, however, we were neglected or abused, or were the victim of trauma, or if our needs were met inconsistently, it is likely that we developed an overall sense of mistrust that will influence our perspective and relationships.

Stage 2: Early Childhood (1-3 Years)–Will

Autonomy versus shame. This stage requires learning skills like walking, talking, feeding ourselves, and toilet training. Given the opportunity to exert our will and individuate, we start developing a sense of self-sufficiency and success. If, however, our efforts are thwarted or demeaned, a sense of shame and doubt begins shaping our identity.

Stage 3: Preschool (3-6 Years)–Purpose

Initiative versus guilt. During these years, we develop a sense of accomplishment and purpose by doing things on our own—getting ourselves dressed, doing simple chores, finishing projects. We discover our abilities and ingenuity. But if we are made to feel badly about making our own choices or doing things imperfectly, our sense of initiative and identity becomes contaminated, overshadowed by misgivings and guilt.

Stage 4: School Age (6-11 Years)–Competence

Industry versus inferiority. This is the beginning of organized competition, comparisons, and hierarchies. We compare our abilities, contrast ourself with others, and evaluate our self-worth in relative terms. If we make good judgments about ourself, are at the top of the list, or are affirmed for our skills, we develop a sense of competency. If we are devalued, go unacknowledged, or don't believe we measure up, we develop a sense of inadequacy and feeling of inferiority.

Stage 5: Adolescence (12-18 Years)–Fidelity

Identity versus role confusion. Teenage years are a time of great questioning and discovery. We attempt to figure out who we are, what we want to do with our lives, and how we fit with our peers and family. If we value our choices, if they are accepted and affirmed, we feel a sense of fidelity that resonates with our individual identity. If, on the other hand, we are denied freedom to explore or are rejected for our choices, we experience a sense of disloyalty that contributes to role confusion and a potential identity crisis.

Stage 6: Young Adulthood (18-35 Years)–Love

Intimacy versus isolation. This first stage of early adult life involves dating, marriage, friendships, and family. In order to experience love and intimacy, we must be able to successfully form loving relationships with other people. If we have sustained developmental injuries in previous stages that undermine our trust or self-esteem, we may have difficulty forming lasting relationships and will feel isolated and lonely.

Stage 7: Middle Adulthood (35-64 Years)–Caring

Generativity versus stagnation. This middle stage of adulthood is a time of work, raising a family, and being productive. It is also the time we begin assessing our accomplishments and level of satisfaction. If we feel fulfilled by the care we have extended to our children and society, we will have a sense of purpose and like the way our life is going. But if we regret our choices, are not investing in others, or are not contributing to future generations as we mature, we can feel stagnant and dissatisfied and may experience a "second adolescence"—a midlife crisis—to prove our life isn't over and hasn't been wasted.

Stage 8: Late Adulthood (65-Plus Years)–Wisdom

Integrity versus despair. In the last stage of life, we review our accomplishments. If we have been true to our values, learned from our experiences, and accept the choices we've made, we live with a sense of contentment that comes with integrity and wisdom. If, however, we are disappointed by the way we have lived, have refused to learn from our mistakes, or have deep-seated remorse about what could have been, we can spend our final years feeling the hopeless anguish of despair.

5.3 | FRANK'S STORY

Every tired human being may regress temporarily to
partial mistrust whenever the world of his expectations
has been shaken to the core.

—ERIK H. ERIKSON

Frank is in his sixties, nearing the later stage of the life cycle,
and is in deep despair. He knows he needs help, and after finding
a phone number for the community clinic, he shows up for a
counseling appointment.

I greet him in the waiting area, where he nervously hands
me his intake forms, and together we head past the front desk
and down the hall to room number three. "How long you been
doing this kind of work?" he asks, as he takes a seat on the
donated beige velour couch and sizes me up.

In my new suit, with the calculated poise of a professional
and the racing heart of a novice, I shut the door, then sit in the
black pleather desk chair, leaning back a bit for effect, and respond,
with the most assuring voice I can muster, "Oh, for a while."

I am ruffled, not sure how honest I should be, not wanting
to undermine my client's confidence, but the truth of the matter
is that I have just finished my thesis and graduated from my
master's program, and am working at the clinic for a little less
than an hour. And as a brand-new intern—continuing my three
thousand supervised hours required for licensure—I am seeing
my first "official" client ever: Frank. And everyone, except Frank,
knows it.

Thankfully, he doesn't ask a follow-up question, seems satisfied with my evasive answer, and together we simply move forward. And though we don't know it, we are about to become teachers to each other: Frank will help me grow more experienced and confident as a young therapist, and I will help him progress through developmental tasks that will bring him greater integration and contentment as a man.

During our first session, I learn about Frank's alcoholic mother, about how he basically raised himself and struggled terribly in school, and about how his father abandoned him when he was just a baby, leaving him without so much as a mental image to hold on to through the years and stages of life.

Frank looks sad and weathered. His hair is shoulder length and dirty, his jeans old, his gaze downcast. He is unkempt and speaks with one hand cupped over a mouth that, I will soon discover, is missing nearly every one of its neglected top teeth. I feel the intensity of Frank's pain as he begins to weep, with a look of embarrassment, and as he wipes tears away, he reveals that he is no longer sleeping, eating, or finding any satisfaction.

He is clearly depressed, and I want Frank to continue being honest, without feeling ashamed by this flood of emotion. But I really am not sure what to do next or how to make it better. What do I say to a man old enough to be my father, one with great sorrow and years of disappointment? Do I become a nurturing mother—one he never had—hand him a tissue, and assure him that it will be okay somehow? Or do I try to cheer him up, tell him exactly what he should do, be the friend or big sister or authority who gives him a pep talk and slew of suggestions about the benefits of exercise, diet, and a daily routine?

"I lost my job 'cause I stopped showing up after my girlfriend took off. I don't have anything to live for," he says, as he points to the green inked letters emblazoned on his forearm

between his wrist and elbow. There, in decorative script, mono-grammed for perpetuity is the name A-m-b-e-r, written next to a blood-red heart pierced by a dark, prophetic arrow.

Hearing the desperation in his voice alerts me to follow a protocol for which all budding counselors are trained: First, we must do no harm to those who come seeking our help, and, above all, we have a responsibility to protect our client's life. The kind of despair that snuffs out a reason to live—phrases like "don't have anything left to live for"—are red flags that we must take seriously. Suicide, a potential risk for anyone with depression, is exceptionally high for men of this age and stage of life who feel a sense of hopelessness. And my job, here and now, is to assess this risk by directly checking it out with Frank and hospitalizing him, if necessary.

With the concern of one human life for another, I begin asking about Frank's safety, about his thoughts and plans for the future, and about whether he has considered, or has tried, harm-ing himself (or anyone else) during this challenging time. I talk directly about depression and despair, voice my most pressing objective to keep him free from harm, and boldly inquire, "Frank, have you had any suicidal thoughts? Have you tried to hurt yourself recently or in the past? Do you have any plans to hurt yourself now?" And then I listen.

"I actually bought a gun about a week ago," Frank confesses. "Wanted to end it all but couldn't. I've been drinking a lot. Haven't really wanted to wake up, but something in me says I better get my act together. Next thing I know, I'm calling this place, and here I am."

We talk about an innate desire to live, about discovering a bigger, divine plan that gives meaning and purpose to our lives, and about Frank's courage to call for help and show up. I need to know that he will be safe, and wonder aloud how he will handle being alone in his trailer with a gun and alcohol—a deadly combination. And, together, with earnest agreement from Frank, we concur to continue working together, exploring the way out of his depression, and adhering to a safety plan, which, at this point, will include a medical evaluation, a daily check-in call, and biweekly appointments.

"I definitely will be okay," Frank commits, as he schedules his next visit with me and agrees to make an appointment with one of the clinic's doctors. "How about if I give my gun to my neighbor who has a safe? I will do that—I'll call, and I will be back. I promise."

I believe him—reassured simply by the confession, sense of relief, and thanks expressed in his eyes and parting handshake. True to his word, Frank calls that afternoon to tell me that the gun is gone, locked away by a friend. Based on the tiniest act of care and thinnest sliver of hope, Frank has agreed to participate, to find a way through his pain. He calls daily and shows up faithfully from that day on—never missing a single one of our appointments—for well over a year.

For the next twelve months, Frank talks, or draws, and I care. And with the developmental stages serving as our road map, we navigate through specific crises, tasks, and virtues, starting with a repair to the very earliest of stages, where hope is born: in a relationship of mutual respect, boundaries, and honesty. And here, within a trustworthy therapeutic bond, Frank shares and revisits childhood, looking at the shame that undermined any sense of purpose or competency early in his life as he grew himself up without parents and spent years doubting himself, feeling inferior and unimportant.

I learn about his teenage years, about how he found a twisted sense of identity by latching onto girls, becoming a "ladies' man," and had a son when he was just seventeen. And how, just like his own dad, he abandoned his infant son and the boy's mother, leaving them without so much as a photograph or forwarding address. We talk about fidelity and intimacy, and how, in an effort to impress his lovers, he hid his thoughts and feelings away, leaving himself feeling lonely and unloved.

Frank's adult life was filled with sexual conquests and addictions. When he met Amber at a bar nearly a year prior, he thought he would be happy forever. "Fun and pretty—a real catch," Amber was nearly twenty-five years younger than Frank and enjoyed what he had to offer. Within weeks of their meeting, she moved in, pledging her devotion, as Frank showed his allegiance with expensive gifts and a tattoo bearing her name.

At the time, Frank didn't realize that he was being taken advantage of, that while he was at work each day, Amber was getting high, watching daytime television, and rendezvousing with old friends, even hooking up with her previous boyfriend. When she told Frank that it was over, he was shocked.

"I felt so betrayed. Then, when I found out that she was moving in with Jason [twenty years Frank's junior], I felt stupid, and old. I just couldn't believe it."

Frank was grieving not just the loss of a girlfriend, but also the loss of a job and yet another unsatisfying season of life. Triggered by early abandonment, lack of trust and autonomy— developmental virtues meant to build a reservoir of internal strength—Frank, once again, doubted his worth, purpose, and even reason to live.

Together, we explore Frank's bucket list—the things he still wants to do with his life—reawakening childhood dreams and discovering how alcohol and one-night stands were attempts to fill the void meant to be satisfied with fidelity, love, and caring: traits meant to be developed and passed along in a personally unique way.

Without a family to care for, Frank spent the middle part of his adult years dating and enjoying the bachelor life in a midlife adolescence that impeded his progress and left him feeling disconnected and dissatisfied. And now, nearing the final stage of life, he regrets choices he's made and feels remorse about what could have been, yet isn't sure how to do it differently or move forward.

In order to alleviate his despair, we concentrate on what's left to do with these important years and find a path to right Frank's story in a way that infuses it with greater love and wisdom. In this stage of integrity versus despair, we celebrate Frank's accomplishments, looking at what he has done well and accepting his experiences—good and bad—as valuable life lessons. And for Frank, as for each of us, acknowledging the whole truth about ourselves is how we get untangled from the destructive shame and self-loathing that arise from our human mistakes and delicate egos.

Frank finds forgiveness and the God of his understanding in Alcoholics Anonymous, where he attends meetings, works the steps, and vows to stay sober. He finds a sponsor and shares his story with an integrity that touches the lives of men of all ages. And in a particularly courageous session with me, he wades into the whirlpool of his greatest pain, deciding that what he'd most like to do with his life today—his greatest act of caring, love, and fidelity—is to locate, and make amends to, the son he abandoned years ago.

Wisdom consists not so much in knowing what to do in the
ultimate as in knowing what to do next.

—HERBERT HOOVER

So how do we ultimately find contentment? What is our intention and purpose? Deciding what to do with our lives can cause confusion, not just for the self-absorbed or misguided, but even for responsible, goal-oriented individuals who want to make a difference with their lives.

After months of honesty, sobriety, and reflection, Frank found that he was moving out of loneliness and stagnation by sharing his experiences, mistakes, and accumulated wisdom with other men in recovery. And, after we've spent nearly a year together in therapy, Frank is convinced that the next step in his evolution is to reach out and find the son he deserted, offering him the love and care Frank was unable to give him years ago.

But before he begins to search for his son, Frank prepares for their meeting by practicing love and care for *himself* first—getting a haircut and a job as a security guard, saving some money, visiting a dental clinic, and eventually getting a new set of teeth. Positioned on the couch across from me, he talks about his plans with enthusiasm, looking healthy and handsome, not at all like the disheveled man who, just a year earlier, sat in the very same seat, contemplating whether to end an unsatisfying life.

We all must find our own way to fulfillment, becoming engaged in life in a way that doesn't leave us feeling defeated by challenges or driven by a ravenous, malnourished ego. Our insecurities, longings, and sentiment of personal failure can become our deepest source of shame and regret or can set us on a pilgrimage to find integrity and wisdom. As adults, we have specific obligations and opportunities within the human community that give meaning to our lives—specified *tasks* that, when attended to, help us to feel balanced, whole, and good about ourselves as social beings and, when neglected, leave us with an insatiable hunger.

The Tasks of Life pose problems and generate questions that must be answered if we are to live a contented, meaningful life.

Just as the developmental stages provide an overview of skills and virtues that can be examined and repaired, so, too, do the Tasks of Life require our consideration and involvement if we are to experience an overall sense of well-being and success. By evaluating our priorities and level of satisfaction in each one of the five tasks that confront us in our adult lives—*love, work, relationship, self-care,* and *spiritual development*—we can gain a personal understanding of what gives us greater contentment and discover where to make a bigger deposit in our own happiness.

And, like Frank, until we engage in life's full spectrum —cultivating social interest and contributing to the welfare of *ourselves and others*—we will likely feel incomplete, unsuccessful, and disappointed without knowing why. And so, by evaluating how satisfied, or dissatisfied, we are with each of life's five tasks, we can become more conscious of whom or what we may be neglecting, and where we may want to invest to create a greater sense of meaning and inner satisfaction, and a better community for friends, family, and fellow human beings.

Love

Love is about our most intimate union, the closest emotional relationship that can exist between two people. Whom we choose to partner with and how we love them spotlights our choices and demonstrates whether we are able to give and take, serve and be served. What we believe to be true about ourself and another gets played out as we commit to vulnerability, expressing our thoughts and feelings, or resort to manipulation, deceit, and power to get our needs met. Whether we have married one partner for life or have been through a series of engagements, sexual affairs, or divorces, the task of love reveals our injuries and patterns, and the honesty and respect we hold for ourself and the partner we purportedly love.

> *What is your history of adult love relationships?*
>
> *How satisfied are you with your current intimate relationship?*
>
> *What are your strengths as a partner? Your difficulties?*

Work

Work looks at how we use our time and talent, and the task of work asks us to consider how we can contribute our share to the planet and our fellow human beings. Meaningful "work" is not necessarily what we do to make a living or pay the bills; it is what we do when we take into account that we live in association with other people and cannot exist alone. Satisfying "work" benefits not just the self but humanity, and is what we generously donate to the world to make it a better place through our occupation, talents, or gifts as a volunteer and altruistic member of the human race.

What is your work history and current job satisfaction?

How are your assets being used in your work/activities in the world?

What is one/some of the most satisfying gifts of time/talent that you have given?

Relationship

Relationship requires that we reflect on the roles we hold as family members—siblings, children, parents, cousins, grandparents, or distant relatives—and evaluate how dependable, loving, and gracious we are with our kin, as well as with those in our inner and extended circles. The task of relationship is about our associations with people, looking at whom we are attracted to, the groups we join, and how we relate with friends and associates. It solicits us to be conscious of the marks we are making in others' lives, the endowments they have deposited in ours, and in whom we want to make a larger, or lesser, investment for greater satisfaction.

Who are your closest friends? When and where did you meet them?

How would you describe yourself and roles as a family member? As a friend?

What are your community/group affiliations? What do you give/get?

Self-Care

Self-care entails clarifying what we have come to believe about ourself, revising what is true, and caring for our mind–body connection in practical ways that enhance our sense of well-being. The task of self-care is about deepening our appreciation for our unique design and personal experience. As we value our whole being, we take charge of our thoughts and physical health, eliminating self-destructive patterns, lessening stress, and creating daily routines that take into account diet, sleep, exercise, hygiene, and overall vitality. Using positive self-talk and affirmations that lead to self-love and acceptance, we embrace our creative gifts, use our desires to set goals, and grow beyond our insecurities and fears.

How are you caring for your mind and body? Self-destructive patterns?

What positive affirmation(s) do you long to hear and believe: "I am _____."

What are some of your strengths/assets? Desires? Goals?

Spiritual Development

Spiritual development takes a look beyond the material realm and pleasures of life that are here today and gone tomorrow. The task of spiritual development requires that we ponder why we are here and raise questions about the mysteries of life, death, and the world of spirit. To be deeply satisfied necessitates that we dissolve fear and pride with rigorous honesty, to humbly open ourselves to grace, forgiveness, and the God of our understanding. Through an inner knowing; the beauty of nature, art, music, and poetry; and soulful practices like dance, meditation, singing, and prayer, we can connect to a Power greater than ourselves, discerning how to rise above earthly pain and circumstances with supernatural joy, peace, and love that surpass intellect and human limitations.

When do you feel closest to God? What practices inspire faith/hope/love?

What was your childhood image of God? Who most influenced your beliefs?

How has your image of God changed? Is your God loving and forgiving?

During our first few weeks together in therapy, I asked Frank to draw a circle—create a pie chart—illustrating what percentage of his time he was spending on each of the five Tasks of Life. Instead of a circle showing a number of different slices, Frank's circular graph, like his life, was devoid of pieces; his *entire* pie was dedicated to a love life that had consumed 100 percent of his time and attention—a visual of an unsatisfying imbalance that would urge Frank to examine, revise priorities, and discover a way to greater personal fulfillment.

Using the Lifestyle Assessment, Developmental Stages, and Tasks of Life as tools in the righting of Frank's story, we witnessed a radical shift in just one year, as illustrated in a second pie chart that was notably different from his first. His final circle was divided into quarters, with one section labeled *work,* another *self-care,* another *relationship,* and another *spiritual development.* Like his first graph, this pie reflected Frank's priorities, showing how he was spending his time in new, more satisfying ways: in his *work* with men in recovery; *self-care* habits that improved his health and self-esteem; *relationship* with his son, extended family, and community; and *spiritual development* that evolved from the program of Alcoholics Anonymous, the Serenity Prayer, church, and a forgiving, compassionate God.

When I think of the renovation that took place that year for both of us, I can't help but recall Frank's depression and my own fears early on, our emotional farewell, and the memorable message that was delivered to the office soon after our last session. Written on a small white card tucked within the blooms of a dozen sunny yellow roses was a profoundly satisfying note of appreciation that stated simply, "Thanks, from Frank."

Solutions arise when we value our gifts and destiny and consider how to make a contribution to the welfare of others.

Frank's transformation and gratitude touched me deeply and have continued to motivate me on many occasions—through difficult sessions, feelings of inadequacy, and codependent struggles. Nearly a year later, I received an inspiring letter from Frank that I keep (with that small white card) locked in a cabinet with files and case notes. I pull it out from time to time, because it's not often that I get to hear what happens after you and I say our good-byes, when the door closes and you leave to find meaning and equilibrium in a world of instability. Usually, I am left to wonder how vibrant and fulfilled you are out there on the other side of therapy, but rarely do I get to know.

Dear Tuya,

I am here in Angleton, Texas. It's a long story, but I wanted you to know. I found my son! The bad news is that he is in prison for three years now. The good news is I work there. I am a guard and see Jim nearly every day. He looks just like me and guess he followed in my footsteps.

I started two twelve-step groups for the men here. Jim comes to them and many others do too. We are getting to know each other. He calls me Dad. I have a grandson and granddaughter that I will meet in just a few weeks!

It's real different here. It's a small town and I don't have no ladies in my life, do you believe it? But I go to AA and a real nice church. I feel good and happy. And I know none of this would of happened if you didn't care. Thank you for being there and helping me get my life back.

Love always,
Frank

So, whenever I need a bit of encouragement—a reminder that one human can significantly impact the life of another, that what I am doing in this room is valuable, and that with therapeutic tools, understanding, and courage, you will find your way from despair to a more balanced life that touches others—I use Frank's own words to replenish my heart with the hope and satisfaction that comes from participating in a burgeoning process that heals, transforms, and ultimately pays it forward.

5.5 | FEELINGS

*No one can develop freely in this world and find a full life
without feeling understood by at least one person.*
—PAUL TOURNIER

Our feelings inform us and, though sometimes
difficult to put into words, provide a relational
language that can be felt and shared with others. Infants
freely express themselves in coos and shouts and tears,
hoping to be noticed, hoping to be *felt* by someone who
can sense whether they are hungry or need a fresh diaper or
an engaging smile. And as we grow, our vocabulary expands,
until we rely less on communicating in feelings and more
on expressing what we are thinking in words and conversations.

But our thoughts and feelings are powerfully linked
and together become the surest way to gain awareness
about the beliefs and principles that underlie and drive our
behavior. Mindfulness is a state of paying attention, and in
order to grow in self-awareness, we must be able to recognize what we are feeling with curiosity and without judgment. To feel understood, to express what we want or need,
we must first know ourself: what we are feeling and why.

With socialization and language, feelings get covered
up, smoothed over, and manipulated. We learn to talk a
good game, put on a layer of verbal padding, and be so
consistently "okay" that we lose a sense of our own internal

temperature—what we are feeling and why we are feeling that way. Once we move past the level of early language and survival, communication evolves more from the head than from the gut, and we can spin words to impress others or hide away difficult emotions, and, in the process, short-circuit our natural ability to check in, to know what we feel and sense what is bothering us or what we want or need.

So, feelings—and the experience of being *felt*—are important here behind the door. Coming out of hiding, unwrapping what we think and feel, and recognizing why it makes sense to feel the way we do reconnects mind and body and offers us a primitive, complex language that allows us to be seen and understood by another person. And the human need to feel understood is intricately linked to feeling *loved*. Love and understanding are so connected that, according to the French psychiatrist Paul Tournier, "we never know where one ends and the other begins. . . . He who loves understands, and he who understands loves. . . . One who feels understood feels loved."

And yet because of our fear of "losing it"—crying, becoming overly emotional, or somehow being inappropriate—deep sharing in our everyday encounters is risky and rare. Sadly, those same concerns apply even in intimate relationships where emotional expression is uncomfortable or unacceptable, or has resulted in our feeling misunderstood, discounted, or shamed. After years of listening to pent-up emotions and the loneliness that comes from holding them away from others, I am fully aware of how uncommon it is to really *feel* understood, even within our marriages and closest friendships.

Looking at an alphabetical list of feelings, a page of cartoon faces, or a variety of words grouped around a central emotion is how we start most early sessions. After taking a calming breath or two, you identify what you are experiencing here and now, sharing what you *feel* before explaining what is happening. *I am feeling X* is the entry point from which you check in and I attempt to relate and empathize.

Though initially it is difficult for most of us to name exactly what we are feeling, it gets easier with practice. So we take our time, using the handy words or faces to recognize what you are feeling—pinpointing at least two specific emotions without judgment—and then exploring what might be activating those feelings.

Saying, for example, "I am feeling *nervous* and *irritated*" invites me to share your mood and level of upset, and also leads us to better comprehend what you might be telling yourself (thinking) about your predicament. Mind reading is unrealistic and rarely successful and is disastrous for relationships. And because thoughts are elusive—mostly out of our consciousness—our feelings provide the most accessible gateway to our interior world.

Prompted with *because* . . . , we connect our feelings with the thoughts that are fueling them. Anxiety—which might be identified as feeling afraid, terrified, nervous, panicked, etc.—is fear that has been severed from its original source into free-floating dread about what could happen in the future. Depression, too, is about a sense of overwhelm in the present—showing up as feeling sad, hurt, discouraged, hopeless, weary, etc.—from things that happened in the past, things that were incubated and kept alive with guilt-ridden, negative messages and regret.

Our feelings create our behaviors.

Actions are driven by our emotions. Our body reacts to

what we feel, and whether we are enraged, afraid, confused, tranquil, conflicted, affectionate, hopeless, playful, or despondent will determine whether we will contract or expand, relax, dilate, engage, recoil, detach, fight, or flee. And our moods and physical reactions, without our realizing it, are all created by our thoughts—yes, by our thoughts. The highly personal way we perceive things—our cognitions and reasoning—is what creates what we feel! We feel the way we do—whether bitter, frazzled, or grateful—because of the thoughts we are thinking in the moment.

Our thoughts create our feelings.

Thoughts create the feelings that result in actions. When we feel depressed, for example—withdrawn, listless, dejected, etc.—our thoughts are being dominated by a persistent negativity because we *believe* it is really as bad as we imagine it to be, and we act accordingly: drinking, lashing out, isolating, cutting, bingeing, etc. If we believe we have no power or there is no way out, we will feel a sense of despair and hopelessness. Tucked behind most thoughts are powerful principles from the past, beliefs that tell us what is "true" about us and the world, though we are likely unaware of them. We construct our reality from our private logic, the deductions we make that are often old, immature, and faulty.

Our beliefs create our thoughts.

BELIEFS ⇨ THOUGHTS ⇨ FEELINGS ⇨ ACTIONS

We can change our moods by knowing our mind. Right or wrong, our beliefs are the bedrock of our reasoning, and, using insight to investigate what we have come to believe—evaluating what is factual and making mental revisions—we can make cognitive shifts that change what we ultimately do. Connecting past and future with the *present* is how we discover not only what is bothering us but also how we can open up to new possibilities and ways of being that reawaken our dreams and take us to places of greater serenity and freedom.

Our stories are revised by recognizing what it is that we feel, think, and believe and deciding—making choices—about what we may want to keep, discard, or edit to improve the story that is ours to live. Freedom, our birthright, is a desire to know our own heart and mind, to be known and accepted by ourself, others, and our God, and shedding whatever is holding us captive so we can freely experience the love, joy, and peace we crave.

5.6 | CAROLE'S STORY

We don't see the world as it is. We see the world as we are.
—AL-ANON

Carole was unable to enjoy much of anything. Palm trees were a nuisance, expensive to maintain. The beach was dirty. And even the celebrated sunsets over the Pacific Ocean weren't able to impress her. Roses had thorns. Food had to be organic, unsalted, and gluten-free. Sweets caused cancer. Nothing was pleasurable, nor should be, according to Carole.

We start our session in the usual way, with forms and consent, as Carole studies the laminated sheets of feeling-words and faces. According to her paperwork, she is coming to therapy "to feel better"; she states that she is suffering from several physical ailments, including fibromyalgia, chronic fatigue syndrome, migraine headaches, and colitis.

As she begins filling me in on the things that are stressing her, I ask her to join me in getting comfortable, looking around the room, allowing her eyes to go wherever they might like to go, and then taking in a few deep, slow, cleansing breaths, in through the nose—into the abdomen, filling the belly and lungs —and then slowly out through the mouth, until she is completely empty.

And after just two of these breaths, Carole seems more settled, willing to identify a word on the list that describes what she is feeling.

"I am feeling nervous, I guess," she tells me.

"Nervous," I echo, and pause, sitting with the sense of what Carole is feeling here, now. "You probably feel nervous . . . because . . ." I say, dragging out the word because to indicate that I am inquiring, curious to learn more about the sensation she is experiencing and the thinking behind it.

"Maybe because I've never been to therapy," she tells me, and I begin getting inside Carole's skin, attempting to relate, letting her know that showing up here—or anywhere we have never been—is a courageous act. She tells me about the medical doctor who referred her to me, and how she has been battling one illness after another, as anxiety and control issues spill about the room in black-and-white thinking that is mostly black, with only an occasional speck of gray.

"And is there another feeling from the list that describes how you feel right now?" I ask.

"Yes, this one here. Disgusted. I'm disgusted," she says in no uncertain terms, as she points to the illustration of a puckered cartoon face wearing a distasteful look of repugnance.

Now, "disgusted" is a pretty intense emotion, concocted with a mix of anger and hurt and outrage, and I want to better understand. So I question where in her body Carole feels disgust. After some hesitation, she puts one hand on her throat and the other on her belly, and I do the same in an effort to imagine, to sit with the feeling and mirror what she has embodied.

"Any idea why you feel disgusted?" I ask, knowing that we are about to unravel the first of many tight knots in Carole's tangled ball of pain.

"Yeah. It's my husband. He couldn't even come here with me today. He only cares about his golf. Doesn't really care about me," she says, with the slightest hint of sadness. Carole uncrosses her arms, and we take a trip into the past: life with an alcoholic father, growing up wanting to be a nun, and regrets about violating her vow of abstinence at thirty-five years old, when she had sex with her fiancé, who is now her husband of twenty years.

I learn about her faith, how life on earth should be spent perfecting ourselves for heaven, and how the world is dangerous and not to be trusted—full of evil and impurity. I witness firsthand the private logic of a girl impacted by her mentors: her mother, who attended confession daily, telling Carole that nuns were the purest of human beings, closest to the angels; Sister Anna, who wore around her waist a rope that she tightened whenever she had an impure thought; and Sister Patrice, who taught that "the devil will gain a foothold" if you dishonor your parents, as a terrified young Carole tried to respect her father, who was regularly in an alcoholic stupor or rant that ended in violence.

Carole had nuns who paddled her for whispering, for not paying attention, for forgetting her homework. Along with other girls in the class, she spent time standing in the corner or hall, had her knuckles bloodied with a ruler, and learned how to qualify for heaven and avoid the fires of hell. Sister Marie taught that penance was required daily, and so Carole found ways to punish herself in her room—biting or hitting or scratching herself with pins and other objects. Sister Helena explained that sex was God's gift for procreation, and that lust or sex for enjoyment was an absolute, definite sin.

Even now, as a grown-up child, Carole feels the need for regular penance, denying herself food and comfort and, of course, sex—which she finds "repulsive." She volunteers regularly at church and confesses to me that she sometimes cuts herself or skips meals for atonement, making it clear just how impressionable our early concepts can be, and how we need to examine and *amend them, if necessary, to find our way to greater acceptance and joy.*

And so Carole and I talk about goals for therapy as she announces that she wants to "feel good: to have fewer headaches and symptoms," and we set about devising a plan of action that will continue into our next session and that will ultimately challenge the thinking and early beliefs that are preventing Carole from feeling . . . good.

We have covered a lot of territory, made a connection, and pick a date to meet in one week. And, instead of reaching for a purse or wallet, Carole reaches into her bra and retrieves a wad of crumpled money, from which she carefully counts and recounts my fee in one-, five-, and ten-dollar bills, stating with conviction, "You just can't trust people when it comes to money. Can't be too careful today."

5.7 | DISTORTED THINKING

You don't have to belong to a cult to become brainwashed.
—SARAH BAN BREATHNACH

So, how do we know if our thinking is skewed, if our beliefs are based in fantasy or reality? How, for example, did Reverend Jim Jones create such panic and confusion in 1978 that he was able to convince his followers to take their own lives and even the lives of their children? By drinking a lethal punch tainted with cyanide and paranoia, 912 cult members died—including 276 of their children—all because of a menacing, delusional "truth" fabricated in the mind of their persuasive leader. How do we know if we, like the victims of the Jonestown massacre, are being deceived—believing wholeheartedly in something, or someone, muddled by distortion, or perhaps not supported by any truth at all?

As with Carole, what we believe *feels* completely true. Our beliefs are ingrained and, as issues of faith, rest heavily on principles that were taught by someone whom we trusted—someone who had influence over us and seemed to know so much more, and much better, than we did. All of us are ripe to become "true believers" who follow along unquestionably, unless we are willing to probe our thinking —what we have caught—analyze it, and *decide* whether or not we want to continue regarding it as our truth.

People often assume that anxiety and depression *cause* negative thinking, but the opposite is actually the case; negative *thoughts* trigger the feelings that build into a state of chronic anxiety and depression. Distorted thinking falls into identifiable patterns that are common in people who routinely struggle with low self-esteem, control issues, compulsions, depression, anxiety, and a variety of stress-related diseases.

When Carole returned for a second session, she was less than eager to look at her thinking. She had decided that prayer was all she, or anyone, needed and that therapy was unnecessary. She wanted nothing to do with poking around early deductions or speculating about the kind of revision that would open her to greater peace; she was convinced, beyond a shadow of a doubt, that the world of spirit was good and the material world—full of forbidden pleasures—was not good at all. And so she left my office after just two sessions, still *believing* that her husband, golf, sex, *I*, and most everything else on earth was as bad as the nuns assured her that they were, and, sadly, I never saw Carole again.

Putting everything into categories of all good or all bad is how we initially reasoned as children, and we often continue to use this same unsophisticated method as adults, determining that what is *good* are those things we accepted early on—rituals and concepts that are familiar and comfortable—and what is *bad* is anything that challenges those early beliefs. But in order to know our mind and transform our lives, we must make sense of what is customary versus what is true, entering uneasy gray areas and looking for thinking that may be causing us distress because it is negative, restrictive, and *distorted*.

TEN COMMON PATTERNS OF DISTORTED THINKING

Black-and-White Thinking

Viewing everything as entirely good or bad, putting people and situations into all-or-nothing categories with little consideration or tolerance for anything in between. "Men are no good." "Eating out is a waste of money." "Poodles are the best dogs." "Blondes are stupid." "Dancing is evil."

Overgeneralization

Taking a negative event and blowing it out of proportion, turning one situation into a never-ending predictor of future events. Exaggerated, critical statements perpetuate a sense of defeat using terms like *never, nothing, everything,* and *always.* "You never listen to me." "Ever since my team lost the pennant, nothing ever goes my way." "After Senator Jones did that, I don't trust politicians; everything they say is a lie."

Filtering

Seeing through a lens that overlooks the positive and focuses on what's negative or imperfect. "I could have had a good report card, but I got a B in algebra." "The wedding would have been nice, but the music was too loud." "She ruined the party by forgetting the birthday napkins."

Discounting

Devaluing positive accomplishments, qualities, and experiences by minimizing their importance or worth. "A lot of people graduate from college; let's see if you can find a decent job!" "So what if she made the honor roll! It's for boring people who have nothing better to do." "Of course you want to open a bakery. . . . Dream on! How about you make some dinner?"

Catastrophizing

Predicting and continually looking for evidence that things are going in a negative direction, or forecasting that they will end badly. "If you don't stop running, you'll break your neck." "I'll just get hurt if I open my heart again." "The way things are going, we will all end up sick or broke."

Judging

Criticizing oneself or others with rigid standards and emphasis on terms like *should, should not, ought, must,* and *have to.* "I should not have gotten my hair cut short/signed up for softball/written the poem, etc.; people are going to laugh at me." "You should know better." "You must keep a stiff upper lip." "You have to try harder." "I ought to be over it by now."

Mind Reading

Making negative assumptions about people's motives and intentions, regardless of any evidence—personalizing and being sure that you know, when you don't. "I can tell by the way Susan looks at me that she is jealous and just doesn't like me." "I know you don't mean anything you just said." "He's mad, or he would have called me by now." "She thinks I'm stupid."

Emotional Reasoning

Interpreting feelings as facts; reality is based on present feelings and results in *decisions* being made based on what is *felt* in the moment. "I feel nervous about the new job/worried about the computer training; I am going to call and quit." "I feel anxious about opening a new business; must be a sign to forget it." "I'm uneasy about meeting new people, so I'll stay home."

Labeling

Using name calling or bad words to brand oneself or another person, instead of describing the mistake or upsetting behavior "You are so *stupid* and *lazy*; how could you possibly have forgotten the directions?" "You are such an *irresponsible loser*." "What a *good-for-nothing brat!*"

Personalizing

Blaming and holding someone (self or another) responsible for something that was not within his or her control. "Why didn't I just cancel my appointment? If I had been home, he might not have gone to the bar and gotten a DUI." "My entrée was too salty, so no tip for that waitress!" "If I had been a better daughter, my parents wouldn't have gotten a divorce."

So how do we determine whether what we believe is actually more about an ingrained, negative way of thinking than it is about the truth? Or how do we know whether what we have accepted from parents, teachers, or religious traditions is based on the faulty, paranoid cognitions of someone else? Along with checking our reasoning for common patterns of distortion, we can also check in to that place of inner knowing where mind, body, and spirit unite.

Beyond skin and marrow, our soul—the eternal essence that arrives with us at birth and accompanies us when we vacate this world—is with us on this mission of exploration and discovery and has the power to direct and inform us. When we open ourselves to beauty and possibility—when we attend to what nourishes our soul—we are expanded with a sense of wonder that generates passion and creativity and resonates with what is good and right.

But if we neglect to feed our soul—overlooking gifts within and around us—we limit ourselves and our destiny. Concentrating only on our adult duties, challenges, and disappointments, we can easily forget why we are here, and that can restrict us from realizing our magnificence and most exhilarating earthly potential. Negative beliefs and messages tend to focus on what is difficult and imperfect—on all that is wrong, bad, and evil in the world—and create an unrewarding perspective wrought with critical judgments, dissatisfaction, and a perverted view of reality.

And by discerning whether our beliefs are producing constriction or freedom—whether our cognitions expand us with hope and inspiration or diminish us with fear, stress, despair, or hostility—we can gain clarity. If our intellect does not point us toward serenity, it is time to question our thinking and reconsider. By paying attention to that ageless time traveler—our soul—we are guided to what is true and satisfying, release negativity that holds us captive, and develop more of the love, joy, and peace that surpass understanding and ignite the spark within our essential natures.

Soul work nurtures body, mind, and spirit, connecting us with what is good and giving us eyes to appreciate the miraculous in the mundane—yesterday, today, and beyond. With soulful consciousness, we can try on different, better ways of being, shaping our feelings and thoughts in an "acting as if" reversal, *doing* things that challenge unhealthy beliefs, stretch us, and germinate the seeds of discovery that produce more light, freedom, and compassion within and around us.

Our convictions shape and color our personal point of view. If, for example, we *believe* people are nasty, we will look for proof and our expectations will be fulfilled; we will notice people who seem rude and unfriendly and who mirror the preconceived notions that have been inputted into our system's database. Cooperating with the mind's eye and messages, our thinking drives our feelings and moods until we act accordingly in behaviors that perfectly reflect our cognitions:

BELIEVE ⇨ THINK ⇨ FEEL ⇨ ACT

Believe: the world is unkind ⇨
Think: people don't care ⇨
Feel: hurt and lonely ⇨
Act: aloof, guarded, unapproachable

However, we have the power to evaluate our internal program, to adjust our worldview and level of satisfaction. Instead of letting old, unfavorable beliefs continue to affect our thoughts, feelings, and behaviors, we have the capacity to revise or reverse them by *acting* in ways that confront old, negative suppositions and set us free:

ACT ⇨ FEEL ⇨ THINK ⇨ BELIEVE

Act: engaged and say "hi" ⇨
Feel: happy and caring ⇨
Think: people are friendly ⇨
Believe: the world is full of loving kindness

According to William James, "We don't laugh because we're happy—we're happy because we laugh." Our *actions* can change our feelings, thoughts, and beliefs. And so, by mindfully trying on behaviors that enliven us with soul-enriching serenity, connection, and happiness, we can *experience* a whole new reality and radically transform our lives.

5.8 | WORDS

Gracious words are like a honeycomb, sweetness to the soul and health to the body.
—PROVERB OF KING SOLOMON

We revise our stories by knowing our minds—recognizing possible distortions and faulty logic, shifting perceptions and taking corrective action that leads us to greater joy and compassion. And the most mindful way to deconstruct thinking that may be negatively impacting our moods and behaviors, and to build thoughts that lead to more of what we want, is to pay close attention to what we say and hear.

Our internal dialogue and every word we speak contribute to our reality and destiny. Our self-esteem and every area of our life depend on how and what we tell ourself. And *words* are the human way we make sense of what we perceive; they are the building blocks used to translate thoughts and feelings into a form that can be received by our minds and communicated with others. And, like a computer, we categorize and store words, using them to run the personal search engine that connects us with the collective World Wide Web.

If we are to obtain accurate information and desired outcomes, the language that instructs our individualized program must be precise. Each word and phrase is significant to navigate to the correct destination, and our input must be without error, or we will not end up where we want to be. Our direction, the results we are hoping to achieve, and even our relationships are dependent upon the words that have been entered into the central processing unit that consciously, and unconsciously, propels us through life.

My fascination with words began years ago, when I tried to rid them from my head (and from earshot of the neighbors) and recognized that once words get into the database, they set in motion a commanding program that can be tricky to eliminate and rebuild. Words, though often taken for granted, have tremendous value and authority. They crystallize our thoughts and allow us to transmit our experiences. And as orators, hypnotists, politicians, and advertising executives know only too well, a well-placed word can effectively mold and change the mind of an individual and influence an entire crowd.

Language, like hypnotic suggestion, is a powerful instrument. It can result in self-sabotaging behaviors that hold us hostage, or it can set us free to realize our potential. And by looking at the words and idioms you use, and listening to what you continue to say and hear, you can unlock and reprogram the unconscious belief systems that may be keeping you stuck. Much of what is whispered inside your head was originally heard on the outside: "You're smart," or "You'll never amount to anything," or perhaps "You'd lose your head if it wasn't fastened to your scrawny little neck."

Words can persuade, evoke action, manipulate, inspire, and defeat us. And according to Yvonne Oswald, author of *Every Word Has Power*, "[s]imply by becoming more consciously aware of the words being used, attitudes change and relationships improve dramatically." With attention to the words we choose and use every day, we can better understand not only the impact of words on our own psyches, but also which words are most effective in getting us more of what we really want.

Certain words—like *imagine, you,* and *because*—are powerful, hypnotic words that activate the subconscious mind and influence us to take action. Other words—like *no, never,* and *not*—confuse the system, because, like a hypnotic induction or a Google search designed to process key words and overlook negatives, "not *bad*" focuses on *bad*; "no *problem*" focuses on *problem.* If, for example, you tell your mind "*not* to think about teapots," or "*don't* focus on the number five, or "*never* imagine a tall pink giraffe wearing a striped T-shirt and sunglasses," what happens? Exactly. You can't help but think about teapots, the number five, and a big pink giraffe in an oversize T-shirt and dark glasses!

Aaron was only seven, but he was already plagued with guilt. After finding one of his father's Playboy *magazines, Aaron became preoccupied with women's breasts. His mother noticed his new, unsettling fascination and, after learning about his exposure to* Playboy, *decided to bring him to see me.*

Aaron was embarrassed about it, as was his mother, and admitted that he had been staring at women's chests and seemed unable to stop: his mother's, his teenage sister's, his teacher's, strangers', and now, no doubt, mine.

"Yes, I've told Aaron that it is impolite," says his mother, "that he should stop thinking about that part of a woman's body —that he should just tell himself not to look there."

"I tell myself that I shouldn't look at their chests, and then I do," he confesses, as he makes brief eye contact with me, before quickly looking away.

Aaron feels bad about this behavior that has recently set itself in motion and is stuck in a thinking loop that is rein-forcing the very behavior he wants to eliminate. And to reprogram, we must effectively replace what not *to do with what is positive and acceptable to do.*

First, the allure of a woman's body needs to be normalized, and the natural curiosity of a seven-year-old boy appreciated. So we talk openly about body parts and the amazing way our bodies have been designed, taking away the stigma that there is something innately wrong with wanting to know more about our own bodies or the bodies of the opposite sex.

After all, women's breasts are magnificent; they are shown in paintings and sculptures at art museums and in magazines purchased by grown men, and come in all shapes and sizes. And they are the source of human milk that nourishes babies and keeps our race alive. There is no disgrace in curiosity; breasts are interesting and quite remarkable! The only thing wrong with wanting to stare at them is that staring, for any reason, makes people feel very uncomfortable.

And so, to change the behavior, I talk to Aaron about how not thinking *about something is problematic—nearly impos-sible—because we teach our brains what to focus on with our words, and when he tells himself* not to look *at a woman's breasts,* looking *will be the very thing that he does!*

"If I say, 'Do not *think about Darth Vader,' what happens?" I ask, as Aaron takes a moment and then lights up with a look of understanding.*

"Or how about 'Do not, *under any condition at all, never, ever imagine a penguin wearing a cowboy hat'? Now what?"*

This time Aaron laughs out loud as levity surfaces, dissipating the heaviness he appeared to be carrying.

"Would you like to try it with me?" I ask.

"Okay," Aaron says, as he takes a moment, then gives the directive: "Do not think about a red car." But, of course, I do—we all do—and the point is made as we laugh about the way our brains work.

"So, instead of telling yourself not to look at someone's chest, what might be a better place for you to put your eyes when you're tempted to stare at a lady's breasts?"

"Her eyes," Aaron says quickly. "I could just look at her eyes."

And so, together, we make a plan that if Aaron starts to talk himself out of a behavior with what he shouldn't do, he will switch from what not to do (negative) to what to do (positive).

"I will tell myself to look at her eyes, or maybe her face, or maybe her hair, or her nose, or her feet, or her teeth . . ." And then we all laugh with relief at Aaron's inside joke, indicating that with the power of language, new insights, and release from shame, he can move forward with his unspoiled, seven-year-old life.

Our mind's mission is to serve and protect us and take our instructions. And, like Aaron, as both the student and the teacher of our mind, we can tune in to the words we choose and can function more proficiently by being mindful of our language—noting whether it is ultimately affirmative and how it might be affecting us and others. Widely read classics, like *The Power of Positive Thinking*, *The Magic of Thinking Big*, *The Secret*, and hundreds of other books through the years, have linked mind and positive language with happiness and success. And today, with mind-science research and advances in energy medicine, we are learning even more about how and why that is so.

In her information-packed book about the power of words, Oswald tells us that optimistic, "high-energy words"—*achieve, beautiful, believe, dream, enthusiasm, family, happy, heart, smart, thanks,* etc.—vibrate at higher frequencies, gener-ating higher levels of thinking and power. On the other hand, negative, "low-energy words"—*afraid, difficult, failure, hate, lose, poor, problem, sick, stupid, worry,* etc.—vibrate at lower frequencies, impeding vigor and confidence and ul-timately decreasing our potential to turn our dreams into reality.

If you tap into your inner dialogue, you will recognize two basic kinds of thoughts: those that are positive and supportive, and those that are not. And *by simply changing your internal and external language patterns*—changing negatives to positives, (switching, for example, *not bad* to *good, no problem* to *fine* or *terrific*) and incorporating more high-energy, constructive words than low-energy words—you will find that your mind can empower you in ways that dramatically shift your outlook and what you accomplish.

Affirmations, as well, are a major programming tool in this process. Positively stated, they are clear and simple declarations meant to provide us with greater assurance, contentment, and well-being. When we state, "I am safe; my world is a place of loving kindness" or "My body is healing itself, and I am well," our mind takes our direction and sets about the task of making our thoughts come true. Conversely, if we feed our mind fear-based messages like "I will fail," "I am getting sick," or "I'm stupid," these beliefs, too, will become our focus and, most likely, our reality.

In words, we have a power source that can bring us more of what we want or can inadvertently demotivate or undermine us in ways we may not realize nor intend. And, in the same way, our words impact and influence those we love, requiring us to be intentional about the words and messages we are choosing to pass along. Our stories are communicated in language, committed to memory, and written in words that get deposited into the annals of history. As Walt Whitman, the American poet, reminds us from the grave, "The powerful play goes on, and you will contribute a verse."

WORDS

Your words are essential to human growth
Ingested and absorbed like a mother's milk;
They become the manual your children carry through life
And the echoes that beckon them back home.
So rock your infants with lullabies
Immerse them in the glorious beauty you see;
Tell them of their precious gifts and possibilities
And wrap them in the language of a warm embrace.
Bathe them in balmy wonders of the universe
Speak of splendor all around and within;
Sing of twinkling stars and moonlit skies
And blanket them in lyrics of enduring love.
Profess your joy at their one-of-a-kind perfection
Marvel at the unrivaled miracles in your care;
Swaddle them with verse and affirmation
And cradle them in a coverlet of gratitude.
Remember always the infinite power of your tongue
Transform its tempests into refreshing breezes;
Cast spells that nourish, rather than curses that destroy
And clothe them in a mantle of confidence and compassion.
Choose your words and use them well
They are being written into sonnets and stories for all time,
Inscribed into epics crafted of flesh and blood
And will be recited, verbatim, for generations to come.

5.9 | REFRAMING

*I will not let anyone walk through my mind
with their dirty feet.*
—MAHATMA GANDHI

What you have been told about yourself is most likely what you end up believing—even if the words originated from someone else's "dirty feet" or polluted mind. Righting and revising that old story—reframing what you believe about yourself *now*—requires that you disinfect yourself and set yourself free from unwanted, soiled messages. And at the core of stinking thinking and its contamination is always an infectious germ of toxic shame.

Guilt is the sense that you have done something wrong —your conscience has been pricked, and you feel bad—and you might not feel better until you do something to fix or amend the situation. Shame, on the other hand, is a feeling that you are bad as you are, that you have little worth—and though you may try to earn it, rarely do you feel better or deserving of good things.

Donna was demeaned as a child. She was called "big boned" and "clumsy" and was an embarrassment to her socially conscious mother and sister, who, according to Donna, were both blonde, pretty, and petite.

"I always felt bad about myself. My mother was clearly ashamed of me; I was the dark-haired, fat one who looked like

my dad and was always on a diet. She never seemed to want me around and would send me to my room whenever she had friends over."

Donna tried to win her mother's approval for years, and finally, at age fifty-two, after a mastectomy and her second chemo treatment, she went to her mother's house for the weekend, hoping for some rest and (long-overdue) tender loving care.

Instead, she got what she always got—a dose of rejection and shame. Her mother showed her to the guest room and callously announced, "If that curly hair of yours starts falling out, use the dustpan; I don't want to find it all over the bathroom floor. Better not rinse it down the drain, either, or I'll have a plumbing problem. And don't use the good towels!"

Losing one's hair after chemo is an upsetting experience for anyone, and while her mother may have been insensitive and extremely practical, her delivery was just plain cruel. During her stay, Donna was ignored as her mother watched TV and smoked cigarettes, telling her that if she wanted something to eat, she should fix it herself. With hair loss and nausea compounding an early wound, Donna felt not only physically ill but utterly abandoned and clear that her mother was never going to extend her the care she so effortlessly offered to her sister, friends, and assorted houseguests.

"It was a low point in my life," Donna told me. "My husband left me a year before the cancer, and it was pretty obvious my mother wanted nothing to do with me. I left after that weekend feeling completely unloved, and considered ending my life."

Donna and I worked together, building a relationship, resurrecting love from the Source, and recognizing the damage that arises from the tactless acts and words of a crazymaker. Donna began valuing herself, recognizing how she had unconsciously educated others—including her ex—about how to treat her and what she ultimately did *or didn't* deserve. She set goals and boundaries, pursued her dream of becoming a hospice nurse, and found people to love and serve—who loved her back.

Donna became aware of her contagious laugh, magnanimous spirit, and exquisite gold-green eyes, and it wasn't long until others became aware of them, too. With greater confidence and self-care, she joined a support group, became more involved with her church, and even began dating a man who appreciated her full figure and fresh sprouts of dark, curly hair. And after hundreds of entries in her dog-eared journal, and nearly a year together in therapy, Donna shared with me the sentiment of liberation from impure, faulty notions in her own stirring, powerful words:

I am learning new ways of being. Of thinking. I am reconsidering and reframing all I have been told about myself, and have begun to experience a slightly different reality of me. I will re-create the person I am; the person I have forever been but have never known. I will reframe myself by discovering what has always been true and dissolving layers of veneer. With God's love, I am finding and recognizing my true self, softening with a new freedom. Reconsidering. Rediscovering. Renewing. Reenergizing. Reframing.

* The stages of human development provide an overview of the skills and virtues we confront as we mature.

* We must resolve specific challenges and opportunities—the Tasks of Life—if we are to find meaning and contentment in our lives.

* Beliefs (though mainly unconscious) create thoughts, which trigger our feelings and behavior.

* Distorted thinking patterns are fear-based, negative, and restrictive.

* Every word in our inner and outer dialogue is a power source that can positively, or negatively, influence us and others.

* By knowing our mind, we can right negative thinking and reframe it with affirming self-love and kindness.

5.10 | YOUR STORY

It's your turn to tell your story. Imagine you're the client.
Get comfortable. Breathe deeply. Use the following prompts to make
discoveries and gain clarity on your way to personal freedom.
Use a journal to capture any thoughts, feelings, or images that come
to mind or talk into a recorder. Welcome to your session ...

What is the greatest life change you are currently facing?

In which stage of the eight stages of human development are you? Do you have gaps in your development?

What skills and virtues need to be revisited or repaired?

How satisfied are you in each of the five Tasks of Life: Love? Work? Relationship? Self-care? Spiritual development?

Which task needs the most immediate attention? What is lacking? How can you attend to this task? What mini-step will you take?

Breathe in deeply. Exhale fully. What do you *feel* right now?

I feel ___x____.

What thought is connected to the feeling:

I feel__x__because _thought____.

What belief may be influencing your thinking and emotions:

I feel ___x__ because_ thought__, and I believe _belief__.

Have you detected patterns of distorted thinking?

Can you identify negative beliefs fueled by old messages?

How will you use your words to positively reframe what you believe about yourself? To affirm and encourage others?

SIX

Transforming

6.1 | GROWING UP

Growth is not always about getting what we think we want. Always, it's about becoming the men and women we have the potential to be: loving, pure, honest, and clear.
—MARIANNE WILLIAMSON

Growth is inevitable. We will all grow. We start as seedlings covered in impeccable skin that is as silky-fresh as the scent of our baby powder. And then, with no effort whatsoever, we stretch up and out, accumulating an array of personal markings—freckles and scars and blemishes—as our exteriors steadfastly morph and expand before our eyes.

Over time, our birth suits lose elasticity, sagging and wrinkling like a poorly tailored unitard in need of a nip or tuck. Our interiors begin to demand attention, too, calling for magnifying glasses and hearing aids, bone scans and blood tests. Surely, years will take their toll, inside and out, as we are offered season upon season in which to grow and mature, and a face that will be rearranged by the steady pull of gravity, and a variety of indiscriminate factors that are largely out of our control.

Some of us will ripen with our lessons and experiences and will gain wisdom during this process, some of us will combat this natural course of events as though we're battling a vindictive contender, and others will just wither and decay without much of a fight or reflection. We can grow old without ever growing up, or we can choose to appreciate this incredible garment that will weather and change dramatically—like it or not—as we travel in it through time to watch, and listen, and learn.

Growing up is not easy; adulthood is a whole different world than the one into which we are born. Dressing up, acting as if we know what we are doing—even when we don't—trying on new roles, falling down, and skinning our knees is tiresome. Even if we were lucky enough to have had supportive parents, they move on with their lives, die, or, at best, take seats in the cheering section as we run the race alone.

The adult realm is the school of hard knocks, car payments, job interviews, and learning how to defer gratification for a future payoff. Aging is about moving through the developmental stages and continually going somewhere we have never been before. It is understandable that the balance between freedom and responsibility can easily get out of whack as we try being big. Leaving youth behind as we transition to this grown-up world is often more stressful and scary than the satisfaction we anticipated.

It is no wonder that, given the chance, we prolong adolescence. Many "teens" have begun living with parents well into their thirties. The number of high school students who are cutting themselves and suffering from depression, eating disorders, addictions, and other symptoms of emotional instability has increased. Colleges are witnessing more mood and adjustment disorders among students, with a rise in extreme cases as troubling as suicide and mass murders on campuses. Transitioning from childhood to the adult realm is a challenge that requires plenty of guidance, encouragement, and healthy models for the younger generation to emulate.

But we have become a narcissistic culture, filled with midlife teenagers, Disneyland dads, trophy wives, and rock star wannabes. We are driven by fear of failure and hefty egos hungry for material success. In a society where appearances and winnings trump a kind heart or sense of integrity, being an elder has lost its appeal. Today, as we elevate toys and triumphs, reality-TV rivalries and overnight successes, nice guys who stay the course often finish last. Humankind has lost its heart as it makes an unsettling tilt toward competition and greed and buys into society's marketable obsession with beauty, instant gratification, and staying young forever.

The world has become lopsided with too few sages and too many indulgent kids. We need more caring leaders with generativity and less self-centered behavior from a glut of overgrown teens. Crossing from childhood to adulthood is the bridge to personal freedom and the way to steady a planet in need of balance. Becoming a grown-up is not just about growing old; it is about shedding faulty logic knitted together in youth and embracing spiritual lessons that direct us to a place where fulfillment, grace, and acceptance flourish.

What keeps many from this passage from youth to adulthood? For some, it is the simple fear of growing old, losing our looks and our vitality, and facing our mortality. For others, it is complicated by a lack of development from addiction, narcissism, or entitlement issues. But, in addition to the obvious reasons for lingering in immaturity, moving on requires a ticket of sorts: a personal dig, without which it is impossible ever to cross over.

Until we are willing to take a good look at our parents —the people who raised us—and see them for who they *really* are, or were, we will stay dwarfed, stuck in the land of childhood, regardless of our age. The fee necessary to become an official adult requires that we take a conscious step to recognize our caretakers as imperfect people—a mixture of good and bad, neither saints nor villains, angels nor demons—just overgrown children themselves.

Like all humans, every parent or caretaker is a flawed product of his or her upbringing, resources, and choices. And like *all* parents, they will have missed the mark to some degree, causing us a certain amount of pain and confusion and leaving us with baggage to contend with in therapy. *Every* child will have issues to deal with as part of his or her developmental process.

Why? It is the human condition, perhaps the only way we expand our characters with the acceptance and loving kindness that heals and grows us beyond our childhood selves. To reach adulthood, each of us must wrestle with hurts and misunderstandings from the past. It is how we beat our wings against the cocoon or peck ourselves out of the shell. We, too, have a way to emancipate ourselves from the confines of our first homes and emerge, with greater strength and vision, to face the next phase of our lives.

While some parents did their personal best, others were inadequate or even cruel. Some left us bruised and damaged. Others gave us all they had to give. But *none* was perfect. Granting them a pardon is a prerequisite, the customary and necessary tariff that allows us to move on. It is our way to release them and to detach ourselves from regrets, shame, and resentments that will hold us chained to our younger selves.

The forgiveness we extend is not about minimizing an offense; it is not about letting an abuser off the hook or forgetting painful injustices. Forgiveness is about freeing ourselves to till and cultivate a healthy sense of self, regardless of our beginnings. We grow bigger only when something shifts in our perspective, when we start to see our parents, and ourselves, in new ways. We accept the reality of who they *were*, not who we wanted them to be. We stop putting energy into trying to please them or change them or the past. We stop trying to be just like them or completely different, and we focus on our unique talents and the remainder of our lives.

Offering forgiveness and making peace with our past is the official place where adulthood begins. So, how will we know that we've grown up? When we cease to overreact—stop punishing or blaming anyone else for what's happening *today*—we will sense a shift and begin seeing things through wiser eyes. We leave childhood when we become autonomous individuals, no longer consumed by transgressions or driven by someone else's approval or lack of it.

By taking responsibility to repair, revise, or forgive what keeps us stuck in childlike dependency, we earn the required fare for passage to a place of grown-up independence and will know we have arrived when we feel the presence of *freedom* there. As unencumbered adults, we can accept God's gifts of mercy, beauty, creativity, and joy and cultivate matters of the heart. And as we find opportunities in change, tend to our leftover regrets, and continue to dream with hopeful curiosity, we can experience the soulful buried treasures that are found in the realm beyond childhood.

From a seed of gratitude for our life and story, we age gracefully, mindful of the generous spirits and unsung heroes who have inspired us along the way. And as elders, we carry on *their* legacy, contented by *giving* love and encouragement, not just getting it. We will know that we are fully grown when we believe it is never too late for us to be our best self and become the mentors who contribute by blessing others—and ourself—with love that nurtures and wisdom that embraces those who show up in our life.

6.2 | HAVING A VOICE

Reckless words pierce like a sword,
but the tongue of the wise brings healing.
—PROVERB OF KING SOLOMON

Sitting here on the airplane, wedged in by a large man filling the center seat and a student sleeping on the aisle, I feel small. Trapped. Leaning against the window, I want to cry. I am mad at myself. "This time will be different," I vowed and had realistic expectations, or so I thought, about this latest visit to see my mother. I'd made it to the finish line without incident, didn't take things too personally, and wasn't even upset when I said good-bye. But now, here in the plane, I feel flooded—overwhelmed, immobilized by emotion.

For years, I have been doing my work: unpacking baggage from the past, lightening my load for today's lessons and adventures to come. I'm a therapist—I help other people do this—and really believed that I was sufficiently detached, finally immune to this growing-backward stuff. But during this trip back "home," it happened again.

It was fine for a couple days, but by day three, I began the regression. The name-calling and incessant talking started getting the best of me, with the predictable commands to do this and not that—"Look. Listen. Stand here. Repeat back: 'Yes, your hair looks good; yes, the food is delicious; yes, that's a nice shade of lipstick'" (whether it's true or not)—over and over.

I feel completely invisible, once again, with a life that seems to be of little interest or significance. My mother tells me what and how much to eat, gets offended if I make any choice that is different from hers, and never asks me a question—except those wrapped with prickly contempt, like "What the hell is wrong with you?" "Don't you have a brain?" "Why would you ever wear that?"

INVISIBLE

*Talked at
And talked at
And talked at.
Commands,
Demands,
Instructions.
Food
And money
And bodily functions.*

*Anger,
Disrespect,
Biting criticism.
Repeated monologues.
Polite silences.
Conversations inside my head.
Stuffed full
But starving.
Screaming, but without voice.*

Strangely, even after a slew of decades, advanced degrees, children, and grandchildren, I can become young instantly from a sharp remark or certain disgusted look from a mother who is much too old to still be hurting my feelings. Through the years,

she has provided many monetary gifts and has "put up with me."
I believe that somewhere deep down, she even loves me, but she
hasn't liked me very much.

To my mother, I have been a nuisance, someone she has had
to care about and look out for. I have made her proud on
occasion, but if she actually kept statistics, the moments I
delighted her—with gifts and awards, dean's lists, school
activities, scholarships, acting, writing, piano recitals, public
speaking, teaching (pretty much everything I could think to do
but stand on my head!)—would be gravely outweighed by the
multitude of letdowns and disappointments she has had to
endure and mentions on a regular basis.

She contends that I have cost her plenty, and she wants me
to know that if there were a running tally, my value remains in
question; I would not measure up to her standards. I get on her
nerves, can't read her mind or seem to make her happy nearly
enough. The crazy thing, after all these years, is that I still try. I
want my mother to actually like me—to be curious about who I
am, ask a legitimate question about my life, maybe even value
my opinion once in a while. But with each passing year and
visit, it's clear that I want something from my mother that she
cannot give. I want her to be someone she is not.

On a good day, I am able to forgive her for sharp-tongued
put-downs and the emotional outbursts she seems unable to
control. I have tried to understand her volatility by imagining a
hurt child buried within this eighty-year-old woman who has
been impossible to please. But on other days, when I forget all
about boundaries and letting go—when I start taking things
personally and grow small in my own estimation—the reality of
the situation gets blurred and I lose sight of my identity as an
engaged, accomplished woman and a caring adult daughter who
is simply undervalued.

I love my mother but hate the narcissism that has engulfed her and darkened my life. As a child, I tried everything to please and developed skills that allowed me to wait patiently, to put myself aside, to be a companion and confidant. I followed my mother's lead and, in the shadow she cast, politely endured her rants and judgments with devotion. But there is a cost—collateral damage—that comes from remaining voiceless.

SCREAMING HEADACHE

MY BODY BECAME MY VOICE.
IT TRIED TO SEND A MESSAGE
RIGHT OUT THE TOP OF MY HEAD,
BUT THE WORDS GOT STUCK INSIDE.
THEY TRIED SO HARD TO SHOUT:
"YOU'RE MEAN. YOU'VE TRIED TO RUIN MY LIFE.
I'VE PAID DEARLY FOR THE DAMAGE YOU'VE DONE
AND NAMES YOU'VE CALLED ME.
YOU'RE A BULLY. YOU'RE WICKED.
YOU'VE SEARED MY HEART
WITH WORD-SHAPED DAGGERS
AND NO APOLOGIES."

YOU'VE MOCKED THIS DEFENSELESS CHILD,
RIDICULED AND USED ME,
CALLED ME NAMES,
AND I HAVE PARDONED YOU.
YOU SHOVED YOUR WILL DOWN MY THROAT
AND MADE ME CHEW AND SWALLOW.
MY VOICE HAS ALWAYS BEEN A WHISPER
THAT YOU CALLED DEFIANCE
OR REFUSED TO HEAR,
BUT MY BODY WILL NOT STAY SILENT.
IT IS CRYING OUT ITS ANGER.
"NO MORE. ENOUGH OF THIS."

THESE MURMURS HAVE ERUPTED INTO A SCREAM
THAT IS SHOUTING WITHOUT SHAME.
I WILL STAMMER BUT NOT BE DAMNED,
TRY OUT NEW WORDS AND TELL STORIES
WITHOUT REPRIMAND.
MY TORTURED SOUL IS NO LONGER
HELD CAPTIVE IN MY ROOM
AS YOUR PRISONER.
I WILL NOT BE SILENCED.
I AM FREE.
MY VOICE HAS FOUND ME
AND I WILL WHISPER NO MORE.

And now, here in my seat, I am trapped, entangled in old connections about the biggest and most aggressive getting their way, held hostage by thoughts and feelings of being unprotected and voiceless—overshadowed and diminished by the rudest and most overbearing. But I have the power to set myself free. *I have a voice, the freedom to use it, and, as an adult, the ability to come and go as I please. I matter, too!*

The wound of a narcissist's child has been torn open, yet again, by the recurring suggestion that I am uninteresting, undeserving, and unlikable at the core. Though I know these deprecating thoughts come from a damaged brain, untreated and unwilling to share the spotlight or put itself in anyone else's shoes, they come with the powerful attachment of a child to a mother, one who declares that any act of separation is a blatant, malicious act of abandonment. And so I find myself caught between jumping for joy at the prospect of returning to my husband, children, and grandchildren and feeling guilty for leaving my mother with her discontent and twisted mind.

And what contributes to my sadness is the realization that even after all these years—and endeavors to appease—I am still unable to lift her spirits. I have only continued to burden her by growing up with a personality and family of my own. And, in order to heal the wound I carry, I have no choice but to hurt my mother by leaving as a betrayer, a full-grown adult who can no longer be accountable for her contentment but am entirely responsible for mine.

Sitting here among travelers from many cultures and family trees, I wonder what private journeys they've been on and where they are going, and whether or not they have found a sanctuary —a distinct space on the planet in which to thrive and grow. I think of my final destination, my loved ones waiting there, and I no longer feel obligated to defer my needs here on the plane or anywhere else. I am not that stifled child anymore—confined and stuck without a voice—in this, or any other, corner. And it is okay—necessary—for me to be good to myself.

So, without apologizing for being a nuisance or an inconvenience, I simply open my mouth and politely tell the passengers in my row that I'd like to get out. We are, after all, a family of growing children here and everywhere we go, tourists with varying wounds, dreams, and biological necessities. Equals. And so, after unbuckling my seat belt—with skillful maneuvering and accommodating smiles—I step into the aisle as a confident, fully sanctioned woman who can express and care for herself without fear of disapproval or reprisal, a grown-up who has liberated her voice to speak on her own behalf, free, and grateful to be coming home.

6.3 | REATTACHING

Soul, the basic substance of the universe,
yearns for connection.
—JOAN BORYSENKO, PhD

The need for connection is part of a design that every soul yearns for, a powerful influence that incites us to attach, be nurtured, and ultimately thrive as human beings. But some attachments can be toxic and so gripping that they hold us captive—tethered to someone whose love we crave—even after history makes it clear that the person has none to give. When a longing for someone's affection becomes a consuming hunger, we can become enmeshed in a sickening relationship in which we allow ourselves to be degraded, manipulated, and mistreated as we loyally attempt to stay connected and earn validation from someone who is unlikely to offer it.

Jurors witness this confounding pattern in cases of domestic violence when abused partners put themselves in jeopardy by returning again and again to be condemned and bruised, as though they have been bewitched. Victims appear to be volunteers who are unwilling to cut emotional cords and release themselves from an unyielding, mysterious bond that keeps them stuck. And sometimes, in an effort to escape—to be set free from the invisible, noxious shackles—they resort to a desperate act of revenge.

The television show *48 Hours* presented the true story,

set in Texas, of one such unwholesome attachment between a father and son. The father was a fun-loving man with wealth and charisma—boats, lavish parties, and a private jet —that impressed and entertained scores of acquaintances. Friends called him a partier who liked women and alcohol, and a few shared candidly about a much darker, *wicked* side. His ex-wife recounted unbearable years of verbal and physical abuse and explained how their youngest son had always been his favorite target, until they divorced and he abandoned the family.

Years later, when that son grew to be an adult, he sought out the dad who had abused and neglected him, and willingly moved into his father's home. The attaching spell, set in childhood, was still reflected in the forlorn eyes of that grown son as he wept bitterly before the camera. From jail, he recalled how a night of alcohol, mixed with the voice of his father's unrelenting rejection and cruelty, pushed him beyond the tipping point. In a drunken frenzy, with pent-up hurt and anger behind each adrenalized blow, he brutally bludgeoned his father to death.

Yes, he had been called disparaging names, had been humiliated and beaten throughout his life. His father continued to remind him regularly just how worthless and disgusting he was as a man. His dad bedded his girlfriends and proudly jeered about his conquests and superiority. His eldest brother had disappeared as a teenager and was found living as a recluse in a shack without running water or electricity. Another brother had committed suicide. Their father had mercilessly bullied them all.

The television interviewer wondered what might propel someone to revisit such a life. When asked why he wanted to live with the abusive father who called him vulgar names, beat him up, and even propositioned his fiancée, he looked genuinely bewildered and merely replied, "I don't know." Sadly, in the end, after viciously attacking his father, he used a cord to dominate and choke the life out of the very man whom he wanted most to please.

All children need to know that they are loved in connections that value them. Personal growth requires that a message of worth be delivered as lavishly as light and water to thirsty sprouts. From the gestures and words of those responsible for our care, we draw our nourishment and earliest deductions about who we are and *whether or not we are lovable.* Even grown children return to a rejecting parent for a smile of approval or pat on the head. Sick as it may be, we are drawn by the hope that maybe *this* time, we just might get to hear the words that we have been waiting to hear for a lifetime.

Jails are crammed with children who got tired of waiting and instead mixed their rage with a drug of choice and an act of violence. All children would rather be good than bad, rather be pleasing than a heartbreak or a screw-up. Impressionable children, and the adults they become, often send coded messages of discouragement in the form of negative, hurtful behaviors that are galvanized by emotional pain and feelings of utter shame or failure.

As the *48 Hours* interview ends from a prison cell, a devastated son confesses to the horrific murder of his own father. Though grief-stricken and troubled by his actions, he takes responsibility for what he's done, admitting through tears and regret that even though he's locked behind bars, he finally feels *free*—for the first time in his *entire life!*

Bonds become sinister entanglements when messages of

a tormentor become the reality of innocent victims. Held fast in binding attachments they seem unable to sever, they are unwilling to cut the cords connecting them to their abusers as they try to counter what they are being told about themselves. Sadly, in an effort to validate their worth, they become prey—sacrificing themselves over and over again—as they strive to win approval or at least be noticed for their patient endurance in a steadfast quest to prove that they are, in fact, good and lovable human beings.

While most of what we learned in our early years was the result of keen observation, there is a major flaw in this method of inquiry. Interpreting nonverbal language and human behavior requires sophisticated expertise, and while we may have been great observers, we were not skilled at making inferences. Consequently, our earliest deductions and private logic were filtered through the eyes of a novice —a child with limited ability to understand and very little life experience.

Without awareness or feedback to correct any of the faulty assumptions we may have accumulated, we incorrectly record misinterpretations as *facts*. It is common, for example, for children of divorcing parents to read the hurt and anger on parents' faces as something *they* contributed to. Children may carry years of guilt because of the mistaken notion that if they had been better sons or daughters —had said or done the perfect thing—their parents might have stayed together. Every child (and adult) of divorced parents needs to be assured that divorce is an adult decision and is never, *ever* the fault of any child.

But if parents neglected to help us assess and correct faulty reasoning or used words that belittled us, we likely hold beliefs about ourselves that are not true. And if our experiences were punitive, we often continue to punish ourselves with self-destructive behaviors; we cooperate by cutting, piercing, mutilating, or starving ourselves. We become perfectionists who can never be satisfied with our accomplishments. We drink, binge, overdose, and even take our own undervalued lives. We long to love the self that we have been taught, by word or example, to loathe.

Once we submit to the notion that we are not pleasing to someone who should have loved us in childhood, we are at risk of becoming that which we *believe* we are: damaged goods, worthless and inferior, deserving of an unfortunate destiny. We *feel* unlovable and live with an unspoken agreement that we have somehow warranted this treatment. From early childhood recollections, we carry a sense of the inadequacy and disappointment we saw registered on the face of a significant adult in our world.

Some stay tangled in these bonds and identify with their abusers. They learned lessons by living them first as an innocent victim. And once they reach a position of authority, they make an unconscious decision to model the experience they know so well, but this time no one will hurt *them*—they will be the one doing the hurting. With insults and aggressive behaviors, they display superiority over their subordinates, in the same way it was demonstrated when they were young.

Many perpetrators started as the tortured soul, caught in a merciless stranglehold. With practice, they learned to defend themselves with a vengeance. Their determination to gain the powerful upper hand repeats the cycle, as they become the next relentless bully who chokes the life out of anyone who shows weakness or helplessly submits. Fear and powerlessness—associated with years of victimization—

become a despicable reminder of vulnerability and feelings of inferiority.

While healthy human development is dependent upon a secure attachment between a growing infant and a loving, responsive caregiver, the model of attachment we experienced in early childhood becomes our norm. We expect to be treated in a certain way that feels familiar. Strong emotional attachments formed in childhood become preoccupations that manifest in other relationships throughout our lives. Whether they were positive or negative, secure or chaotic, patterns of thinking about ourselves were set within those early bonds. And what may seem normal and instinctual to us can look completely neurotic to an impartial observer.

Staying connected to someone who denigrates or assigns negative motives to our behaviors causes upheaval that can feel both crazy and just like home. For those who grew up in environments that were rejecting and hostile, life without this drama can feel oddly out of sync. Most victims from these backgrounds carry an observable weight of sadness. They are disappointments. Blatantly told, with or without words, they accepted the reproach of an unhealthy adult who told them that they did not, and never could, measure up.

The first five years of life are critical, yet most of us do not remember them in any detail. We piece together our experiences from photos, vague memories, and hearsay, and as adults, we disclose the story of our formative years in our ability to trust ourselves, others, and our world; our mysterious beginnings resonate through time to reveal our self-image and impact the relationships in which we choose to live our lives.

When the words of our mentors do not match with their actions, we grow up not knowing what is true. If there was hostility, addiction, abuse, or mental illness in our home, mistrust reigned. We did not know whom or what to believe, and though our models may have been damaged and confusing, we likely ended up mistrusting *ourselves*. When perceptions are distorted in childhood, we can begin life with a crisis of identity that can develop into a troublesome pattern of self-doubt and inferiority.

Regardless of who the adults were in our young lives, or what they espoused, we relied on their words and values and gave them greater clout than even they imagined. We were tiny. They were enormous. They had authority and we had none. We attached to them for our sustenance, and they held the power to nourish, force-feed, or starve us. And they told us what was "absolutely true" about the world and about us—our worth and lovability—and we believed them.

But to grow up and experience the fullness of life requires that we leave childhood and detach from the messages and people who are unhealthy for our development. To reach our highest potential, we must reconnect to our starting and ending place, attach once again to the Source of Truth that frees us from shame and injustice, where our soul—body, mind, and spirit—can be lifted and nourished with essential love that heals wounds, validates, and satisfies our deepest longings. And that process begins with *willingness* to move beyond the ego in an honest assessment of who we, and others, really are—naked and without masks or secrets—before our God and fellow human beings.

It takes an attitude of openness, a conscious shift

toward love in all our affairs. And it starts with the desire to surrender, to detach from what has been critical and self-depreciating—though familiar—and reattach to what is good and *true*. A spiritual awakening allows us to see beyond blind spots and character defects. It illuminates troublesome relationship patterns and survival skills—drives and delusions and addictions—that have been our unique attempts at being good enough and lovable at the core.

Truth with a capital T is disclosed by a Higher Power, the Source of love and forgiveness that transcends egos and limited human perspectives. The secure attachment we long to have with another human being—the model of grace and acceptance—can be found in our connection with the compassionate God of our understanding, the bond designed to reveal our soul's essential nature and lovability and ultimately empower us to live our fullest, least deluded, and most contented life.

6.4 | CARING

Without a sense of caring,
there can be no sense of community.
—ANTHONY J. D'ANGELO

Our souls are not satisfied by stuff, though our egos strive to acquire assets and look good in a world of trinkets, hierarchies, and winners. But what we really long for—what deeply gratifies us—is to be in relationships in which we are seen, understood, and cared about. And though we are social beings needing connection, we can be derailed by fear and pride, driven by our egos to become *superior* to others—to come out on top, amass prizes, fortunes, and victories—to prove our worth and *hide our insecurities.* Caring is a spiritual act that opens us, makes us emotionally vulnerable, and connects us with our true natures—our soul essence—and what matters most.

While the ego seeks to protect and elevate only *me,* an individual, the spirit provides what is best for *all of us* to thrive and coexist and guides us to a perception of reality based on love. In its self-centered drive, the *ego* will <u>e</u>dge <u>G</u>od <u>o</u>ut, in an effort to mask feelings of inadequacy and shame—pushing spirit away—and will strive instead to gain possessions or an image of success to fill the void. To invite God back into our lives creates a spiritual awakening that values intrinsic gifts—love, joy, peace, kindness, goodness, faithfulness—that fill and nourish us from a source beyond what narcissism, power, and money can buy.

When we feel connected and cared about, when we trust the universe to support us and our place in it, we feel neither *inferior* nor *superior* but precious and equal with other human beings—not better than or less than, but irreplaceable, with a matchless destiny to fulfill. Feelings of worth come from an enlightened spirit and a balanced ego that overcome an innate inferiority complex, assuring us that we are good enough—valuable *just as we are*. With faith in a Power greater than ourselves, we return to love at the core of our being, growing in compassion for our own astonishing design, as well as that of our fellow human beings and all of creation. A spiritual perspective soothes egos and doubts, allowing us to be more caring and humble individuals, admittedly less-than-perfect people who need neither to impress nor to surpass but fully appreciate ourselves and others for who we are, where we've traveled, and the lessons we've learned.

To connect openly and honestly in our relationships with God and others—to feel seen and understood—requires vulnerability and courage. Brené Brown, author of *The Gifts of Imperfection*, says, "Comparison is the thief of happiness." Sure to steal our joy, comparing is an attempt to measure up and feel good about ourselves. But in the process of evaluating our status, we are likely to stimulate shame and critical assessments, often focusing on flaws and appearances, as we attempt to convince ourselves that in order to be good enough, we need to be *perfect*, or at least *better than someone else*.

But true connection is not about winning approval or being admired; it is about coming out of hiding and *being known*, defects and all. It rids itself of comparisons that produce feelings of pride or inferiority, and equates success with growing, learning from our mistakes, and developing spiritual gifts that bring more genuine care into our lives and into the lives of others. It recognizes that we are each a blemished individual, divinely constructed, with a unique temperament, personality, and experiences that can be known and felt only through the filters of our own pores and senses, in personal ways that are difficult to communicate.

A spiritual awakening changes us into human beings who feel guided and encouraged to move toward wholeness, to give and receive love more freely—and generously. We recognize that we are all alike and yet so different, designed to perceive through our set of eyes. We accept the fact that we can never fully know another, nor grasp the full impact of living apart from our own bones and biases, yet we need not be stifled by the dread of loneliness or the threat of being misunderstood. Authenticity—the truth of who we are—comes with a spiritual awakening that frees us to be *real* and shapes our relationships with greater transparency, honest sharing, and gratitude for the beauty of individuality and our unique contributions.

As our perceptions begin to shift, we experience more serenity and a healthier self-concept. We stop isolating and defending our exclusive view as the *only* way and realize that although we will never actually share a common skin with anyone, we each have a significant slant—breadth and depth—that can enhance one another's life and brilliance. Reality is multifaceted, balanced and increased in clarity by bits of wisdom that come from sources and experiences beyond our own. We all have egos to tame and a bigger truth awaiting us if we are willing to expand our consciousness with courage, compassion, and *connection*.

With appreciation and care for one another, and a Power beyond us, our minds and hearts are renewed as we begin to see with more acuity. And like the lion and the mouse in Aesop's fable, we gain a perspective beyond that of our limited field of vision and solitary spark when we implement the adage that, despite the odds, "no act of kindness, no matter how small, is ever wasted." A spiritual process enlightens us with a broader, brighter flame of understanding and compassion that absolves us of shame and bitterness, opens our eyes to the healing power of forgiveness, and illuminates the soulful path to freedom and spiritual gifts that matter most.

6.5 | RITA'S STORY

We are afraid to care too much, for fear that the other
person does not care at all.
—ELEANOR ROOSEVELT

Rita arrives hopeless, with the kind of discouragement that
affects sleep and appetite, creates depression, and convinces us
that we will never be okay ever again. Though she is under the
care of a doctor and is taking prescribed medication, she is
continuing to lose weight, is sleep deprived, and is filled with so
much anxiety that she feels physically ill. She can't remember
the last time she felt joy or cared about much of anything.

"The problem began two years ago and is just getting
worse," Rita tells me, "and there's really nothing anyone can do
about it."

She doesn't cry or show much emotion as she talks about the
presenting problems that began after her son and his wife
abruptly banned her from seeing her grandchildren.

"They tore out my heart, and I don't even know why. My
whole life revolved around my two grandsons until my
daughter-in-law decided I couldn't see them anymore. And I
haven't even met my new granddaughter."

Rita is suffering terribly, feeling punished and rejected, and
has considered legal action . . . or maybe just moving on and
caring less. But I know that cutoffs and hardening our hearts to
those we love doesn't bring the kind of healing we long for. And
the power and anger we use to win legal battles in our rela-

tionships often backfire, leaving us feeling even more bruised. There's a deep, painful story here, a gaping wound that ultimately needs to be sutured by hope and compassion. But, as always, to really understand the story—and the ache—we start at the beginning.

As a child, Rita spent a lot of time with her younger brother, or alone in her bedroom, rocking and singing. Often, there would be a fight going on downstairs as her dad drank one beer after another and got more belligerent as the night wore on. So Rita found creative ways to distract herself from the bickering and neglect by writing stories, making up songs, or visiting a neighbor with a piano that she learned to play, and love.

Like all little girls, she wanted her daddy's affection but couldn't seem to get a second glance. Sometimes she would dance, sing, or read him stories she had written, hoping to gain admiration for her accomplishments, but he'd usually just laugh hysterically (though her performances were never meant to be funny) or dismiss her and go back to watching television before she reached the all-important finale. Once, in a bold move, she asked him if he thought she was pretty, to which he replied, "You might be someday. After you grow up."

It didn't help that her mom was busy trying to make ends meet and had an active social life that kept her out of the house much of the time. Rita remembers wearing the same dirty clothes to school over and over, trying her best to rotate the few things she owned. Once, thinking that she was being clever, she wore a pajama top for a blouse, but her classmates noticed and made nasty remarks. Even her teacher laughed, leaving her to feel ashamed, misunderstood, and all alone.

Maybe that's why Rita was so attracted to Jim—he paid attention and told her she was pretty, and he was so much like Dad: older, but with money that bought her jewelry, pretty clothes, and even a piano. They married as soon as she turned eighteen, then moved out of state to be close to his family, and it wasn't long until Rita was pregnant. Jim would leave in the morning to tend to business and go out drinking with his buddies at night. And when he did come home, he was usually drunk and belligerent . . . and Rita was lonely, turning to her piano, singing, and writing for solace. Déjà vu.

When Jimmy was born, he was the love of Rita's life, but she was still a teenager who needed support and attention. Jim's mother helped once in a while, and when Jimmy was only six months old, Rita's mother was diagnosed with terminal cancer and her dad began showing signs of dementia. So she packed up herself and Jimmy and moved back to her childhood home to help her parents, with the idea that Jim would join them on the weekends—but he never did.

Within weeks, her mother died, Dad began soiling the bed and running away, and Rita was diagnosed with mononucleosis. In tears, she recalls having felt alone and exhausted. Her brother had his own alcohol problems by then, and she describes what happened next as "the biggest mistake of my life." Not knowing what else to do, she called Jim to come get Jimmy, placed Dad in a nursing home, and checked herself into a hospital.

"I had a nervous breakdown or something. I was so sick. Didn't get out of the hospital for weeks. And what I didn't know is that while I was attempting to get well, Jim and his family hired a lawyer. Jim wanted a divorce—already had a girlfriend —and they all wanted to keep Jimmy . . . and get rid of me."

While Jim's family had plenty of money for attorneys, Rita couldn't find a lawyer, or even a friend, to fight on her behalf. Still exhausted, with no resources and medical bills she couldn't pay, she agreed to have scheduled visits with Jimmy in exchange for living expenses that would allow her to get an apartment and move on with her life. And move on she did, right to New York City, where she got a job as a waitress and took classes in music and dance—and excelled.

For the first time ever, Rita was noticed for her talents, for her dancer's body and her beauty. She not only earned a master's degree but even landed a few parts in musicals and had no shortage of men giving her time and attention. She accepted a teaching job at the college, felt in charge, and depended on no one but herself for her livelihood and success. And when Jimmy came to spend the summer or holidays with her, they'd have a great time exploring New York City and making memories.

But something happened when Jimmy hit his teens, when he decided that he had been abandoned by a mother who cared more about being a star than she did for him. "He resented that I 'ran off to New York' and had other men in my life. His stepmother probably filled his head with nonsense. I'm not sure what changed, exactly, but we reconnected after I got married, moved to Holly-wood, and Jimmy got to know Leo. He liked him."

Jimmy eventually married, too, and had children of his own. By then he wanted his mother to be a part of his family and generously bought her a condo nearby (with a piano) to use whenever she and Leo came to visit. Jimmy ran the family's lucrative business and had a lakefront home, a well-kept wife, and everything else that money could buy.

"It was the best time of my whole life. We had so much fun together, and I was finally part of a family again; the grandkids would come over, and we would sing and make up stories and dance. We were so connected. They were naturally musical, and I adored them. And they loved me, too."

Rita claims to be clueless about what happened that changed it all, though she admits that, from the start, there was tension between her and her daughter-in-law. She couldn't recall a specific incident, but what she remembers most is that horrible day, "out of the blue," when her son announced that the condo was being sold and that she needed to pack up her things and wasn't even allowed to say good-bye to her grandchildren.

"I know my daughter-in-law, Erin, was behind it all. I really think she's a mental case. She always acted uppity and rarely talked around me. The latest thing I heard is that I ruined their wedding somehow, too. My son told me they are going to therapy now and he refuses to be in the middle. And he suggested that I write her an apology. Can you believe it? Like it's my fault! His wife always seemed intimidated by me. Didn't like the fact that the kids wanted to be with me. Erin has no musical ability. I never could see what he saw in her; she's not even pretty."

I hear the disdain, the ache and rejection, and I want Rita to feel supported and understood. As a therapist, I join with her by acknowledging her pain, agree that her daughter-in-law is being vindictive—possibly sick—and am appalled at how badly she is being treated. I empathize, with the wounded heart of a grandmother, aghast at the cruelty that is keeping Rita from a relationship with her grandchildren. And from my experience as a grandchild who adored my grandmothers, I voice my sympathy for the grandchildren who have been deprived of the generous gifts and love that only Rita can add to their young lives.

I know that the first order of business is for Rita to feel heard, to have a safe place to deposit years of sadness. And while good therapy ultimately results in our taking responsibility for our reactions and behavior—not focusing on what was done to us or staying stuck in the unfairness of it all—becoming our best self is always the ultimate goal. But without a spiritual *awakening that restores hope to the hopeless, our fears, discouragement, and regrets can easily convince us—like Rita—that life is cruel, that maybe we are being punished or are unlovable, or are destined to be unhappy and get less than we deserve.*

6.6 | RECOVERY

There is a soul force in the universe, which, if we permit it, will flow through us and produce miraculous results.
—MAHATMA GANDHI

Hope springs from a belief that *good* things are possible, even when life looks precarious or confusing, and that there is a soul force in the universe—a Power beyond us—that is somehow at work *on our behalf*. And this conviction, more than any other, affects our serenity and ability to trust, soothing despair and lifting anxiety as it shapes the way we approach life in general, offering peace in the face of difficulties that are out of our control.

According to Albert Einstein, the first and most basic question *all* people must answer for themselves—"the most important question facing humanity"—is this: "Is the universe a friendly place?" And from our response to this simple question, we uncover private logic that is radically impacting our reality—the answer determining not only how we think about life but also how we live and ultimately *feel*, and whether or not we will face our days with hope.

Hopefulness flourishes with a notion that we are not alone in a cosmos that is *friendly*, with a benevolent force in control and capable of flowing in and through us—and that *good* is probable and we are deserving recipients of the abundance this universal Power has to offer. But too often, like Rita, children raised in homes with addiction or neglect or abuse spent years holding it together when there was no one else there to help—or care—and grew up feeling abandoned, alone in a universe that was *not* friendly, wondering if they were, somehow, unlovable or undeserving of those *good* things.

Having spent years relying on herself, Rita felt no support, no net, and had a sense that if she fell, it would be the end of her. Independent and extremely competent, she built a successful life and made a name for herself, until, as she says, "it all came crashing down." And, now, feeling totally alone and hopeless, she doubts herself and her lovability, wonders about the point of it all, and is gravely in need of a good night's sleep and a faith journey to examine, and perhaps reconsider, how she wants to answer that all-important question about the universe and her purpose in it.

When, as adults, we feel disappointed and have little hope, we continue operating in the same self-protective ways that seek to *prove* we are desirable and deserving, while distorted logic from childhood continues to suggest that we are not. But hope isn't simply about adopting a positive attitude or becoming an optimist. Hope comes from a *decision* to believe in something beyond us—a soul force capable of flowing through us, enlightening and bettering our lives. "Within each of us is a spark," says Bernie Siegel, the holistic medical doctor and author of more than ten transformational books about healing. "Call it a divine spark, if you will, but it is there and can light the way to health."

A glimmer of hope can open the door to a perspective and spiritual awakening that redefines what is possible and what we can and cannot control. We consider trusting that somehow, beyond our limited thinking, our challenges can work out in the long run, that blessings can come from situations that look bleak, or even from the bad things that happen to good people and innocent children. And with a leap of faith that unwraps denial and dysfunctional patterns, we begin to notice that love can triumph, move us toward serenity, and flow through us in ways that heal us and resonate with that inner spark of knowing.

But until we transcend our egocentric natures by turning our lives and wills over to the God of our understanding, we are not plugged in to the energy Source from which love, respect, and goodness flow. An essential part of recovery is to seek and connect with that divine spark and humbly surrender egoistic control. Then, with greater insight, we are able to recognize our self-defeating patterns and shortcomings, let go of self-protective behaviors, and reclaim our most healthy selves—spiritually, emotionally, and physically.

Recovery, like all change, happens little by little. It starts with hope's promise that good is being worked out within us, with a willingness to "let go and let God," as they say in twelve-step meetings. "There is no life without a spiritual life," says Oprah Winfrey, "and spirituality is like a muscle. It must be fueled." With faith, there comes a shift as our capacity to trust steadily grows and our ability to love and receive love gradually increases. And like any real change, the process of recovery—healing and renewing— requires us to be patient and persevere through our growing pains; it takes time and the courageous discipline of vulnerability to allow others into our lives to encourage and hold us accountable as we mend.

With a connection to the Source of love and goodness, our ego and own lovability issues begin to diminish. With new vision, we are able to acknowledge the error in our own thinking, recognizing that the sins of those who missed the mark in our young lives were not personal affronts—not facts about our worth—but were *their* human failings. And we begin a spiritual process of reparenting the child who felt lost and abandoned. With greater self-love and new appreciation for our strengths and weaknesses, we humbly embrace our talents, mannerisms, and story as part of a beloved, miraculous design beyond that of our human psyche or personal drives.

As we develop greater understanding and compassion for ourselves—accepting limitations and imperfections—we have less trouble being fully honest. Our ego is less threatened, less apt to elevate or hide regrets and insecurities under a blanket of false pride that arises from inferiority. Without the narcissism that focuses on comparisons and pushes us from an intrinsic *inferiority complex* to a more comfortable position of *superiority*, we can open ourself to being more fully known—and truly loved—by others.

But it takes courage and humility to move beyond the influence of a shame-based egocentric system, with a spiritual connection that helps us experience love and recognize that in*fear*iority is an essential part of our *human* nature and drive to survive, and that instead of marching through life, elevating and overcompensating whenever we feel a deep-seated uncertainty about our worth or safety, we can plug into our *spiritual* nature, balancing the ego's tendency to push us to compare, to measure up and become superior, in a misguided effort to win the affection and esteem we crave.

Whenever there is an excess of arrogance, perfectionism, or an obsessive drive to dominate and excel, it is likely that an overactive ego is covering up a deeply hidden burden of self-doubt that is pushing to find a way *to be better than*—and worthy. Without a spirit of humility, we are blind to our own self-protective devises. According to *A Course in Miracles*, a change in perspective is nothing short of a miracle. And in order for true and lasting change to occur, we must be *willing* to discover the error of our ways and then *ask God* to remove those dysfunctional patterns—the beliefs, defenses, and behaviors that at one time may have contributed to our survival but are now causing us and others pain.

And Rita was willing to do just that. She took a personal inventory and went on a faith journey, exploring various religions, attending a few different churches and temples. She read, attended Al-Anon, and began working through the twelve steps with a sponsor. She went on a spiritual retreat, regularly meditated and took walks at the beach, and journaled daily about what was stirring in her soul. And within about a year, Rita surrendered in faith to a Higher Power, asking the God of her understanding for greater peace, better sleep, and a change in perspective.

THE TWELVE STEPS OF ALCOHOLICS ANONYMOUS

(which are adapted and used in Al-Anon,
Adult Children of Alcoholics, Overeaters Anonymous,
Narcotics Anonymous, Codependents Anonymous,
Sex and Love Addicts Anonymous, etc.)

1. We admitted we were powerless over alcohol [or any substance or behavior spinning out of control] —that our lives had become unmanageable.

2. Came to believe that a Power greater than ourselves could restore us to sanity.

3. Made a decision to turn our will and our lives over to the care of God *as we understood Him.*

4. Made a searching and fearless moral inventory of ourselves.

5. Admitted to God, to ourselves and to another human being the exact nature of our wrongs.

6. Were entirely ready to have God remove all these defects of character.

7. Humbly asked Him to remove our shortcomings.

8. Made a list of all persons we had harmed and became willing to make amends to them all.

9. Made direct amends to such people wherever possible, except when to do so would injure them or others.

10. Continued to take personal inventory and when we were wrong promptly admitted it.

11. Sought through prayer and meditation to improve our conscious contact with God, *as we understood Him*, praying only for knowledge of His will for us and the power to carry that out.

12. Having had a spiritual awakening as the result of these steps, we tried to carry this message to others, and to practice these principles in all our affairs.

With a hopeful shift in energy, Rita trusted *good* to balance her heartbreak; she began playing and composing music again and started a blog to share with and encourage others estranged from their children and grandchildren. She published two children's books dedicated to her grandchildren and was willing to examine whether there were any offensive ways in *her*—focusing on herself and cleaning up her side of the street.

And she courageously pushed past her ego to look for traces of *superiority*—ways in which she may have presented herself that could have seemed adversarial or intimidating to the "competition"; after all, Rita and Erin were vying for the affection of the same man and children. Willing to step into her daughter-in-law's shoes, Rita saw herself from a different vantage—as an accomplished woman with advanced degrees, experiences, and skills that Erin *didn't* have.

She delved into how she might have elevated herself when feelings of inferiority pricked at her lovability and worth, asking herself, for example, if she tried to appear *more* intelligent, beautiful, competent, artistic, extroverted, or witty, or even more pious and self-effacing. Because whatever form our attempts at superiority take when we *doubt ourselves*, rather than making us *more* lovable—more talented, perfect, or right—they unwittingly create the opposite effect; instead of feeling connected and loved, we set ourselves apart and feel less accepted for being the insecure, fallible person we *really* are.

Slowly, as more was revealed, Rita gained wisdom, began sleeping better, and, amazingly, in place of feeding her anger and retaliating, sought ways to extend loving kindness. She lit candles and prayed for herself and her family, *including her daughter-in-law*, steadily replacing feelings of hatred, fear, and rejection with compassion. With greater clarity, faith, and hope for reconciliation, she was able to reach out to Erin and her son, humbly apologizing and expressing a desire to be a part of their lives again, to which she got no response—dead silence—for a long and painful six months. But we can be responsible only for ourselves—becoming honest through a searching inventory that uncovers our hurtful behaviors—when asking for forgiveness and attending to *our* amends.

Whenever we operate from defenses and an elevated place of superiority manufactured by our self-protective ego, we will only activate the ego in others. Likewise, when we surrender in faith, operating from the spirit within us, we will call up the spirit in others. "Switching from fear to *love*," as Rita was able to do, not only is contrary to our human nature but also, according to *A Course in Miracles*, is the kind of "change in perspective" that invites healing, forgiveness, and reconciliation that is truly "a miracle."

6.7 | FORGIVENESS

To err is human; to forgive, divine.
—ALEXANDER POPE

Every one of us has been offended and likely deserves an apology that we will never get (and probably owes one that we will never give). In the world of ego, criticism and negative voices cause injury, casting doubt about our worth and, unfortunately, playing most loudly in our heads. And in this egocentric domain, it is only natural that we take things personally, feeling wrongly accused and misunderstood on a regular basis, though other people's hurtful behavior is usually less about *us* and all about *them*; hurt people hurt people. But it's hard to fathom, and without the help of spirit, it is nearly impossible to discern this truth or have the capacity to let go of the pain people have caused us—by offering forgiveness.

But a life of love and serenity requires that we forgive, not just for the offender, but for *us*—the offended—so we can evolve. We need to forgive them, whether or not they deserve it. Many don't. Some of them consciously abused, neglected, or used us. Many repeated what was done to them. Some didn't know any other way. Others did but chose to be selfish or cruel, or numbed themselves with substances that impaired their judgment and behavior. Though we have been injured and suffered, still, a life of peace requires that amends be exchanged and accounts settled.

Though it is not easy to forgive another person or to admit to our own transgressions, it is our responsibility to right our story—to concentrate on the "log" in our eye, rather than the "speck" in theirs. We are each responsible for writing chapters that address healing and freedom. And *forgiveness sets us free.* We all have the task of liberating ourselves from entanglements that choke us and make us soul-sick with infections that stunt the growth of *our* bodies, minds, and spirits. Some of us choose to cut ourselves off from our offenders as a simple solution, but that alone will not necessarily free us. Unless the anger and bitterness of an offense is released, it continues, like a noxious poison, to sicken the life of the person who carries it.

As for perpetrators, it is rare that they seek our forgiveness, and even when they do, it is one of life's most difficult tasks to actually extend the hand of reconciliation. Whether a reformed, sorrowful human being asks us for atonement, or whether we must contend with someone who defensively denies or minimizes the hurt they have caused, we must still find a way to forgive *for our own well-being.* Holding on to the injury, carrying resentments, or plotting to get even only diminishes *our* health, *our* peace, even our beauty. The painful burden we carry eventually finds its way to turn down the corners of our mouth, furrow our brow, and raise our blood pressure.

Wanting to punish someone who has hurt us is natural, a common response to having been victimized. And, while "an eye for an eye" seems like the fairest way to settle the score, payback misses the mark. Even after revenge, the wrongdoer is not erased from our memory and the wrongdoing is not forgotten. Without a serious brain disorder, people simply cannot "forgive and forget." It is rare to forget what has been done to us, or the people who have done it. But we do not have to try to wash anything away from our memory; forgiveness is not about forgetting.

By definition, forgiveness is an act of contrition sought by a penitent offender and granted by the offended party. But what happens in cases where there is denial of guilt or lack of remorse on the part of the perpetrator; why should we forgive someone who doesn't ask or even seem to care? In order to be set free from the sorrow that breeds resentment, we must pardon even those who do not ask for our forgiveness, so that we can cut them loose and let go of the emotional pain that festers into dis-ease and the corrosive malice that eats away at *our* body, mind, and spirit.

We release the condemned from our hearts by giving up our need to personally sentence them for the crimes they have committed. We do not pardon to absolve them of guilt or injustice; we pardon in order to turn a case over to the God of the universe and set ourselves free from the responsibility of judgment. When we grant a pardon, we are released from the powerful hold of enmity. We willingly relinquish our personal connection and potential resentments by removing the case from our hands and sending it on to another department.

In some situations, it may actually be a case for the courtroom, and in others, for the loftier courts of heaven. Either way, the sentencing of our offenders rests with a higher authority. Our job is to *let it go* and trust that ultimate justice lies beyond our scope and jurisdiction. And, when we release our wrongdoers, we allow them freedom to spend their lives in whatever way they will. Unless it is an actual legal matter or presents a danger to victims who need to be warned or protected, their fate and life choices will no longer be our concern. We cannot mitigate the past or control how they choose to behave, but we can liberate our spirit by allowing ourselves to give it up.

If we want to experience serenity and know joy, we must till the soil of our own garden. We tend to our brambles and hurts: forgiving those we need to forgive, expecting less of those who seem incapable of loving well, and pardoning those who refuse to acknowledge their transgressions. And as we weed umbrage and bitter roots from our lives, we *set ourselves free* to grace the earth with compassion. We open spaces for seeds of mercy to bloom, reseed, and grow the kind of merciful understanding that promotes peace and blesses generations to come.

But forgiveness is not a onetime event. It is a process that involves working through our repressed feelings and anger. It takes time for our shock, outrage, and broken places to heal. And while forgiveness can't be rushed or offered lightly before the inner work is done, our job, first and foremost, is to be *willing* to forgive. And by opening ourselves to the possibility, we allow the spirit of love to guide us through our pain—the anger and tears—to soothe and transform us, until, in due time, we arrive at a super-natural place of acceptance where we quit trying to fix, undo, or repair.

We stop blaming them or shaming ourself, and we become aware that a burden has been lifted and something inside has mended. Forgiveness is not about forgetting; it's about *loving*. Whenever we forgive, we are conduits to the divine love that frees us from the slavery of antipathy and releases us from bondage. And with curative power that transcends our ego and injuries, we are infused with greater attention and gratitude for what is good *today*. Rather than ruminations that waste our time punishing perpetrators or wallowing in the pain of their transgressions, our energies and desires are redirected toward a life of passion and beauty.

Living well truly is the best revenge, certainly the only one that does not sacrifice our time, contentment, or anyone else. Forgiveness proves that love can overcome iniquity with an amazing grace that nourishes and alters us and is sown lavishly into every pardon and amend. By overlooking imperfections, forgiving offenses, and focusing on moving forward, we give ourselves the gift of a liberated spirit that lightens our days and encounters and cultivates a legacy of love.

6.8 | A STRANGER'S STORY

Life is an adventure in forgiveness.
—NORMAN COUSINS

Walking into the small café, I notice her right away. What a striking woman, *I think, as I make my way to an open table and take a seat near the window. Something about her captivates me. Tall and willowy, especially for a woman who appears to be in her seventies, she is a tasteful blend of maturity and sophistication, adorned with strands of sterling and Indian turquoise, classic black, and high-heeled, tall leather boots.*

Her hair is completely white, yet unusual for a woman of her decade. It is neither fried by a tightly curled perm nor chopped off at the nape of the neck, as many women decide to do when they've decided that hair is nothing more than a nuisance. Hers is full of life, styled into a silky wedge that frames her delicate face and moves as gracefully as she does.

Settling into my chair, I can sense something happening in her direction. I have no intention of participating in this stranger's world on the other side of the room but can't help myself from noticing what is directly in my view. The therapist in me has a way of tuning in to other people and dialogues, pulling them into the portable office inside my head, even when I don't want to, even when it is none of my business. So here I am, hoping to enjoy lunch with a most special guest, my grandson, but instead I am using precious moments, and the corners of my eyes, to discreetly study someone I will likely never meet.

I simply cannot avoid detecting the shift in energy and emotions building on this woman's face as her snow-white skin turns fiery red and, in a flash, she explodes with a burst of fury. Her mouth contorts as her body pitches forward over the table she shares with someone I can't see. Bewildered, I watch clandestinely as she wags her finger in ferocious outrage at the person on the other side of the booth. Scolding and flinging her head in dramatic gestures that send every strand of that pristine hair flying about like feathers in a storm, she is full of anger, clearly upset about something.

The recipient of this pent-up aggravation must be her husband. What a creep, *I decide.* He probably is a difficult man who is getting the earful he deserves. *Maybe he discounted her for decades and, after years of cruelty, she is giving him an overdue ultimatum. Maybe, in the confines of this restaurant, he has disclosed what she has been dreading to hear: He is leaving for a younger lover. Or, could it be that she has been the demanding one? Maybe she is an ungrateful, pampered beauty, a prima donna who has always been impossible to please. Or perhaps she is the disgruntled, aging mistress.*

For a moment, she stops her tirade as the mystery person on the other side of the booth leans forward to take a sip of soup. What I see shocks me; from the shadows emerges a quivering spoon connected to a small, wrinkled hand, as a shriveled old woman, likely in her nineties, gradually appears into the spotlight and my field of vision. Not much taller than the table, she is frail, and moving ever so slowly, as she attempts to control the annoying tremor that would make it nearly impossible to get the soup from the bowl to her lips.

Here, face-to-face, sits a mother and daughter with a personal history and a universal story. With this restaurant as our backdrop, a scene is unfolding from a most common human drama. Staged before me is the dilemma we confront as a parent or grown-up child. It is the performance each of us will give in a different setting and another time.

I marvel as I quietly take in what is happening before me. In this moment, a daughter is livid about who knows what. Years have been invested in this anguish that is playing out across the room. Perhaps it has something to do with the details of a will, or maybe it hinges on that one certain comment her mother always makes in that predictably irritating tone.

Maybe it is related to dementia, or to a forbidden family secret that has finally been revealed after a lifetime of dishonesty and shameful abuse. But whatever the case—whatever was said, or done, or avoided—the daughter is enraged and relentless in her vicious attack. And the mother, costumed in elderly innocence, takes it all without a single word in her defense. In that booth where mother and daughter share more than a bite to eat, there is silence—dead, cold silence.

Oh, there is talk after that, as the daughter turns her attention to the waitress and even to the young couple at the next table. She smiles pleasantly and engages in conversation as she turns her body out to the center of the restaurant, leaving her mother with an icy shoulder and a bowl of soup that grew cold long before it was ever touched by that shaky spoon. The two of them speak not a word but communicate plenty.

The daughter finishes her sandwich and rises with the beauty and ease of a dancer, while her mother, head down, digs carefully through the swollen white handbag on her lap. Reappearing with a walker that has been stored behind the hostess stand, the daughter arrives as her mother unearths a crumpled tissue and dabs at the corner of one eye. Without an utterance or a second glance, the daughter deposits the walker at the edge of the table, pays the check, chats with the cashier, then abruptly walks out the door.

With arms folded and a look of disgust, the stunning woman who had first captured my attention is now pacing just outside the window beside me. As if the curtain has opened to scene 2, the character who had once appeared so lovely is transforming; her beauty is fading away, dissipating, like that of a queen who has sipped a bitter potion. Given the disturbing scowl that distorts her face, her black garb and pointed boots, I almost expect a wart to suddenly grow from her nose as she peers angrily into the glass to watch what is happening from afar.

Inside, her mother uses the table for support as she laboriously moves one knuckled hand and then the other, pulling herself to the end of the bench, where the trusty walker is waiting. Reaching its handles, she cautiously raises herself bit by bit, until she can rely on its four strong metal legs to bolster her own. With great effort, she steadies her hunched and twisted shell, gathers her belongings, and sets off. Shuffling ever so slowly, with her pocketbook dangling from her spindly forearm, the old woman clings awkwardly to the walker as it carries her fragile frame to the door.

I guess I will never know who these women are or what caused such pain between them. Am I the daughter and this my mother? If so, this woman has misunderstood the longings of a daughter who tried to please her for a lifetime. Nothing was ever good enough, and after years of unrelenting criticism, a wounded child withdrew from the mother who never asked, never listened, never spoke an encouraging word. Or am I the mother who did the best she could but never got it right? She gave everything she could give, only to be told she never listened, never did enough. Even after years of devotion, she is abandoned, unknown, by the very daughter she loved for a lifetime.

Who knows how the story goes? Apparently, it is not for me ever to know, nor to judge. Family dynamics are intricate, to say the least. But as a witness there that day, I watched as resentments eroded all traces of peace and tenderness in a lovely lady. Bitterness devoured her empathy and soured her beauty. As in a fairy tale, a grievance of old entwined itself around her heart, until her blood turned cold and her face hard. And like the message of those tales from childhood, this enactment served as a glaring reminder that genuine, lasting beauty radiates from a warm and merciful spirit.

This scene of a mother and daughter is a story of the ages, a photo from every family album. It is the snapshot of our grown-up longings and unmet dreams and the imperfect parents we idolized, who never fully got to know us, or we them. It is a lesson about growing up as we grow old on love's journey through disappointments, forgiveness, and acceptance—to eventually arrive at a place where we can appreciate what we've learned, and have, *today.*

Our peace is inextricably linked to our most valuable relationships. In them, we invest our beings, and through them we reveal ourselves and gain a clearer image of our character. We all have work to do, hurts to mend, accounts to settle. Each of us has an ego to tame and loved ones who have let us down. Regardless of the score, we have all made mistakes that beg for accountability. The greatest wisdom we can gather comes from the connections that showcase our true natures and remove the facades that we erect for the rest of the world to see.

Then, there in the glass, I see my own reflection: another aging woman—a grandmother—with time slipping by. I think about the years that brought me to this place and the chair that I now occupy. Here, at the table, with my daughter's son, are two of us sharing a similar story. Ours is also a tale of a mother and daughter, of disappointments, tears, and letting go. And like all real stories of love, ours, too, has had its share of misunderstandings, conflicts, and wounds that needed apologies and the healing touch of time and grace.

I look at my grandson, wearing my daughter's eyes, and appreciate the gift of reconciliation extended through new chapters and next generations. With a smile, I acknowledge the sanctity of the moment, aware that all of our stories are penned from the words and pages of these everyday opportunities and simple conversations. "So, how's it going at school?" I ask with renewed interest. "Tell me about your day. . . ."

6.9 | LOVE

Love is a fruit in season at all times,
and within reach of every hand.
—MOTHER TERESA

Love is a gift, one we want and need more than any other—the soul food that nourishes our mind, body, and spirit. According to Dr. Brian Weiss, a prominent psychiatrist and best-selling author, "[l]ove is the most basic and pervasive energy that exists. It is the essence of our being and of our universe." It is at the core of our design, essential to our growth and well-being, and is always within our reach.

But love is a *spiritual* gift, connected to the universal power—the God of our understanding—that gives us life and breath. It is part of the unseen realm that collides with earthly hierarchies, suffering, and anger. Love is, however, always present, ours for the asking. And when we surrender to its source and powerful energy, even in the midst of pain or conflict, it can heal and alter us with a generous infusion of peace or forgiveness or joy that is difficult to explain or comprehend, and radically changes the way we perceive things.

My greatest heroes are regular people who have chosen love over fear, or hatred, or defeat. Though they faced their dark nights of the soul—their terrors, losses, and grueling challenges (and may have buried their head in the sand, had

panic attacks, or even curled up in bed, wanting to die)—
with prayer, they were able to muster up enough valor,
sometimes in one fell swoop, sometimes in itty-bitty
micro-movements, to move into unfamiliar territory and
replace their dread or hostility or cynicism with love.

It takes courage to love, particularly in situations and
relationships that activate our ego injuries and anxiety. But
we grow stronger as we allow faith to move us toward
mercy, one deep breath and daunting step at a time. It is
not always easy to say "I love you" through good times and
bad, or to extend grace in our everyday speech and behaviors. It takes stamina, and a spiritual connection, to
continue caring for others for the long haul. Love requires
us to let go of grudges, forgive regularly, and enter into the
world of others with compassion, even when they are
reluctant to enter into ours.

Love is less about being admired and validated and
more about focusing our attention on developing loving
feelings *within* us and *toward* others, and ridding ourselves
of toxic shame and condemnation. It is not about being a
doormat, nor is it about sacrificing ourselves to elevate
someone else; love persuades us to value our own precious
self, too, to pursue our destiny and develop our gifts, and
use them in actions that engender honesty, respect, and
intimacy in our everyday encounters and relationships.

But in some relationships, love gets confused with
romantic passion, though they are not the same. When love
moves from the realm of spirit to the domain of romance,
passion is easily mistaken for love as it courses through our
veins like adrenaline, jump-starting hormonal batteries and
setting us ablaze. A definite high, passion is the heartthrob
of a new romance and the stuff that sex addicts get hooked

on. It is the sexual tension that sleeps with a best friend's wife or propels balding men, cougars, and high school teachers to run off with neophytes half their age. And with its powerful, compulsive drive, amorous passion can convince us that a steamy affair or midnight Internet hookup is a rendezvous with an *authentic* soul mate.

Love, on the other hand, evolves over time in *actions* that sometimes require us to defer gratification or make sacrifices. As passion is lived in profound sensations and moments that are *experienced* and labeled as "love," true love is lived in daily behaviors that change diapers, take out the trash, or patiently work through painful misunderstandings. The emotional ecstasy of passion has no obligations, no burden of history, no resentments, because passion lives for today, in emotions ripe with the illusion and possibility of what we imagine unspoiled—unconditional—real love *should* be.

The feel-good hormones that keep passion alive fire up a euphoria similar to the kind that cocaine produces. PET scans indicate that the area of the brain stimulated by cocaine is actually the same brain region that lights up at the start of a new romance. Like a drug, hormonal chemicals contribute to creating a fabulous honeymoon every day, until their surge is over. And here lies a major problem: Passion generated by an invigorating, fresh connection has a shelf life of just a year, maybe two. Apparently, our amazing bodies have been biologically programmed for sexual attraction to entice a potential mate and partner.

While passion fuels relationships with excitement and vibrant sensuality, it loses potency and wanes, leaving many couples to question their original pronouncements of loyalty. Often, they come to believe that they have "fallen out of love," when it is not love that has "died" but is, more accurately, the original dose of passion's organic brain cocktail that has expired. Passion and love are meant to go together; while passion is the spice that can begin and infuse a relationship (and needs to be replenished), love is the meal that sustains it. Though they are intertwined, many relationships fail because they confuse the two.

Love is foundational—respectful, patient, and kind. Above all, it values the relationship more than money, power, or image. There is no refuge on earth like a dedicated love that does not abandon. It is the treasure we crave as grown adults and wounded children. We long to know that we are chosen and lovable. And studies suggest that, even with divorce at its all-time high, married—committed —couples live longer and are eventually happier than their uncommitted counterparts. Though we claim to want love more than commodities or anything else, we often accept substitutes because genuine love carries a hefty price tag.

There is no shortcut or discount; love requires a commitment in which one person gives wholeheartedly to another for the long haul. It demands our investment even when there are passionless days or arid seasons that yield few dividends. Unlike passion, love is unnatural, a *spiritual gift* that is nurtured by faith and devotion. And though it must be tended with care, love's fruit can grow from the seeds of passion, a dutiful heart, or even an arranged marriage to a stranger. But it is an endowment that many are just not willing to make.

Love is imperfect, like people—full of flaws and ambiguities. There is no such thing as unconditional love between imperfect human beings. But with empathy come awareness and a richer truth, as we curiously look through the eyes of another, seeing the world from a distinctly different perspective. With regular lessons in acceptance, compassion, and forgiveness, we quiet our selfish egos and open ourselves to the spirit of grace that keeps love from growing sour or running away. And if it does not give up, true love will never really fail us; the act of loving another —a partner, child, parent, sibling, or friend—while a difficult task, is our greatest teacher and ultimate reward.

We are children of God, and love is our birthright, ours for the asking. Through the lens of faith, the Source of compassion can be made known to us in a connection that rearranges our sensitivities and attitudes and moves us from a milieu of anxiety and despair to one of gratitude and love. But if our life circumstances or the conditions in which we were raised make it difficult even to imagine a *merciful* Higher Power, with willingness—prayer, meditation, and the boundless beauty of creation—we open ourselves to a love and energy that can heal and transform us.

And though it takes courage to love freely and nobly, without fear that we won't be loved in return or get our fair share, by plugging in to the Source, we gain spiritual insight with fresh vision and verve. Those daring enough to open their hearts to divine love, to let go of their fear of abandonment and its scorecard, to share themselves with others—to move beyond the ego, beyond fears and doubts and insecurities, to forgive regularly and *love anyway*—are our guides on a path that leads to fulfillment, joy, and freedom and are our least celebrated, grandest heroes.

* Becoming an adult requires that we stop punishing or blaming anyone else for what's happening today and take responsibility for our life: forgiveness or pardon, and making peace with our past, are prerequisites.

* Emotional maturity is a process of shedding faulty logic knitted together in our youth and implementing spiritual lessons that open us to greater compassion and acceptance.

* Authenticity—the truth of who we are—comes with a spiritual awakening that frees us to be real and shapes our relationships with greater transparency and appreciation for our individuality.

* The twelve steps are used to break dysfunctional patterns and recover the wisdom and serenity that come with a spiritual perspective.

* Holding on to emotional injuries affects our health; a life of peace requires that we make amends when possible, settle accounts, and let go.

* Love is at the core of our design, essential to our growth and well-being, and always available if we plug in to the Source.

6.10 | YOUR STORY

It's your turn to tell your story. Imagine you're the client.
Get comfortable. Breathe deeply. Use the following prompts to make
discoveries and gain clarity on your way to personal freedom.
Use a journal to capture any thoughts, feelings, or images that come
to mind or talk into a recorder. Welcome to your session ...

How would you describe your earliest bond?

How has that connection repeated itself in other relationships?

How have you been wounded, intentionally or not, by a parent or caretaker?

How have those injuries made it difficult for you to grow up?

Whom do you need to forgive/pardon so that you can move on?

What regrets, grudges, or blame are still getting in the way of your growth?

Have you connected with a Higher Power to gain a spiritual perspective?

Do you feel absolved of shame, blame, and resentments?

Is anyone currently treating you in a rejecting, hostile manner? Who? What can you do today to care for yourself?

What steps are you taking to have a voice and recover self-esteem?

How do you compensate for feelings of inferiority?

When you feel vulnerable, how might you take on an air of superiority?

Do you have a sense of hope—a belief that good can prevail?

Are you consciously switching fear-based beliefs to more loving thoughts?

How do you show/express your love to others? Yourself?

Who needs more of your compassionate understanding?

Do you have a spiritual practice/tools to connect with the Source of love?

What are you doing to develop greater serenity in your life?

What are you most grateful for today?

SEVEN

Taking Flight

7.1 | HEALING AND HAPPINESS

I believe that satisfaction, joy, and happiness are the
ultimate purpose of life. And the basic sources of happiness
are a good heart, compassion, and love.
—DALAI LAMA

For those who come to therapy looking for relief from debilitating symptoms and stating a desire "to be happy," love tells us that we have headed in the right direction. But without an infection to eradicate—a fever that breaks or a rash that disappears—how do we actually know when we are happy enough, or whether we have been cured of our dis-ease? Does mental health occur in ten sessions or in ten years? "To see takes time," says the artist Georgia O'Keeffe, and in order for psycho-clarity to bring us the insight and conditions that foster joy and satisfaction, we need determination, *time*, and a knowledge of what it is we are looking for so that we will know when we've found it.

Mental health and emotional maturity are demonstrated in our ability to handle situations—by reacting constructively to changes and difficulties that come our way, and by interacting with compassion in our relationships. Charles Menninger, MD, who cofounded the Menninger Clinic in 1919 with his two sons (all three psychiatrists), "had a vision of a better kind of medicine and a better kind of world." Today, the Menninger Clinic continues to be a leader in the field of behavioral health, providing patient services, a training school, a wellness center, and a nonprofit foundation at the forefront of psychological research, education, and social outreach. And from the famed Menninger Clinic comes a picture of well-being in the form of a checklist by William C. Menninger himself:

THE CRITERIA OF EMOTIONAL MATURITY

* The ability to deal constructively with reality
* The capacity to adapt to change
* A relative freedom from symptoms that are produced by tensions and anxieties
* The capacity to find more satisfaction in giving than receiving
* The capacity to relate to other people in a consistent manner with mutual satisfaction and helpfulness
* The capacity to sublimate, to direct one's energy into creative and constructive outlets
* The capacity to love

But how much growth can we expect? When, exactly, does therapy end, and how do we know whether or not it has been successful? Here—behind the door—we mark our progress by examining our goals and determining how far we've come in the therapeutic process and whether we've achieved the written, *personal* objectives that we formulated together. Frank, for example, had goals related to his safety and, early on, realized that effective treatment would require him to "see a doctor," "get a job," and "go to AA."

Within a year, Frank met all of his original goals and added new ones, like "exercise daily," "fix my teeth," and "find a Higher Power." In doing so, he moved beyond his addiction and suicidal depression to discover a life of purpose with his son and other men in recovery. Faye met goals to alleviate anxiety, as well as to "get conscious about my patterns with men" and "identify red flags in my dating choices," and with determination and insight was able to embrace the frightened young girl—and woman she had become—to "love myself more" and eventually find the kind of partner with whom she felt valued, safe, and understood.

Katie was able to "get help for my family," "do better in school," and "gain five pounds"; Linda stopped having panic attacks after she found her voice and was able to "express myself to my husband" and, in her resolve to "find something meaningful to do," found fulfillment volunteering in the neonatal unit of a local hospital. Greg purposed to overcome his fears, to "stay out of bed during the day," and stepped up to the plate, literally, by signing on as an assistant coach for his son's Little League team.

Dolores got up enough courage to "get out of the house by myself" and did something that she had always wanted to do—began singing in the church choir. Over time, Rita was able to "sleep through the night without nightmares" and, after "detaching with love," found greater creative energy and compassion to extend to others and to her music. Marie was able to "lose twenty pounds" after attending Weight Watchers and developed a latent gift after daring to "sign up for an art class" that filled her with excitement and joy. Maureen continued sharing in her women's group, fostering friendships, and noticed that, in time, she began to "dissociate less," connect with others, and "feel less lonely." And with tools and attention to somatic symptoms, she began having "less anxiety and more fun."

Like Hannah, Carlos began replacing grief and compulsive behaviors with compassionate understanding and loving affirmations, and his bald patches eventually filled in with hair. Donna was able to "stop obsessing about my mother and my ex" by revising internal messages that reframed what was true—and lovable—about her. And Winnie, by sharing a secret that had burdened her for years, was able to rid herself of the toxic shame that had eroded her joy, allowing her to finally "stop crying . . . and enjoy life again."

While, ultimately, health and emotional maturity come with insight that heals, alleviates symptoms, and betters our relationships, how does *happiness* actually develop? Or is happiness something that we are born with—a sense of wonder and delight that tarnishes from years of disappointment or erodes beneath the dirt of condemnation or self-protective secrets? Getting conscious of our thoughts and feelings, learning to express what it is that we feel, think, and believe, is how we rid ourselves of the emotional pain, guilt, and shame that contaminate us and rob us of valuable energy and contentment.

And as we unearth and let go of our afflictions, trusting that *good* can prevail beyond our limited understanding, we begin to sense a shift and experience life differently, seeing through soulful eyes of wisdom. Like the advice of Anne Frank, a child of the Holocaust who was wise beyond her years, we recognize that happiness is dependent on our attention, even in the midst of life's most tragic challenges. "Think of all the beauty that's still left in and around you, and be happy," Frank tells us. With greater love and less shame, we can value our essence and unique journey, cherish what is right and lovely in our lives, and realize that, in the process, we have cleared a fertile space for compassion and joy to bloom.

7.2 | FINDING JOY

It's never too late to have a happy childhood.
—CLAUDIA BLACK

Though everyone wants to be happy and says so, happiness typically peaks and wanes as a result of our circumstances—things outside us—that are often beyond our control. Joy, however, is the kind of happiness that develops *inside* us, a contentment that endures regardless of our situation, disappointments, or difficulties. And cultivating a joy-filled life, like love, requires a spiritual connection and awareness that grows stronger with time and practice.

But to right our story and experience a happy-childhood ending filled with the kind of restorative "happiness" and delight we long to feel—again or for the first time ever—we need to know joy. And, like love, it is a gift that flows in and through us, nourishing our body, mind, and spirit, *if* we are willing to create a space to get still, cultivate seeds of consciousness, and plug in to a Higher Power.

"The joy of Being is the joy of being conscious," states Eckhart Tolle in *A New Earth*. It requires that we awaken and pay attention with an intelligence *beyond* that of our ego, because if we look only to the ego-driven world to bring us happiness, we will be regularly frustrated and disappointed. Unhappiness is not just a feeling that happens because of situations and outcomes; unhappiness develops because of our focus and *what we tell ourselves* about what is happening to us. "Emotion in itself is not unhappiness," says Tolle. "Only emotion plus an unhappy story is unhappiness."

Happiness that supersedes our circumstances and story requires a spiritual awakening that moves us beyond our human drives and self-absorption—beyond an earthly realm that can be fickle, constantly dissatisfied, and inept at truly validating our worth. Joy arises with increased clarity that life is fundamentally a *good gift* from God. And by embracing joy and its source, we are lifted from the darkness of adversity with a radiant energy that can heal *our* depression and anxiety and enlighten the planet.

Joy is an aliveness that comes from letting go of outcomes, valuing who and where we are in this very moment; it comes from being fully present, awakened to a creative force flowing in and all around us in a state of consciousness that accepts wholeheartedly the beauty of the present moment.

And like the Hebraic gift of manna meant to be gathered and consumed *daily*, joy is a treasure that cannot be purchased or stockpiled; it lives in the *now*, meant to be received and relished in *this* instant.

Mindfulness practices, called GEMS, are powerful, simple treasures that we can apply in our daily lives to move toward a life rich in joy. With soulful awareness and inspiration, these personal habits direct us to the bedrock of contentment and infuse our lifestyle with authentic happiness.

GEMS

Gratitude . . . for all that is good in your life

Notice five specific items during the day for which you are thankful. List them each evening in a gratitude journal. Write a thank-you note. Express your appreciation. (When you can't find something to be grateful for, check your pulse.)

Expression . . . of what you are experiencing

Journal thoughts and feelings without judging or editing. Paint, dance, sing, write a poem, create freely. Share your thoughts and feelings with another person. (Years of impression, without expression, result in depression.)

Mindfulness & Mercy . . . that lead to peace

Take five minutes to be still. Pay attention to your breath and senses. Close your eyes. Breathe. Meditate. Consciously let go. Accept the gift of *now*. Extend compassion. Learn from past failures or regrets. Set yourself free by forgiving yourself and others. (Be better, not bitter.)

Steps . . . toward a life of balance and abundance

Take walks with breath and senses activated. Play often. Engage in actions that invite consciousness and inspiration. Take love in—with self-care, creative excursions, beauty, nature. . . . Let love out—with gifts of self, a random act of kindness, a smile . . . (Fill up/let love *in*; spill over/let love *out*. Refill regularly.)

An abundant life of joy lets go of fear and control and allows God to run the universe. Its trademark is *gratitude* that sees and appreciates what *is* in the present moment, awakening us to love, beauty, and our many blessings. "The man who forgets to be grateful has fallen asleep in life," said Robert Louis Stevenson, the inspired adventurer and novelist. Gratitude, more than anything else, is the key that unlocks joy, waking us up to what is right in front of us. It can instantly shift negative energy to positive energy, open our hearts, and change our perspective, making victors out of victims, a home out of a modest shelter, or a celebration out of just another day.

Joy *notices* and is grateful for all that we have, including our unique being, endowed with traits and talents in a combination unlike that of any other. And with *expression*, we share our thoughts, abilities, and feelings in personal ways: writing, painting, singing, acting, sewing, building, cooking, dancing, etc. As we connect with our imagination and ingenuity, we unite with our gifts, our Creator, and our very essence; we draw close, as cocreators, experiencing the originality and enthusiasm that comes from *being* wholly ourself. And with these discoveries and offerings, we clear shame with vulnerability that invites others to know and support us as we grow to realize our purpose and possibilities.

Mindfulness takes time out to pay attention, to reflect on what is right in front of and *within* us. We look, and with prayer and meditation, we speak and listen in stillness. Connected to the Source, we let go, releasing anxiety and upset and filling with breath and energy from a place beyond our finite power. And as we calm our frantic efforts to earn our worth or regulate what is not within our control and just *be*, we are awed by a sense of acceptance and *mercy* that flood us with greater peace and joy and prompt us to share compassion and hope with others.

Practicing a life of joy requires action *steps* to regularly replenish ourselves with light and everyday doses of inspiration. Without sustenance to support our whole being, we will wither away or end up gorging ourselves in bulimic agitation. Without joy from a source beyond our ego, we are destined to struggle, doomed to fill ourselves with stuff—the jewelry, the job, the affair, the candy, the looks, the titles, the awards—that never completely satisfies. A healthy diet provides nutrients to sustain our body and food to nourish our mind and soul as well.

We must value ourselves enough to make time for actions that refresh us and renew our energy—healthy pleasures and activities that balance our stressful responsibilities and routines. With mindfulness, we can take a simple walk, visit a museum, build a snowman, see a movie, plant a garden, swim, eat a meal, listen to music, offer a smile, or spend time in nature, *en*-joy-*ing* the beauty of the moment by immersing ourselves in delight and gratitude that can enrich our lives and hearten others'.

Yes, we need to attend to the essentials of a healthy life and make choices that contribute to living well. Simple as it may seem, we need to evaluate whether we hold limiting beliefs about *deserving* a healthy life by evaluating *how* we actually treat ourself on a regular basis: Do we drink plenty of water, get enough sleep, eat nutritiously, exercise in ways that feel good, and connect with the Source of energy that enlivens us? And if we don't, why not? By defining what a healthy lifestyle looks like, envisioning it for ourself, and deciding that we are actually worthy of living that way, we can start creating a life that reflects it.

With a spiritual connection, we find priceless treasures available all around us, delightful jewels that satiate our human hunger and generate abundance. Our physical, emotional, intellectual, and spiritual selves need goodness and love to thrive. And by concentrating on what is healthy for our body and mind and feasting on God's provisions—ingesting morsels of grace, beauty, and truth in our daily lives—we can be filled to overflowing. Then, with love and joy that spill into our relationships, families, and acts of service, we gain a heightened sense of fulfillment and freedom to be the person we were born to be.

7.3 | SETTING FREE

Then you will know the truth, and the truth will set you free.
—JESUS

Freedom comes from knowing the truth: What is *true* is ultimately liberating. When we experience the love and joy that lead us to a place of acceptance—for what is good today, what we've gleaned from yesterday, and what tomorrow will bring—we become unshackled by the awareness that life itself is precious and that *we* are valuable and beloved. We find ourselves released from shame and inadequacy as we accept this love, rewrite the internal messages that have diminished and confined us, and right our stories with truth that restores our confidence in positive outcomes and unforeseen possibilities.

With peace that comes from surrendering to a Power beyond ourself—letting go of ego-driven control and shame —we experience divine love that keeps our soul steady and rooted, even in the most challenging of circumstances and environments. And though nothing can grow in soil that has been parched and depleted from years of neglect and abuse, adverse conditions improve and become growth opportunities with the light of wisdom, faith, and the fresh air of a *true*, changed perspective.

Like the prayer that has helped millions find peace in twelve-step and other support groups, the words of empowerment and surrender of the Serenity Prayer (by Reinhold Niebuhr) conclude self-help meetings around the world and change millions of lives by subduing overbearing egos and creating an environment in which seeds of tranquility can bloom:

"God, grant me the serenity to accept the things I cannot change, the courage to change the things I can, and the wisdom to know the difference."

Without cultivating a connection to a deeper, more noble truth, we can be overwrought by a sense of our own inadequacy, tyrannized by an ego trying to prove our worth, or enmeshed in a thicket of cynicism growing from a bitter root that chokes our hope and happiness. To be set free from our distress, we must recognize how anxiety and shame distort the truth and delude us, and we must *accept life as it is*. We need to weed out unrealistic expectations and faulty notions about controlling things, people, or situations over which we are powerless and attend instead to the unhealthy knee-jerk reactions that we are capable of evaluating and changing.

Anxiety is set in motion when we try to manage outcomes or burdens, especially those beyond our scope and power. Often, the things that weigh us down are not within our control, but we worry about them anyway. While worrying spends time ruminating about things we *cannot* change, peace concentrates on the things that we *can*: our responses and attitudes. But worry and peace cannot coexist; where there is worry, there will be no peace. Like any repetitive behavior pattern, with mindfulness, the worry habit can be broken, replaced with serenity that comes from entrusting a Higher Power with the issues and fears that are beyond the reach of humankind.

The dis-ease of worry, discouragement, and suffering comes from *thinking* that somehow we can or *should* control other people and situations. But the truth is that life is an adventure over which we have limited control. And when we *choose* to be at ease with *what is*—concentrating less on what we can't control and more on what we *can*—we develop a more relaxed attitude that increases our well-being. So regardless of whether we win the lottery or the favor of another person, or whether life is going the way *we think* it should, we can experience greater peace by focusing on loving more, laughing more, and stressing less—intentionally letting go of anxiety and control—by allowing a Higher Power to run the universe.

And while the search for God is made beyond the door and scope of therapy, it is a lifestyle decision that enables us to discover more of the contentment and serenity that we come to therapy to find. If we choose to fill our hearts and minds with the things of God, we experience refreshment and healing energy flowing into us like water into thirsty ground. With regular feedings of gratitude, creativity, mindfulness and mercy, and with actions (GEMS) that fill us with a renewed sense of grace and fulfillment, what is planted inside us is nourished. Warmed by the Source, what lies dormant starts to germinate, as dreams and desires push through the darkness of our insecurities, grievances, and shame.

With affirmations of love and wisdom from the God of our understanding, we feel and see differently, accepting with greater conviction that "I am loved . . . free . . . gifted . . . pardoned . . . doing the best I can . . . a child of God . . . precious . . . creative . . . a masterpiece . . ." And as these truths resonate deep within us, they awaken hope and passion, ridding us of doubt and judgments that discourage, fester into loathing, and steal our joy. Beliefs that are *true* will set us free from fear, from animosity, and from the torturous thoughts and behaviors that confine us to an existence wrought with misery.

Peace is a by-product of love and forgiveness, and the result of right thinking. Until we free ourselves from toxic fallacies and fill our minds with what is *true*, peace, love, and healing will elude us. The National Alliance on Mental Illness (NAMI), a leader in education and advocacy for mental health, uses information from *Peace, Love and Healing* in its Family-to-Family program to describe tenets of well-being and inner peace. Written by Bernie Siegel, MD, a distinguished pioneer and author in the field of body-mind communication and a renowned practitioner of holistic medicine, the book outlines the following:

SYMPTOMS OF INNER PEACE

* Tendency to think and act spontaneously, rather than from fears based on experiences from the past
* The ability to enjoy each moment
* Loss of interest in judging self
* Loss of interest in judging other people
* Loss of interest in conflict
* Disinterest in interpreting actions of others
* Loss of ability to worry
* Frequent episodes of appreciation
* Contented feeling of connectedness with others and nature

* Frequent attacks of smiling through the eyes of the heart
* Increasing susceptibility to love extended by others, as well as the uncontrollable urge to extend it
* Increasing tendency to let things happen, rather than to make them happen

By trusting enough to let go, enjoying the moment, and connecting with love and appreciation, we offer ourself and others greater empathy to *be* and correct critical messages of condemnation and beliefs that focus on inadequacies, comparisons, and imperfections. We can look back and learn from the past, but we aren't trapped there. Righting our wrongs and seeing ourselves, and others, through eyes of compassion, we accept our human condition, discarding unnecessary baggage by receiving forgiveness for our own defects and offering grace and forgiveness to others for theirs.

Created for love, our individual journeys are the stories of our longings, our strivings, and our discoveries. Along the way, we attempt to *feel* worthy and satisfy an inner craving to find meaning and purpose. But when mistakes and self-doubt convince us that we have missed the mark and that we are *less* than lovable, we conceal our true nature in costumes to make us appear more desirable—more perfect, brilliant, powerful, talented, or prettier than our neighbor—or we immerse our feelings of unlovability in impressive accomplishments, glittery possessions, or harmful addictions to drown our qualms and disgrace. But until we accept love's tender mercies to satiate our innate insecurities and empower us with affection that emancipates us from our critical judgments and cover-ups, we will continue to thirst for authenticity that drives us to know the truth and its source.

The truth is that love heals. It is essential for human health and wholeness. It is at the core of our design and at the foundation of all good gifts and self-worth. We spend our days on earth trying, in our own way, to discover this truth. And as we pay attention, growing in psycho-clarity, we come to acknowledge that there is no truth more simple, or profound, or life altering; love is what we are looking for and need if we are to heal ourselves and our planet and experience our greatest sense of well-being and inner peace.

Freedom comes from connecting with love that casts out fear and knowing that regardless of our mistakes, our imperfections, or judgments—or those of someone else—we are valuable and cherished. By looking at life through eyes of wonder and appreciation, we experience the gift of divine love that ultimately heals, convinces us that we are beloved, and liberates us from the roles we play and the masks we wear to be *enough*. Our purpose and destiny is to accept this love, to experience the affection and mercy that change us on the inside and get channeled as compassion in our interactions, our relationships, our world.

As Dr. Bernie Siegel says, "We are here to contribute love to the planet—each of us in our own way." And with this insight and truth, we relinquish our burdens and self-doubt, accepting our purpose, our inner wisdom, and the skin we're in, to travel with greater curiosity and ease. Transformed by the renewing of our minds, the refreshing of our bodies, and the reawakening of our spirits, we become our most healthy, authentic, and compassionate selves.

7.4 | SAYING GOOD-BYE

*The embrace that sets us free
is the embrace of the divine in us.*
—MARIANNE WILLIAMSON

Freedom from distress—anxiety, depression, compulsions, addictions, fears, grief, obsessions, and self-doubt—is what brings us to therapy. And what we search for here, in this room behind the door, is a way to be released from our loss, from injustices, and from the confusion and shame that bind us. What we find, and what ultimately sets us free, comes from our willingness to be fully known in spite of our neediness and imperfection. What heals, through our vulnerability and courage, is the rediscovery of who we are and have always been on the *inside*, with a corroboration of the truth by a witness who sees a spark of the divine in us until we, too, recognize and embrace it.

We come in need of encouragement and validation, triggered by betrayal, abuse, and disgrace; we feel unappreciated, worn out, and despairing from tragedies that have wounded us, from reproach for hurts we've inflicted on ourself or others, or from regrets we have about choices we wish we'd never made. What we discover, after a soulful dig, is that beneath layers of contempt, upset, or human shortcomings lie forgiveness, vindication, and a perfectly lovable child within who still embodies hope, inspiration, and our long-forgotten dreams. And as we reawaken this essential part of ourself that time has preserved, we unearth wonder and enthusiasm and bring to life that which has been waiting to be valued and fulfilled.

What we have shared has pushed beyond inadequacies and pretense and into an intimate connection rich with sincerity and grit. Our time together has uncovered stifled emotions, deeply held secrets, mistaken notions, and whatever else was needed to meet your specific goals. As satisfying as it has been for me to watch you grow in inner wisdom and self-respect, ultimately, we will part ways. Closure is the last phase of therapy—the point at which you have implemented insights and tools and are ready to go off on your own. So we evaluate what you will take with you and determine whether you'll need additional resources or referrals before you go. We revisit what brought you here and the progress you've made and reminisce about our journey. Then, inevitably, we will say our good-byes and I will be left behind.

For months, and sometimes years, we've walked together in what seems like the closest of relationships. I've listened and learned about your family, your greatest fears, your joys and sorrows. I've seen you cry, laugh, and get angry and have experienced many of those feelings myself as I nurtured you with confidence and encouragement. I have loved the person you've shown me, until that love could make its way into the fractured heart of your own narrative. Yet, ironically, this has never been a *real* relationship; it is a professional one—a "therapeutic bond"—that a code of ethics has tailored and carefully structured for *your* protection and healing.

Saying good-bye is bittersweet. Fulfilled that our time

together yielded a strong alliance and a healthier perspective, I am greatly satisfied by the work we have
accomplished. With one last handshake or hug, you will
leave empowered, with greater self-esteem and clarity. But
I am fully aware that once we say our farewell, there will
likely be no contact between us ever again. Occasionally, I
may receive a random voice message wishing me a happy
New Year or a quick hello in the aisle of a grocery store.
Sometimes there is a follow-up appointment, a periodic
check-in and fine-tuning, but our "relationship" is dictated
by your needs, and confined by confidentiality, to be
cherished in memory only.

We won't be exchanging friendly texts or "wish you
were here" postcards. There will be no meeting up for
coffee, no shopping at the mall. Ethical boundaries advise
me simply to let you go, knowing that I will probably
never see or hear from you again. It is clearly a one-sided
relationship. As a matter of fact, you will likely leave here
knowing very little about *me*: my favorite foods, my birthday, where I was born, the names of my children.

Over a period of more than twenty years, there have
been many hellos and an equal number of good-byes, and I
am not very good at them. Truth be told, the routine,
inevitable good-bye makes me sad.

Plus, lately, something has been awakened in me, the
person whom no one gets to know for *real*. I am good at
listening, tuning in, and giving attention to what someone
else might need, comfortable at championing others with
skill and devotion that have given me a sense of purpose.
But I have begun to feel a shift happening, an inward
glance and a potent desire to value myself and all that I have
collected and learned, and to make myself *visible*: expand

the walls, shine a light on my own interests and creativity, and say good-bye to the confines of this chair and office. Maybe I will leave for good, take a sabbatical, or be redirected elsewhere, but, as with each person who has matured in this room, it is now time for me to go out into the world, equipped and grateful for the privilege to have grown and healed here, too. It is time for closure.

I will be closing the program that keeps my mind in gear, idling on high alert and homing in on signs of sorrow and distress. It's time to shut down the analyzer of erratic behavior, turn off the inquisitive brain that looks for awkward smiles pasted over heartbreak, for evidence of incongruence in subtle movements—diverted eyes, a raised voice, enlarged pupils—or from words that are spoken and those that are not. I need to stop the flow that has made me an ardent studier of people, put the brakes on the survival skills and hypervigilance that were set in perpetual motion to protect me years ago but get in the way of my living fully *today*.

Change has begun and is happening now, uncomfortable in its uncertainty yet necessary for growth. After nearly a lifetime in the trenches, scrutinizing and evaluating, I no longer feel the need to keep this search alive; I have found what I've been looking for. The honest truth beneath the surface of every faith journey and story, including my own, is that no matter how raw or tragic our experiences or discouragement, what we want to know is that we matter, that we are and have always been *valuable*—loved and lovable at the core.

Regardless of what we've endured in this universe that is much too big for us to comprehend or manage, what we long to believe is that we are worthy as we are, an underlying theme in this room where deep connections and miraculous renovations have taken place with the tender mercies of compassion and resilience of the human spirit. The thought of reaching for the doorknob, amid all the life that's been here—the tears, discoveries, and transformations —makes it hard for me to leave, to let go and say good-bye. But, like the growing of wings, this is a transition in the making, the uncomfortable process of exiting the sanctuary of the familiar and entering the mystery of the unknown. And it's clear, from watching others make this passage, that to move forward, something must be left behind; it is the nature of all change.

While it is sure to feel like the kind of loss that persuades all of us to cling to the old and revere the past, transitions are our opportunities to appreciate where we've been *and* where we're headed, stretching us to rewrite stories and conclusions that open us to accept the *whole* adventure. So, even though I don't know exactly where I am going and I can't see around a blind corner, I can enjoy the anticipation of new stages and breakthroughs. And with the persistent urging of expectancy, a steady inner voice keeps telling me that it is okay to close the door, that in saying good-bye I am taking an important step to invest in my own health and relationships and acknowledge a creative child who has been waiting patiently for a long time.

I feel a flame of enthusiasm coming to life from an ember that could not ignite in childhood but has begun burning with new energy and empowerment. This is the next phase of my story, an extension of all my experiences and lessons, and a culmination of wisdom garnered from the sacred stories and divine sparks of fellow explorers who passed through this same door to face their new chapters and possibilities with daring. I'm not sure what I'll discover, and with my radar intentionally altered, I feel a bit out of sync. But I'm excited about desires I can't deny, enlivened by a sense of regeneration and serenity that assure me I am heading in the right direction.

Curiously, faces lit with joy seem to be showing up everywhere I go. Something has shifted in this season, where I find myself surrounded with people and muses I never saw before. I feel a tug encoded in effortless delight that pulls me to listen in with fascination on tales of vision quests, creative dreams, and inner peace, recognizing that I am still on my pilgrimage, meandering on a soulful path where there are many more stories to be heard, more for me to learn, and much, much more to experience.

And so it is my turn to say good-bye, to leave this place and take flight, blessed by the treasured connection and insights we've shared, and by the spiritual gifts that have convinced me of the magnificence, and inherent value, of *every* human being. Liberated by the embrace of love, joy, and peace, which are always available, we can all adjust our customized lenses to unlock the self-limiting beliefs, shame, and cover-ups that have darkened our days with needless suffering. Enlightened by a spark from the Highest Source, we can write our final chapters with truth that sets us free to celebrate our remarkable journeys, our evolution, and the remainder of our precious lives.

* Mental health is demonstrated in our ability to handle change and difficulties and interact with compassion in our relationships.

* Joy is an aliveness that comes from letting go of outcomes and accepting what is: valuing who and where we are in the present moment.

* Gratitude is the key that unlocks joy and instantly shifts negative energy to positive energy.

* To be set free, we must correct unrealistic expectations and faulty notions about controlling people or situations over which we are powerless—accepting what we cannot change and changing what we can.

* Our purpose and destiny is to be transformed by divine love and to find a way—with our unique gifts and service—to channel it into our relationships, interactions, and world.

* Closure is the last phase of therapy, when personal goals have been met and an inherent sense of worth sets us free to live our lives with more love, joy, and inner peace.

7.5 | YOUR STORY

*It's your turn to tell your story. Imagine you're the client.
Get comfortable. Breathe deeply. Use the following prompts to make
discoveries and gain clarity on your way to personal freedom.
Use a journal to capture any thoughts, feelings, or images that come
to mind or talk into a recorder. Welcome to your session ...*

Through the pages of "Your Story," what has been
unlocked? Are you still hanging onto secrets? Shame?
Self-limiting beliefs? Unrealistic expectations?

By knowing your mind, have you gained enough clarity to
improve negative behaviors? Do you need to reach out
for more support?

What is something you did this week to lift your spirit?

What are you grateful for *today*, regardless of current
difficulties?

Which mindful practices (GEMS) will you continue to
apply to:

. . . fill up with joy and love from the Source?

. . . spill over with love that you can share with others?

. . . nourish your mind? Body? Spirit?

When you are troubled by anxiety or self-doubt, which
loving affirmations most validate your worth and set you
free? Remind yourself:

I am_____. I am_____. I am_____.

In exchange for more peace, and with the help of the
Serenity Prayer:

What are you willing to accept? What are you going to change?

What are you noticing about your courage and personal growth?

What single step (bold or tiny) will you take now to continue writing your story in a way that celebrates who you are, validates your gifts and purpose, and channels more love into the world?

POSTSCRIPT

Therapy is not about casting blame; it's about our mistaken ideas, toxic shame, and personal journeys to freedom. I forgave my mother years ago, though she was never actually aware that she had been pardoned (or needed to be). And though her behavior changed very little through the decades, I was able to spend her last years in a relationship accepting who she was, without personalizing her impulsive outbursts or expecting her to give more than she was capable of giving.

Though her parenting was hurtful and unpredictable, I am not sure that her intentions were; she was a wounded child who likely was repeating what she had witnessed growing up. And as I look back, it's clear that she set out to give me more than she had been given, though she was limited by a mental state and addiction that were sure to cause damage, and certainly did.

However, I have always loved my mother dearly, with a quality of compassion that deepened after I stopped needing her as a parent. And though much of what she did was harmful to me as a child, she did shower me with material possessions throughout my life—things she would have loved—and I am grateful for every one of the many gifts she gave to me.

The very best by far was what she, as the daughter of immigrants, passed along to me in her appreciation for the English language and where it could take people who learned to use it well. My ability to express myself in writing, with attention to grammar and nuance, was developed under her critical eye, and I discovered that what she said was absolutely true: language *is* powerful. Unfortunately, not only do words have the capacity to inspire, but they have the ability to destroy as well.

And so, ironically, the tools I used to write this book are endowments from my mother, though she will never read it. Most of us take for granted what we received as children, and rarely as parents do we fully understand what we have passed along to our heirs—from both our strengths and our weaknesses. It is a generational system of flawed people, lessons, and second chances.

But my point in telling my story, and those of my clients, is not to blame my mother—to betray her or anyone else—but to show how our earliest connections, our experiences, and our own private logic powerfully impact us. And that, no matter how we began or what we are currently facing, with the power of love and forgiveness, we can accept where we've come from and how we've grown; we can hold on to the good and leave the rest behind, and free ourselves to enjoy what's left of our imperfectly wonderful life.

ACKNOWLEDGMENTS

To all who have shared your stories with me, who have mentored and awakened me to beauty and joy in the here and now—my dearest friends, family, clients, authors, artists, and healers—thank you for embracing me with your truth and wisdom.

To my traveling companion, who has patiently encouraged me to grow wings and try them out—my rock and hero on this grand adventure through the ages—thank you for years of laughter and devotion, no matter what.

To my children and grandchildren, who have taught me the meaning of amazing grace—the wildest, truest teachers of forever love—thank you for stretching, stirring, and continuously filling my heart.

And to She Writes Press and its community of talented writers, who offered me the privilege to open the door to therapy, to illustrate the healing process, and to share what happens when we dare to tell our stories . . . thank you for the extraordinary opportunity.

ABOUT THE AUTHOR

TUYA PEARL is a psychotherapist from Southern California. With twenty years of clinical experience, and many more as a wife and mother of a growing family, Tuya is a masterful therapist, skilled at helping people develop and find personal freedom. She has treated individuals, facilitated groups and retreats, and in *Tell Me Your Story: How Therapy Works to Awaken, Heal, and Set You Free*, has opened the door to showcase the healing process that happens within and beyond the walls of therapy.

Connect with Tuya Pearl at:
www.tuyapearl.com